THE MERGER & ACQUISITION LEADER'S PLAYBOOK

THE MERGER & ACQUISITION LEADER'S PLAYBOOK

A PRACTICAL GUIDE TO INTEGRATING ORGANIZATIONS, EXECUTING STRATEGY, AND DRIVING NEW GROWTH AFTER M&A OR PRIVATE EQUITY DEALS

GEORGE B. BRADT
JEFFREY P. PRITCHETT

WILEY

Published by John Wiley & Sons, Inc., Hoboken, New Jersey.
Published simultaneously in Canada.

Library of Congress Cataloging-in-Publication Data

Names: Bradt, George B., author. | Pritchett, Jeffrey, author.
Title: The merger & acquisition leader's playbook : a practical guide to integrating organizations, executing strategy, and driving new growth after M&A or private equity deals / George B. Bradt, Jeffrey Pritchett.
Other titles: Merger and acquisition leader's playbook
Description: Hoboken, New Jersey : John Wiley & Sons, Inc., [2022] | Includes index.
Identifiers: LCCN 2022019976 (print) | LCCN 2022019977 (ebook) | ISBN 9781119899846 (cloth) | ISBN 9781119899877 (adobe pdf) | ISBN 9781119899860 (epub)
Subjects: LCSH: Consolidation and merger of corporations.
Classification: LCC HG4028.M4 .B68 2022 (print) | LCC HG4028.M4 (ebook) | DDC 658.1/62—dc23/eng/20220603
LC record available at https://lccn.loc.gov/2022019976
LC ebook record available at https://lccn.loc.gov/2022019977

Cover Design: Wiley

SKY10035423_072222

CONTENTS

ACKNOWLEDGMENTS

The number of people who have had an impact on this book is enormous. It ranges from those like Wiley's Richard Narramore, who had the idea for the book and invited us to bring his idea to life, to all those who taught us lessons throughout our careers.

Somewhere in that continuum fall all of George's partners, colleagues, allies, supporters, and clients at PrimeGenesis and Jeff's colleagues, allies, and supporters at Cerberus Capital Management L.P. and its portfolio companies, as well as all those involved with CEO Connection in any way.

We're grateful to the editing teams at Wiley and Forbes who have sharpened our thinking through the years, all the guest contributors, and friends and family members who support us in their own ways.

Jeffrey P. Pritchett:

To the countless mentors, family members and friends who have pushed, supported, advised, guided, and cheered for me throughout my life and career—thank you.

To my parents, Dr. Judy and Mr. Terry Pritchett who have been and continue to be my closest advisors and biggest supporters, I'm forever grateful for all you have done, and continue to do, for me and our family. To the Chambers family: my sister Jennifer, brother-in-law Dennis, nieces Alyssa and Addison, for our tight, enduring and ever-strengthening bond.

To Chan Galbato, my friend and mentor who has been and continues to be instrumental in my personal and professional development.

To my dear friends, George and Meg Bradt for everything we have done and will do together.

I would not be at this point without all of your influences.

EXECUTIVE SUMMARY

Those leading through a merger, acquisition, or the like do so to create more value faster. They look for revenues to double or more on the way to returning many times their initial investments. Maybe you're driving or leading the investment. Maybe you're leading the business itself or playing a supporting role. In any case, you need a leadership playbook for the merger or acquisition.

This is that playbook, the one we've used as investors, leaders, and supporters. It gives you the frameworks, tools, and sub-playbooks you need to create that value faster. Our overarching approach is to work through customers, capabilities, and costs—in that order. First, figure out how you're going to win with customers. Then build the leadership, team, and capabilities required for that. Fund those efforts by cutting less valuable efforts and their associated costs.

This is how we've created value faster against a backdrop of others failing to deliver the desired results 83 percent of the time. In a *Harvard Business Review* article, Kenny Graham noted that "between 70 and 90 percent of acquisitions fail."[1] A KPMG M&A study found that 17 percent of deals added value, whereas 30 percent produced no discernible difference and 53 percent destroyed value.[2]

This book lays out the seven sub-playbooks and a prototypical order that comprise the M&A leader's complete playbook. We also include summaries of tools to help along the way, each of which has an editable download available at www.primegenesis.com/tools.

The seven sub-playbooks are:

1. The Strategic Playbook
2. The Commercial Playbook
3. The Operational Playbook

[1]Graham, Kenny, 2020, "Don't Make This Common M&A Mistake." *Harvard Business Review* (March 16).

[2]KPMG Mergers and Acquisitions: Global Research Report 1999.

4. The Financial Playbook
5. The Governance Playbook
6. The Organizational Playbook
7. The Change Management Playbook

As this is inherently a non-linear process, parts of each of these playbooks need to be deployed at different times in different mergers or acquisitions. With that in mind, adapt this prototypical order for your particular situation.

Concept => Research => Investment Case => Negotiation => Deal/ Due Diligence => Contract => Close => Integration => Acceleration => The Next Normal => The Next Chapter

	The Strategic Playbook	The Commercial Playbook	The Operational Playbook	The Financial Playbook	The Governance Playbook	The Organizational Playbook	The Change Management Playbook
Concept Research Investment Case	The Investment Case	Organic Revenue Growth	Cost Optimization	Deal/ Due Diligence	Regulatory	Culture Incentives	Integration Leader Change Management
Negotiation Deal/Due Diligence	Focus		Operational Excellence: Supply Chain, Distribution, Continual Improvement	Financing	Financial	Leadership	Communication
Contract Close	Plans	Customers		M&A	Board	People	Announcement
Integration Acceleration Next Normal	Innovation	Marketing & Sales	Technology			Politics	Adjustments

The Strategic Playbook

Be clear on what you want out of an acquisition or merger, how it would fit with what you've already got, and what you're willing to give up to get it. Then broaden your perspective to look at different possibilities before narrowing on the few best candidates and putting together investment cases for them.

Before you attempt to acquire and integrate another entity, it's best to know your own entity first. When leaders have in-depth knowledge of their own core focus and strategic, organizational, and operational processes as well as their culture, they are far better positioned to leverage and blend the combined strengths of their own and other entities.

Align on the core focus of the new organization: design, production, delivery, or service (see Figure I.1). That choice dictates the nature of your culture, organization, and ways of working.

FIGURE I.1 The Core Focus

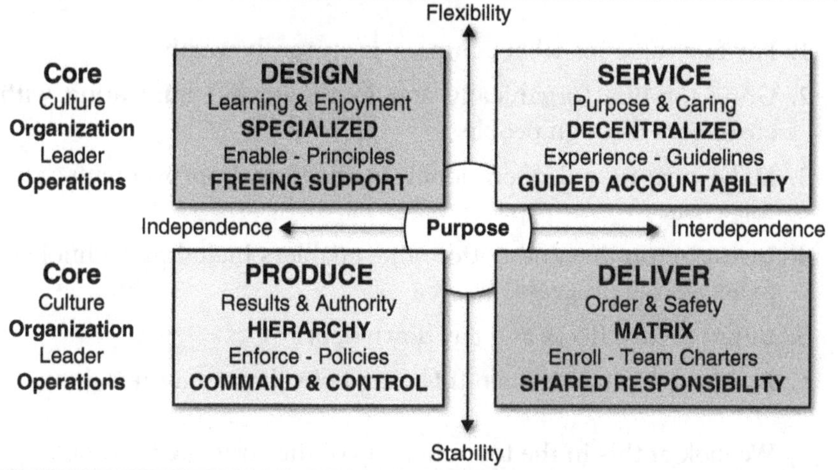

Similarly, understand the business context in which you're operating. Your strategy revolves around a set of choices about the markets, segments, and customers you'll serve. Know and understand them better than anyone else.

The fundamental U-shaped profit curve for almost every industry is that the vast majority of profits accrue to the most innovative who sell fewer "units" at higher prices and margins at the top and to the low-cost producers who make higher than average margins at the "market" price.

Choose whether your innovation will drive higher prices—most likely in design or service-focused organizations—or drive down your production or delivery costs.

If you can't define the value you are seeking to create, it doesn't exist. Get clear on the desired outcomes for your markets, segments, customers, organization, shareholders, and people—as well as *how* new value is going to be created with choices around where you will:

- **Win** by being predominant/top 1 percent, superior/top 10 percent, strong/top 25 percent

- **Not lose** by being above average/competitive, good enough/ scaled, or
- **Not do** by outsourcing or not doing at all

Play this out through the investment case fundamentals:

1. Pay fair value for what company is currently worth.
2. Grow top-line (organically and inorganically) innovating with customers through people.
3. Make operational–operational engineering improvements, cutting costs.
4. Invest in top-line and bottom-line enablers including technology to accelerate progress.
5. Improve cash flows and pay down debt.
6. Exit or recapitalize when this round of value creation is done.

We look at this in the four chapters of the strategic playbook:

Chapter 1: **The Investment Case:** The Heart of the M&A Leader's Playbook
Chapter 2: **Focus:** It Drives Everything Else
Chapter 3: **Plans:** Strategy Precedes Execution
Chapter 4: **Innovation:** A Fundamental Strategic Choice

The Commercial Playbook

One private equity firm looked at its 25 years of deals across its eight separate funds. They calculated that 30 percent of their portfolio companies' revenue growth over time had been organically fueled by their own innovation, marketing, and sales while 70 percent came from further acquisitions. In most cases you'll need both. Organic revenue growth is harder and riskier, but you keep all of it.

There's an important difference between value creation and value capture. Value is created when a customer pays someone for a product or service that costs the supplier less than the price paid. This is why you have to think customer-back to create value by innovating to provide more valuable products and services than your competitors do.

Don't read this wrong. There's nothing wrong with capturing value from competitors—generally by undercutting their price to take market share. This is why the price of everything gets competed down to its marginal cost over time. You don't want to be the ultimate winner of the race to the bottom. But you can make a lot of money winning some of the stages along the way.

We didn't include marketing and sales in the core focus chart shown in Figure I.1. That chart is derived from Michael Porter's value chain work in which he suggests every company designs, produces, sells, delivers, and services.[3] It turns out the most successful companies focus on one of design, production, delivery, or service in addition to marketing and selling.

We look at this in the three chapters of the commercial playbook:

Chapter 5: **Organic Revenue Growth**: So Valuable

Chapter 6: **Customers**: From Which All New Value Flows

Chapter 7: **Marketing and Sales**: Which Every Organization Must Do

The Operational Playbook

The operational processes that worked before your merger or acquisition may not be adequate to deliver your future ambitions. Maintain and evolve the best of your current processes while leveraging innovation and technology to layer in the new processes required to deliver the needed cost reductions and fuel revenue growth.

Essentially, you're going to need to craft, implement, and manage four plans concurrently:

- Resource allocation and plan (requirements, sources, application): Human, financial, technical, operational
- Rules of engagement across critical business drivers
- Action plan (near-term and long-term): Actions, measures, milestones/timing, accountabilities, linkages
- Performance management plan: Operating and financial performance standards and measures

---

[3]Porter, Michael E., 1985, *Competitive Advantage: Creating and Sustaining Superior Performance* (New York: Simon and Schuster).

We look at these in the three chapters of the operational playbook:

Chapter 8: **Cost Optimization:** To Free Up Resources to Fuel Commercial Growth

Chapter 9: **Operational Excellence:** Supply Chain, Distribution, Continual Improvement

Chapter 10: **Technology:** Because All Companies Are Technology Companies Today

The Financial Playbook

Do the deal in a way that reduces your risk of being part of the 83 percent of mergers and acquisitions that fail to deliver the desired results. The first of the many investments you need to get a return on is the purchase price. It is better not to pay enough and lose a deal than to over pay and "win" one of the 30 percent that take a lot of work for no gain, or, even worse, one of the 53 percent that actually destroy value.

The starting point for your deal should be a fair value for what the company is currently worth based on current cash flows. This would reward the seller for what they've built and give you all future value creation. Of course, in the real world, others may be willing to give the seller a portion of the estimated future value. Couple that with some overestimation of possible future value and ego, and it's easy to see how people bid more than they should to "win" bidding contests.

Your real investment is different depending on how you finance the deal. Consider options for funding beyond cash, including equity, seller funding or earnout, and debt in the form of loans, bonds, credit lines, bridge financing, mezzanine, or subordinated debt.

Due diligence is your chance to check your assumptions. If you put a breakup fee in the deal, you did that to allow you to walk away if appropriate. Historically, 83 percent of the time others should have done that. Do due diligence in multiple phases to manage resource allocations (e.g., time, costs, opportunity). Do some before negotiating, some while negotiating, and some between contract and close to avoid wasting much time and resources on low probability or low-impact deals.

Learn as much as you can about the strategic, organizational, and operational processes and culture of the entity you're acquiring.

Don't just take third parties' opinions; be active in learning as much as you can—as soon as you can.

1. Check your assumptions about the value creators that can enhance competitive advantages, increase impact, and enable top-line growth with *customers*.
2. Check your assumptions about cultural compatibility. Because if you can't make the *people* work, nothing else matters.
3. Check your assumptions about synergistic *cost* reductions that can fuel investment in the value creators.
4. Look for other *investments* that will be new and needed for the combined company and need to be planned for and part of the strategy.
5. Then make a go or no-go *decision* being clear on the advantage of cutting your losses before they become material.

We look at this in the three chapters of the financial playbook:

Chapter 11: **The Deal/Due Diligence:** Iteratively

Chapter 12: **Financing the Deal:** The Different Options

Chapter 13: **Further M&A:** Enabling Commercial and Operational Success

The Governance Playbook

You need a license to drive a car. And you need licenses to do mergers and acquisitions. Those licenses come from government regulators, banks, and other investors and get translated and managed by your board.

We look at this across the three chapters of the governance playbook:

Chapter 14: **Regulatory:** And the License to Play

Chapter 15: **Financial Governance:** Always Necessary

Chapter 16: **The Board:** And Its Multiple Roles

The Organizational Playbook

The root cause of many mergers' success or failure is culture. Choose the behaviors, relationships, attitudes, values, and environment (BRAVE) that will make up your new culture. Make sure you are encouraging helpful things and discouraging unhelpful things with your incentives and other tools. Also, as you're choosing key leaders and the broader team, keep in mind that you are inviting people into the new culture, noting who really accepts your invitation in what they say, do, and are.

Take a hard look at the combined organization's skills and capabilities through the lens of the new core focus and strategy to determine if any critical capability sets are missing or misaligned. Not only look at the people, plans, and practices, but also pay particular attention to how well you are performing in the markets, segments, and customers you've decided to pursue. Quickly move to bridge any gaps that exist.

Start by defining the right structure and roles to execute on your mission. Be specific about talent, knowledge, skill, experience, and craft requirements for success in each key role, and then match them with the right people.

- *Innate talent*: Either born with or not
- *Learned knowledge*: From books, classes, or training
- *Practiced skills*: From deliberate repetition
- *Hard-won experience*: Digested from real-world mistakes
- *Apprenticed craft*: Absorbed over time from masters with artistic care and sensibilities

We look at this across the five chapters of the organization playbook:

Chapter 17: **Culture:** The Underlying Root Cause of Nearly Every Merger's Success or Failure

Chapter 18: **Incentives:** Show Me How They're Paid and I'll Tell You What They Do

Chapter 19: **Leadership:** Starting with the Core Leadership Team

The Change Management Playbook

We've all seen organizations acquire other organizations and then run them as wholly owned, separate entities. You can't possibly realize synergies out of separate organizations. Synergies must be created together by teams looking beyond themselves to new problems they can solve for others. This is why a deliberate and detailed integration plan that spans across organizational, operational, strategic, and cultural issues is essential.

All lasting change is cultural change in attitudes, relationships, and behaviors following a point of inflection change in environment or situation and ambition and objectives. Manage that cultural transformation purposefully, deliberately, actively, and in detail. Have a cultural transformation plan in place. When you merge cultures well, value is created. When you don't, value is destroyed.

Implement systems to track, assess, and adjust daily, weekly, monthly, quarterly, and annually: Don't confuse communication with operating cadences. Avoid the public company sprint to do things just ahead of quarterly earnings calls, instead staying ahead of the curve at all times.

- Balanced scorecard (e.g., financial, customer, internal business processes, learning and growth)
- Finance (e.g., revenue, cash flow and cash conversion cycle, earnings before interest, taxes, depreciation, and amortization [EBITDA], return on investment)
- Customer (e.g., sales from new products, on-time delivery, share, customer concentration)
- Internal business processes (e.g., cycle time, unit cost, yield, new product development)
- Learning and growth (e.g., time to market, product life cycle)

We look at this across the five chapters of the change management playbook:

Chapter 22: **Integration Leadership:** Start Here
Chapter 23: **Change Management:** Leading Through the Point of Inflection
Chapter 24: **Communication:** Everything Communicates
Chapter 25: **Announcement Cascade:** Emotional, Direct, Indirect
Chapter 26: **Adjustments:** Because You'll Need Them

Prototypical Order

Chapter 27, "Prototypical Order," covers the last step: preparing for further growth and transformation like the next exit or other "event" as a platform company or bait for strategic buyer. When preparing for an exit, get the story right:

- Strategically: Organic revenue growth; Other M&A
- Organizationally: Buyable management team; Capabilities valuable to others
- Operationally: Buyable infrastructure (Assets, data, IT systems, financial reporting;) Processes; New product development capabilities
- Personally: Making yourself invaluable to the next owners

What really matters is how you influence others and the impact you all make together. Do start with the context and industry landscape. Do align people, plans, and practices around a shared purpose to create commercial and other value. Do the cost-cutting required to free up the resources you need to strengthen the combined entity's culture and strategic, organizational, and operational processes. Do that, thinking customers, then capabilities, then cash, and the merger and acquisitions you lead will go well.

PART I

The Strategic Playbook

CHAPTER 1

The Investment Case: The Heart of the Merger and Acquisition Leader's Playbook

	The Strategic Playbook	The Commercial Playbook	The Operational Playbook	The Financial Playbook	The Governance Playbook	The Organizational Playbook	The Change Management Playbook
Concept Research Investment Case	The Investment Case	Organic Revenue Growth	Cost Optimization	Deal/ Due Diligence	Regulatory	Culture Incentives	Integration Leader Change Management
Negotiation Deal/Due Diligence	Focus		Operational Excellence: Supply Chain, Distribution, Continual Improvement	Financing	Financial	Leadership	Communication
Contract Close	Plans	Customers		M&A	Board	People	Announcement
Integration Acceleration Next Normal	Innovation	Marketing & Sales	Technology			Politics	Adjustments

The first component of the strategic playbook is the investment case. It guides every other part of the investment playbook and every other playbook. The first, fundamental questions go to what you want out of an acquisition or merger, how it would fit with what you've already got, and what you're willing to give up to get it.

What You Want

Synergy happens when two or more people or businesses work together to create new value, capture existing value, or prevent or slow the destruction of value. That leads to some of the different types of mergers and acquisitions and the different reasons to do them:

- Merging organizations with complementary capabilities and strengths to create something that no one else can do, like Stanley merging its hand tool and construction strengths with BLACK+DECKER's power tool strengths.
- Adding innovation or technology capabilities, like Disney buying Pixar to leverage its technology across all animation.
- Gaining access to a new market with a new business model or new Internet protocol, like Google buying Android to give it an operating system.
- Expanding product and service offerings, like executive search firm, Korn Ferry's string of acquisitions to add other human capital consulting offerings.
- Shoring up a weakness to stop destroying value, like Philip Morris buying Kraft foods and merging it with General Foods so the Kraft management team could provide needed leadership to General Foods or the second reason Disney bought Pixar, which was to acquire new leadership for Disney Animation.
- Repositioning a company in a new category (with higher multiples) like Delux's move from being a printing company focused on printing paper checks to merging into payment technology companies.
- Leveraging costs across the platform, like Coca-Cola's master bottlers swallowing up smaller bottlers to further increase their economies of scale.
- Creating critical mass for a platform company to enable future value creation, like regional companies merging to create a national or international footprint so they can expand geographically and serve national or international customers.
- Scaling the platform, where there are economies of scale, perhaps in an industry consolidation like Disney buying Marvel and then Lucas Films/Star Wars and then Fox after buying Pixar.

What You Are Willing to Give Up

You have to give up something to make any merger or acquisition work, whether it's cash or just a dilution of your control. You'd never do this if you didn't believe there would be a positive return on your investment (ROI) in an appropriate time frame.

If you're a public company, you'll need to manage that ROI in your quarterly and annual earnings announcements. Many public company investors will want to see accretion to earnings per share (EPS) every quarter. You will need to think about this aspect and ensure messaging and expectations are clear on when the merger will add to EPS. If you're a private equity firm, you'll need to manage that ROI within the time frame of the appropriate fund. If you're a family or family office, the ROI may be associated with generational wealth creation. Your ROI can be positive if you pay or contribute less or receive more for an asset than it's actually worth. In that case, there's a transfer of value between past and future owners with no need to chase synergies.

This book and this chapter focus on mergers and acquisitions (M&A) in which the combined parts are worth more together than they were separately—creating top-line and bottom-line growth through synergies.

Which Opportunities to Pursue

Knowing what you want and what you're willing to give up to get it points you in the right direction to consider all the alternatives, taking into account overall risks at a high level and how you might mitigate those risks.

British philosopher Carveth Read taught us "it is better to be vaguely right than precisely wrong."[1] Others encourage divergent thinking before converging on a solution. When it comes to looking at merger or acquisition targets, they are the same idea: Expand your thinking to look at vaguely right possibilities before narrowing in, getting more precise at each step.

In any case, make sure the opportunities tie directly into your strategic plan, building strategically important capabilities. Mergers and acquisitions are tactics, not strategies. Not thinking this way is one of the main reasons so many mergers fail.

---

[1]Read, Carveth, 1989, "Logic: Deductive and Inductive," Grant Richards, London, June.

There are four basic things private equity investors do to earn money:[2]

- *Raise money* from limited partners (LPs) like pension and retirement funds, endowments, insurance companies, sovereign wealth funds, and wealthy individuals as well as the private equity (PE) firms and their partners' contributions to the deal(s)
- *Source, due diligence, and close* deals to acquire companies
- *Improve* commercial, innovation, and technology strengths and operations, cut costs, manage risks, and tighten management in their portfolio companies
- *Sell or recapitalize* portfolio companies (i.e., exit them) at a profit

When PE firms analyze companies for potential acquisition, they will consider things like what the company does (their product or service and their strategy for it), the senior management team of the company, the industry the company is in, the company's financial performance in recent years, emerging technologies, industry trends, risks, opportunities, the regulatory environment, reputation, potential competitive response, products and services, customers, and the valuation and likely exit scenarios of the company.

The main sources of value capture at exit include market share growth, growing revenue (and therefore earnings before interest, taxes, depreciation, and amortization [EBITDA] and cash flow) substantially during the holding period, cutting costs and optimizing working capital (and therefore increasing EBITDA and cash flow), selling the company at a higher multiple than the original acquisition multiple, and paying down debt that was initially used to fund the transaction.

This leads to a framework for the investment case—simplified by design. Your actual investment case will include several layers of detail below this overarching framework.

---

[2]Chen, Andrew, "What Do Private Equity Investors Actually Do?" InterviewPrivateEquity.com.

The Path to Value Creation

As McKinsey's Andy West and Jeff Rudnicki laid out in their podcast on "A Winning Formula for Deal Synergies,"[3] the highest synergy potential is found in industry consolidations, capability-led roll-ups, and geographic expansions. Small product tuck-ins, corporate transformations, corporate-led white-space acquisitions, new business models, and IP acquisitions may also be strategic fits.

Think through the core focus, overall strategy and posture, strategic priorities, enablers and capabilities, and organizational and operating priorities for the investment based on a fact-based assessment of the situation.

The 6Cs situation assessment is a framework for understanding the business environment by looking at:

1. Customers: first line, customer chain, end users, influencers
2. Collaborators: suppliers, allies, government and community leaders
3. Culture: behaviors, relationships, attitudes, values, environment
4. Capabilities: human, operational, financial, technical, key assets
5. Competitors: direct, indirect, potential
6. Conditions: social, demographic, and health; political, government, and regulatory; economic, technical, market, climate

Think:

1. What: Objective, scientific truths—facts
2. So what: Subjective, personal, cultural or political truths, opinions, assumptions, judgments, conclusions
3. Now what: Indicated actions

Customers

Customers include the people your organization sells to or serves. These comprise direct customers who actually give you money, as well

[3]West, Andy, and Rudnicki, Jeff, 2020, "A Winning Formula for Deal Synergies," Inside the Strategy Room Podcast (May 8).

as their customers, their customers' customers, and so on down the line. Eventually, there are end users or consumers of whatever the output of that chain is. Additionally, there are the people who influence your various customers' purchase decisions. Take all of these into account.

FedEx sells overnight delivery services to corporate purchasing departments that contract those services on behalf of business managers. But the real decision-makers have historically been those managers' executive assistants and office mangers. So FedEx targeted its marketing efforts not at the people who write the checks, not at the managers, but at the core influencers. It aims advertising and media at those influencers and has their drivers pick the packages up from the executive assistants personally instead of going through an impersonal mailroom. FedEx trains its frontline employees on customer service and how to interact to retain business and grow share.

Collaborators

Collaborators include your suppliers, business allies, and people delivering complementary products and services across your ecosystem. What links all these groups together is that they do better when you do better. So it's in their best interest, whether they know it or not, to help you succeed. Think Microsoft and Intel, or mustard and hot dogs, or ketchup and hamburgers—though never mustard and hamburgers, of course.

Just as these relationships are two-way, so must be your analysis. You need to understand the interdependencies and reciprocal commitments. Whenever these dependencies and commitments are out of balance, the nature of the relationships will inevitably change. Think through your customer's purchasing cycle. Who comes before you? Who comes after you? If you're in corporate real estate, a relocation expert you can vouch for and trust is an obvious ally. In the M&A advisory business, attorneys, bankers, and other professional services firms pull in complementary firms to create the best outcome for their clients. However, a printing business could be your ally as your customer will need new letterhead and business cards to reflect their new location.

Collaborators are strategic partnerships whether that's intended or not. So, think strategically. The less resources you control in-house, the more important this is.

Culture

Some define *culture* simply as "the way we do things around here." Others conduct complex analyses to define it more scientifically. Instead, blend both schools of thought into an implementable approach that defines culture as an organization's behaviors, relationships, attitudes, values, and the environment (BRAVE). The BRAVE framework is relatively easy to apply yet offers a relatively robust way to identify, engage, and change a culture. It makes culture real, tangible, identifiable, and easy to talk about.

Capabilities

Capabilities are those abilities that can help you deliver a differentiated, better product or service to your customers. These abilities include everything from access to materials and capital to plants and equipment to people to patents. Pay particular attention to people, plans, and practices.

Competitors

Competitors are those to whom your customers could give their money or attention instead of to you. It is important to take a wide view of potential competitors. Amtrak's real competitors are other forms of transportation like automobiles and airplanes. The competition for consumer dollars may be as varied as a child's college education versus a Walt Disney World vacation. In analyzing these competitors, it is important to think through their objectives, strategies, and situation as well as strengths and weaknesses to better understand and predict what they might do next and over time.

Conditions

Conditions are a catchall for everything going on in the environment in which you do business. At the least, look at sociodemographic, political, economic, technology, and climate trends and determine how they might impact the organization over the short, mid-, and long term:

- Social, demographic, health
- Political, government, regulatory

- Economic
- Technology—emerging innovation and trends
- Market—including consolidations and cross-vertical expansion
- Climate, weather

Pull these together into a Porter's Five Forces[4] or a strength, weakness, opportunity, and threat (SWOT) analysis or the like and use that to inform your choices, starting with your core focus. Michael Porter's Five Forces are:

1. Bargaining power of suppliers
2. Bargaining power of buyers
3. Threat of new entrants
4. Threat of substitute products or services
5. Rivalry among existing competitors

SWOT is a way of combining internal strengths and external opportunities into key leverage points and internal weaknesses and external threats into business issues. See Chapter 3 for more explanation and a SWOT tool.

For years, United Sporting Goods exploited its relatively strong bargaining power with suppliers and buyers to set market prices as the largest distributor of guns in the United States. It had no single supplier or buyer that accounted for more than 5 percent of their business. The threats of new entrants or substitutes was low, and its existing competitors were dramatically smaller than they were. Its Five Forces analysis was favorable. However, they completely missed the impact of Donald Trump's election on the gun market. United Sporting Goods expected Trump to relax constrictions on gun sales, leading to a market expansion, so it increased its inventory. Instead, it faced "slowing sales after Mr. Trump's election as worries about gun control ebbed among firearm enthusiasts."[5] This is why it needed to look at its SWOT.

---

[4]Porter, Michael E., 1985, *Competitive Advantage: Creating and Sustaining Superior Performance* (New York: Simon and Schuster).

[5]Gibson, Kate, 2019, "Gun Seller United Sporting Goods Bust, Partly Blaming Trump's Election," CBS News MoneyWatch (June 11).

FIGURE 1.1 Core Focus

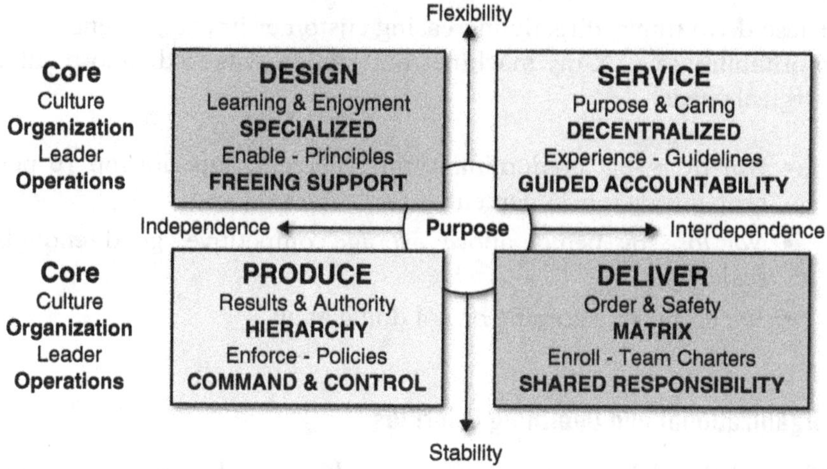

Core Focus

The *core focus* of an enterprise depicted in Figure 1.1 informs its overarching strategy, culture, organization, and ways of working. Understand whether your new, combined organization's core focus is design, production, delivery, or serve. That choice dictates the nature of the culture, organization, and ways of working and flows into your overarching strategy and posture, strategic priorities, and enablers of those priorities, which then guide your organizational and operating priorities.

Overarching Strategy and Posture

Two things drive fundamental choices around the creation and allocation of resources to the right place in the right way at the right time over time in line with your strategic priorities:

- Drive customer impact and profitable commercial growth through product/service development, new offerings, innovation and technology, pricing, marketing, business development (markets, partners, etc.), increase sales to existing and new customers
- Enhance operational rigor and accountability through supply chain, production, distribution, service optimization

Strategic Enablers and Core Competency and Capabilities

These drive things directly increasing customer impact, revenue, and profitability (e.g., X-ray machines and radiologists to diagnose ankle surgical needs).

- *Win* by being: predominant/top 1 percent; superior/top 10 percent, strong/top 25 percent;
- *Not lose* by being: above average/competitive, good enough/scaled, or;
- *Not do* by: outsourcing or not doing at all.

Organizational and Operating Priorities

These help deliver the strategic enablers and competency and capabilities.

People

- The board
- Senior leadership (commercial, operations, tech and information technology, finance, human resources [HR], legal, research and development, M&A)
- Middle management
- Individual and team strengths including project management and transformation
- Incentives

Infrastructure

- Governance including board and systems
- Brand positioning and marketing materials, collateral, tools (e.g., websites)
- Financial reporting, tax, accounting, and compliance infrastructure
- Data, technology, IT, and security infrastructure
- Operational infrastructure including procurement and supply chain
- Organizational and HR infrastructure
- New product development infrastructure

Innovation and Technology

- Revolutionary invention
- Evolutionary steps
- Next version of product or service with what the customer wanted or did not even know was possible

Systems and Processes

- Enabling commercial growth and operational rigor

Balance Sheet and Cash Flows

- Deferred maintenance and modernization investments
- Growth-oriented capital spending
- Technology investments
- Back office: finance, tax, HR

Mergers and Acquisitions

- Bolting on to foundational platform for:
  - Industry consolidation
  - Capability-led roll-up
  - Geographic expansion
  - Product tuck-in
  - Corporate transformation
  - Corporate-led white-space acquisition
  - New business model
  - Intellectual property acquisition
- Taking into account competitive landscape and potential reactions

Fundamental Investment Case Model for a Merger or Acquisition

Step 1: Pay or Contribute Fair Value for What the Company Is Currently Worth.

Begin with the current value of the enterprise you're considering acquiring or merging with based on its current cash flows, when there is current cash flow. There are early-stage growth businesses and businesses in need or restructuring and transformation that are not producing cash flow today. In these cases, you need to think about the future value of the business, based on the current commercial success, once scale is obtained or the value the PE firm or acquirer can bring to these businesses and derive a fair value for these businesses. A couple of things that do *not* go directly into this calculation are:

- Their claimed *EBITDA*: Different organizations do different things with financing and interest, taxes, depreciation, and amortization. Get to the current ground truth with cash flows.
- Their future *projections*—current, not future value
- Possible *synergies*—current, not future
- Improvements to the commercial or operations of the business

This is, of course, not what you're going to end up paying or contributing. But it's important input. The number you do care about is what you think you'll have to pay or contribute.

If you did pay or contribute fair value for what the company is currently worth based on current cash flows, you would reward the seller for what they've built and keep all future value creation. Of course, in the real world, others may be willing to give the seller a portion of the estimated future value. Couple that with some overestimation of future value creation and ego, and it's easy to see how people bid more than they should to "win" bidding contests.

You'll need an expected transaction price for your investment case. Pick a most likely number somewhere between "fair value" and "must have at any price." Then bracket it with best-case and worst-case scenarios. Add in some financing assumptions for leverage and you're ready to go to the next step.

The next steps get at future state value creators: top-line growth, operational efficiencies, technology innovation, and the investments required to enable them.

Step 2: Grow Top-Line (Organically and Inorganically).

Project the *organic growth* that can come from synergies between the two enterprises. In general, these come from getting new customers or getting current customers to buy or pay more. But, for this exercise, take into account only increases that would not happen without the merger or acquisition.

Of course, you're going to consider opportunities and risks like general market growth or market consolidation and the competitive landscape that will impact everyone—including the value of your enterprise.

It is critical to think through what emerging technologies are possible during your expected hold period that could benefit or materially harm the future value of the firm. Amazon's growth has been a major benefit for a number of players in the value stream, including corrugate manufactures and shippers. On the other end of the spectrum, auto suppliers with key components tied to the combustion engines have seen valuations fall as electrification continues to grow, even a decade before the conversion happens. But they impact buyers and sellers whether or not they merge.

Classic synergistic revenue enhancers include:

- Cross-selling existing products or services to the formerly separate entities' customers either in the same or new markets.
- Getting existing customers to use current products or services in new ways—thereby purchasing more.
- Creating and then selling new products or services (that could not have been created without the merger or acquisition).

Then, separately, project the *inorganic growth* enabled by the merger or acquisition. These might include acquisitions, mergers, or joint ventures with other companies, brands, technologies, systems, and the like layered on to the new, combined platform—especially in a relatively fragmented market.

Step 3: Make Operational Improvements and Operational Engineering.

As we've said, this is what most people think of when they think "synergy." While there is often the opportunity for some quick wins falling out of eliminating redundancies, the really valuable operational improvements don't "fall out" of anything. They require real work by people with real strengths.

Look at these in five buckets across the operating flow from procurement to intake to processing to inventory management to distribution:

- Operations strategy, which starts by asking where to play and then (1) doing the most important value-creating operations yourself and (2) outsourcing the less important and less efficient operations.

- Operational jump-shifts to improve quality and reduce waste and costs, perhaps fueled by new technologies, digitization, tools, systems, processes, footprint realignment, unlocking stranded capital, or scale. Scope is a function of resources (including levers) and time.
- Elimination of redundancies: They will be there. Take them.
- Cash and working capital management, especially the lag between money out (accounts payable) and money in (accounts receivables) and also opportunities to generate cash like contracting out unused production capacity.
- Lean, continuous, and incremental improvements, which may take longer to realize but create real value over time.

Step 4: Invest in Top-Line and Bottom-Line Enablers.

What you pay for an acquisition or merger is your first investment, but not your last. Step-changes in top-line growth and operating efficiencies won't happen without investing to realize them. Some of the enablers are more general, and some are more specific.

Think in terms of putting in place a full management team capable of managing another doubling of revenue for the next owner.

Governance engineering can also make a big difference. Think in terms of management equity, debt or leverage, board participation, all securing the license to operate legally, ethically, socially.

Strengthening brand differentiation with prospective and current employees, customers, suppliers, allies, influencers, and the communities in which you operate is always important.

Strengthening go-to-market capabilities through the sales pipeline: generating awareness, fueling interest, and then activating desire helps drive topline growth.

Financial engineering, arbitrage, or balance sheet and cash management including foreign exchange opportunities and risks all directly impact profitability and enable other growth drivers.

At the same time, make sure you're establishing the required infrastructure. For organizations focused on *design*, this might look like a new product development factory—like Michael Eisner and

Frank Wells's reboot of Disney's animation studio when they took over because they decided the core of the company was in animated film design; or efficient procurement and *production* machines—like Disney's development company because Eisner and Wells wanted to capture more of the share of wallets from theme park visitors; or a *distribution* network or ecosystem—like Disney stores to sell Disney character-driven merchandise; or *service*-delivery differentiators—like Disney hotels as part of capturing more of the guests' wallet share and better controlling their overall experience; all supported by:

- IT systems including enterprise management and business intelligence, customer relationship management
- Financial reporting systems
- HR management systems

Step 5: Improve Cash Flows and Pay Down Debt.

While this may fall out of successfully implementing steps 2-4, do calculate this and cash flow sensitivities into your investment case. Some deals will involve some creative financing approaches as well, generating their own synergies and value. And yes, you will need to do a bridge from current revenue, EBITDA, and cash flows to those in your future case, taking into account all the things that help and hurt.

Step 6: Realize Value in Increased Earnings or by Exiting or Recapitalizing When This Round of Value Creation Is Done.

You make investments to earn returns—the "R" in ROI. Sometimes the return is realized in increased earnings. Sometimes it's realized in an exit or recapitalization. Calculate that value one way or another. Bonus points for writing the investment case for the organization eventually buying your new, combined entity—whether or not you think you'd ever want to sell. Write their future investment case, and then make it happen.

Note the most up-to-date, full, editable versions of all tools are downloadable at primegenesis.com/tools.

TOOL 1.1

Investment Case

Core focus of enterprise:

Overarching strategy and posture:

Strategic priorities:

Strategic enablers and core competency/capabilities:

Organizational and operating priorities to help deliver the strategic enablers, competency, and capabilities:

- People:
- Infrastructure:
- Systems and processes:
- Balance sheet and cash flows:
- Mergers and acquisitions:

Fair value of target company:

Target company's perception of its fair value:

Possible acquisition prices:

Organic growth drivers:

Inorganic growth drivers:

Operation improvements and operational engineering:

Investments in top-line and bottom-line enablers:

Projected improvements in cash flows to pay down debt:

Projected realized value in increased earnings or exit or recapitalization:

CHAPTER 2

Focus: It Drives Everything Else

	The Strategic Playbook	The Commercial Playbook	The Operational Playbook	The Financial Playbook	The Governance Playbook	The Organizational Playbook	The Change Management Playbook
Concept Research Investment Case Negotiation Deal/Due Diligence Contract Close Integration Acceleration Next Normal	The Investment Case Focus Plans Innovation	Organic Revenue Growth Customers Marketing & Sales	Cost Optimization Operational Excellence: Supply Chain, Distribution, Continual Improvement Technology	Deal/ Due Diligence Financing M&A	Regulatory Financial Board	Culture Incentives Leadership People Politics	Integration Leader Change Management Communication Announcement Adjustments

The second component of the strategic playbook is focus. It guides plans and innovation choices.

There are four primary areas of *core focus*: design, produce, deliver, or service (Figure 2.1). Most organizations do all four to one degree or another in addition to marketing and selling, which all must do. Pick one as your main strategic focus and primary differentiator, with other activities and your culture flowing into or from that.

Value is defined as the customer's view of the relation between your perceived, relative benefits and your perceived, relative costs.

- Design-focused organizations win by imagining new valuable things—brand-new things and next versions of great products and services.
- Production-focused organizations win by making valuable things out of disparate elements.

FIGURE 2.1 Core Focus

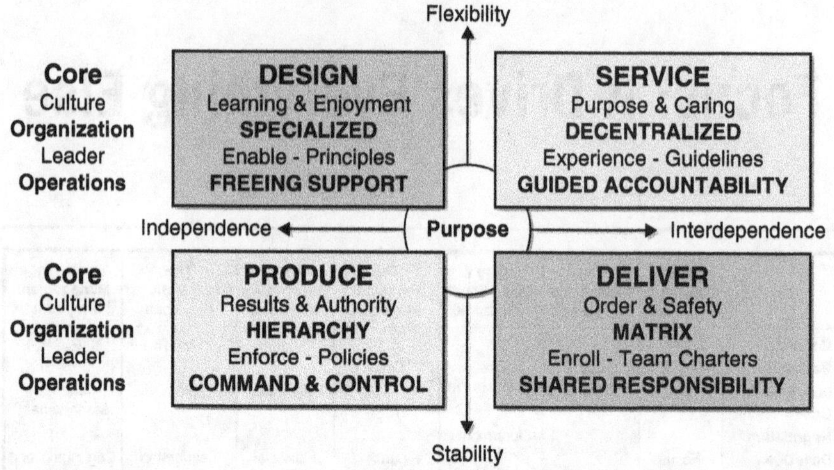

- Delivery-focused organizations win by conveying valuable things from one party to another.
- Service-focused organizations win by valuably enhancing their customers' experiences.

While most organizations do some level of design, production, delivery, and service and all must market and sell, the most successful organizations have a clear focus on one of the first four areas.

Design-Focused

To focus on design is to create, adapt, or arrange something new.

- Create things that did not exist before and are new to the world.
- Adapt things that did exist, modifying them to make them fit for a new use—next version.
- Arrange things by putting them into proper order or into a correct or suitable sequence, relationship, or adjustment, so the new whole is greater than the sum of the parts.

Design Culture

A design-focused organization's main cultural driver should be independence. Its designers should feel free to get their inspiration from anywhere they can. Flexibility, learning, and enjoyment support that. But independence rules.

Specialized Organization

A specialized organizational structure works especially well in design-focused organizations. Designers and inventors have special and often rare strengths. The rest of the organization has to nurture and protect them, minimizing unproductive distractions so they can spend their time creating, adapting, and arranging.

CEO as Chief Enabler

In an organization basing its success on its ability to nurture and protect its designers, the chief executive officer (CEO) has to be the chief enabler. Great leaders bring out others' self-confidence. They do this in large part by emphasizing confidence-building in their approach to the direction, authority, resource, and accountability aspects of delegation. This is especially important when it comes to designers.

- *Direction:* Emphasize the problem you need solved or the opportunity you can take advantage of. Then give them as much freedom as you can about how they solve it. The more they can think with the mind of a child, the better.
- *Authority:* Give them the authority to experiment. By definition, the "new" won't match what you currently have and do. Note the authority to experiment is not the authority to implement.
- *Resources:* This one is counterintuitive, but adding constraints increases innovation. It's helpful to think in terms of scope, time, and resource constrained creative sprints instead of never-ending quests.
- *Accountability:* The key here is assuming success. Have confidence in your designers. Recognize and reward them for their achievements at the end of creative sprints along the way to bring out their self-confidence.

Operate with Freeing Support

Design behavior is fragile. All need to give it freeing support to keep it going. The ABCs of changing behavior apply: antecedent, behavior, consequences.

The antecedent is prompting designers to create, adapt, and arrange as part of your approach to delegation. Assuming you've got the right people with the right direction and support, they are likely to do what you ask them to do.

The trap here is consequences, and especially unintended negative consequences for positive behavior. Make sure you and everyone interacting with your designers are:

- Positively reinforcing desired behavior (creating, adapting, arranging)
- Discouraging undesirable behavior (outside acceptable norms)

Change the way you:

- Positively reinforce undesirable behavior
- Discourage desired behavior (by applying others' standards to their output)

You may have success by leading with principles (as opposed to more rigid policies or more directional guidelines). Principles help people come to their own decisions in a way that fits your vision and values.

George Lucas and team created *Star Wars: Episode IV—A New Hope,* and Steve Jobs and team created Apple's first iPhone, which were amazing first versions. Their subsequent companies have created numerous versions of those core products with even greater success leading with a design-focused organization.

Production Focused

To focus on production is to create a competitive advantage in reliably and repeatedly bringing disparate elements together into something with more value.

Production Culture

A production-focused organization's main cultural driver should be stability. People should know what they are expected to do and get it done consistently and reliably. Although that suggests a degree of independence and there should be a clear focus on results and respect for authority, stability rules.

Hierarchical Organization

Hierarchical organizations work especially well in production-focused organizations. Production is all about bringing disparate elements together. Individual performers should follow the direction of first-line supervisors in working on their pieces. Those higher and higher in the hierarchy will have broader and broader views of how things fit to optimize how they are all pulled together.

CEO as Chief Enforcer

In an organization basing its success on its ability to produce reliably and consistently, the CEO should be the chief enforcer. If everyone is looking up in a hierarchy, they are ultimately looking up at the CEO. Any wobble there can destabilize everyone in the hierarchy below the CEO—which is everyone.

Lead with policies mandating definite courses or methods of action that all must follow.

- Policy: mandatory, definite course of method of action that all must follow
- Guidelines: preferred course or method of action that all should generally follow
- Principles: ways of thinking about action

Operate with Command and Control

For production-focused organizations, policies inspire and enable. Producers find clarity inspiring. Tight swim lanes enable them to do their job.

- Producers work best with swim lanes separated by solid walls topped with barbed wire.
- Deliverers working across a matrix want to know where various players' swim lanes intersect.
- Servers focused on customer experience need flexible swim lanes so they can go wherever required to satisfy their customers.
- Designers and inventors don't even want to be told they have to swim, let alone have swim lanes.

Producers love enforcers. Others in the organization won't be so sure. Those who value independence will see the organization as too controlling. Those who value flexibility will see the organization as too rigid.

If you're leading producers, be unapologetic about your policies and controls. Those who choose not to follow those policies and live with those controls should choose to work elsewhere. Or you should make that choice for them. The number-one regret experienced leaders have looking back on their careers is not moving fast enough on people. In a hierarchy, people will look to the leader for examples of leadership. In these cases, some early public hangings can send exactly the right signals to those looking for stability and clarity.

Note the hierarchy could be a double hierarchy in a helix. As De Smet, Kleinman, and Weerda describe it, the helix is a substitute for a matrix.[1] Each person has a capabilities manager and value-creation manager. As they describe:

> The *capabilities manager* oversees the employee's long-term career path, has the power to hire or fire, and drives performance evaluations with input from value-creation managers.
>
> The *value-creation manager* sets priorities, provides day-to-day oversight, and ensures that the employee meets business objectives.

When George was in China with Coca-Cola, the concentrate plant in Shanghai reported to him as its value-creation manager. But the plant was a production machine and really took its direction from the global head of production who made sure the global policies were

[1]De Smet, Aaron, Kleinman, Sarah, and Weerda, Kirsten, 2019, "The Helix Organization," *McKinsey Quarterly* (October 3).

followed completely. No one on the planet thought George had the authority to tinker with Coke's secret formula.

Delivery Focused

To focus on delivery is to build a competitive advantage in conveying valuable things from one person, place, or thing to another. SIPOC (supplier, input, process, output, customer) helps:

- Your *supplier* (person, place, or thing) supplies you with →
- The *input* (what you will deliver), which you run through your →
- Delivery–distribution/conveyance *process* to get →
- The *output* (what you will deliver) to →
- Your *customer*

Note in this case, the input and output are the same. You're not involved in design—imagining valuable things. You don't produce—making valuable things out of disparate elements. And you don't do after-sale/after-delivery service. Of course, delivery is a service itself. But your focus is on conveying your input safer, faster, and less expensive than others—not on the experience of the people or things you are conveying. That's the fundamental strategic choice guiding your allocation of resources.

Delivery Culture

A delivery-focused organization's main cultural driver should be interdependence. Its people should think about the ecosystem first and ask how to make the system work better every chance they get. Stability, order, and safety matter on the way to creating scalable, repeatable processes. But interdependence and connections rule.

Matrix Organization

Matrix organizations work especially well in delivery-focused organizations. This forces the supplier and customer-focused groups within the organization to work with the functionally focused groups. Matrices work when everyone buys into shared objectives and goals and fail when people try to protect their own turf first.

CEO as Chief Enroller

In an organization basing its success on its ability to enroll suppliers, allies, customers, and clients who can benefit from each other's offerings, the CEO has to be the chief enroller. The CEO's job is to bring people into the ecosystem and get them to collaborate with each other.

Operate with Shared Responsibilities

Delivery-focused organizations succeed only when people accept shared responsibilities. They live in the world of handoffs. Things have to be ready to go when people are ready to pick them up. People have to be ready to pick things up when they are ready to go. That is the foundation of shared responsibilities.

The main trap for delivery organizations is diversification. Many get fooled into thinking they can create more value and make more money by dialing up their services. The U-shaped profit curve rules. Supermarkets deliver large quantities of acceptable flowers to their customers at relatively low prices. Flowerbx delivers smaller quantities of near-perfect flowers at relatively high prices. They both win. Hallmark tried to charge higher prices for barely acceptable flowers and lost.

Know what you do. Know where you play on the U-shaped profit curve. Focus to win. Or dilute your efforts and lose.

Team charters are especially useful in matrix organizations. Use them to get team members aligned around their purpose, objectives, context, approach, guidelines, and implementation accountabilities. (See Chapter 9 for more on team charters.)

Service Focused

Service is ultimately about how you make your customers feel. Design, production, and delivery matter. But they only matter as platforms on which to build the experience.

Service Culture

A service-focused organization's main cultural driver should be flexibility. The frontline people interacting with customers must have the flexibility to meet their needs and exceed their expectations on the spot. Interdependence matters because the frontline people will need to leverage the rest of the organization to help customers. Purpose and caring matter a great deal in uniting all around customer service. But flexibility should rule.

Decentralized Organization

Decentralized organizations work especially well in service-focused organizations. This is inextricably linked to flexibility. Drive decision-making as close to the customer as possible.

The fundamental difference between a decentralized organization and a matrix organization is control of resource allocation decisions. In a matrix organization the geographic or customer-facing people share decisions with functional leaders. For example, the Florida state manager and national marketing manager must agree on the Florida advertising spend. In a decentralized organization, the geographic or customer-facing people make their own decisions, like the Florida advertising spend.

This makes for faster, more flexible, more customer-experience focused decisions.

CEO as Chief Experience Officer

In an organization basing its success on its ability to create superior experiences for its customers, the CEO has to be the chief experience officer. They own the vision and the values, and they must live customer experience in everything they say, do, and are. If they don't fundamentally believe, they will get caught.

Just as Ben Hunt-Davis and his teammates evaluated every choice with the question, "Will it make the boat go faster?" on their way to Olympic rowing gold in 2000, the chief experience officer should evaluate every choice with the question, "Will it improve customers' experience?"

Jim Donald has taught the value of the customer and experience first approach for service-focused organization throughout his stature career in hospitality, retail, and grocery. He successfully guided Starbucks as CEO and Albertsons as president and then cochair, among other great businesses with a similar methodology.

Operate with Guided Accountability

Great customer service organizations operate with guided accountability. Everyone holds themselves accountable for how they make each and every customer they come in contact with feel.

Clear guidelines are critical. Think Goldilocks. Policies—mandatory, definite courses of action that all must follow—are too strict. Principles—ways of thinking about action—are too loose. Guidelines—preferred courses or methods of action that all should generally follow—are just right, freeing people up to act in the best interest of the customer with the guidance they need to make decisions on the spot.

If you're leading a service organization, both parts of guided accountability are critical to effective decentralization. Decentralizing without guidance is abrogating your authority. Guidance without accountability turns the guidance into theoretical gibberish. Only by letting people take up true accountability for the customer experience within agreed guidelines will things go the way you want. Though, if you've read this far you know that it's not about what you want. It's about what the customer wants.

CHAPTER 3

Plans: Strategy Precedes Execution

	The Strategic Playbook	The Commercial Playbook	The Operational Playbook	The Financial Playbook	The Governance Playbook	The Organizational Playbook	The Change Management Playbook
Concept **Research** **Investment Case** **Negotiation** **Deal/Due Diligence** **Contract** **Close** **Integration** **Acceleration** **Next Normal**	The Investment Case Focus Plans Innovation	Organic Revenue Growth Customers Marketing & Sales	Cost Optimization Operational Excellence: Supply Chain, Distribution, Continual Improvement Technology	Deal/ Due Diligence Financing M&A	Regulatory Financial Board	Culture Incentives Leadership People Politics	Integration Leader Change Management Communication Announcement Adjustments

The third component of the strategic playbook is plans. These flow directly from the investment case and focus choices. Let's start by defining the terms:

- *Strategy:* The single overarching choice
- *Strategic priorities, enablers, and capabilities:* in line with the strategy
- *Culture:* The behaviors, relationships, attitudes, values, environment of the organization

Strategic planning is about generating and selecting options to close gaps between objectives and current realities. It is about the creation and allocation of resources to the right place, in the right way, at the right time, over time to overcome barriers and deliver what matters. Strategic planning is also deciding what you will and will not do.

FIGURE 3.1 The Value Chain

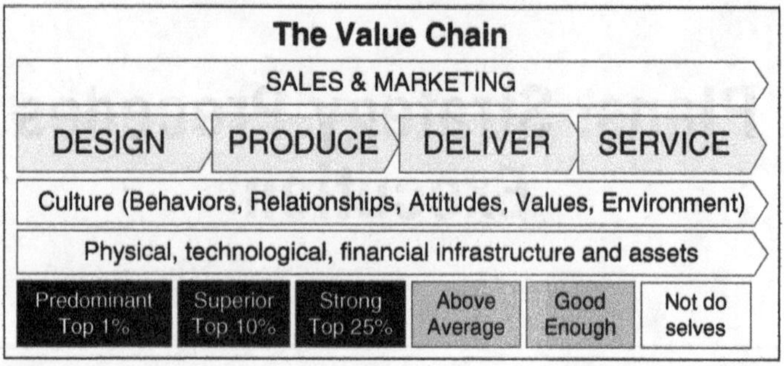

Michael Porter suggests that almost any value chain includes design and invention, production, delivery, and customer service and experience in addition to marketing and selling.[1] Your single, overarching strategy should identify the right way to build and leverage differentially valuable advantages versus competitors at one of the first four while also marketing and selling—which every organization must do one way or another and is discussed in the commercial playbook (Figure 3.1).

Strategic priorities focus people on the most important areas:

- *Hardware and software enablers* like systems and processes, infrastructure (data; information technology [IT]; other technology; security; operational including procurement and supply chain; organizational and human resources [HR]; financial reporting, tax, accounting, and compliance; new product development), balance sheet and cash flows (modernization and growth-oriented capital spending, back office) enable delivery of priorities.
- *Organizational capabilities* across senior leadership (commercial, operations, information technology and other technology, innovation, finance, HR, legal, research and development [R&D], mergers and acquisitions [M&A]), middle management, and individual and team strengths including project management and transformation are those required for the enablers to work.

[1]Porter, Michael E., 1985, *Competitive Advantage: Creating and Sustaining Superior Performance* (New York: Simon and Schuster).

Example:	Apple	Coca-Cola	Walmart	Four Seasons
Manner:	Proactive	Fast-follow	Coordinated	Responsive
Culture:	Independent	Stable	Interdependent	Flexible

365-Day Plan Elements

The starting point for developing your 365-day plan is your investment case (Chapter 1). Essentially, this is your chance to turn that theoretical construct into real actions to grow the topline and make operational improvements behind investments in enablers.

Do understand you may not be able to get everything done in a year. The bigger and more complex the merger, the longer it's going to take to complete. So just as the things you do in your first 100 days set up what you're going to get done in your first year, some of the things you do in your year 1 set up year 2 deliverables.

1. **Grow top-line (organically and inorganically).**

   Gain new customers. Get current customers to buy or pay more.

   Classic synergistic revenue enhancers include:

   - Cross-selling existing products or services to the formerly separate entities' customers either in the same or new markets
   - Getting existing customers to use current products or services in new ways—thereby purchasing more
   - Creating and then selling new products or services (that could not have been created without the merger or acquisition)

   Establish go-to-market and end customer market pursuit strategies including your marketing, communications, and customer interface; sales model and organization; customer profitability and cash flow cube; end-market analysis and go-to-market strategy; and acquisitions or mergers with other companies, brands, technologies, systems, and the like.

   Marketing, Communications, and Customer Interface

   - Discuss current mission statement and go-forward strategy.
   - Agree on internal and external communication preferences and strategy.

- Enhance website for use as both a marketing tool and current customer tool.
- Assess and build out digital marketing presence.
- Consider establishing customer experience lead (if not already in place).

Sales Model and Organization

- Build out customer relationship management (CRM) focused on pipeline, forecast, customer profitability, and estimates.
- Assess existing sales model and determine if a strategy focused on specific industry verticals or regional or geographically focused model would be more appropriate.
- Determine go-forward customer growth strategy and balance of focus between new customer pursuits and upselling existing customers.
- Determine incremental sales resources required to pursue new customers, expand point of sale and point of purchase service offering, and execute go-to-market strategy.
- Assess current sales commission plan and align with sales targets, organizational strategy, and industry standards.

Customer Profitability and Cash Flow Cube

- Prepare a customer profitability and cash flow cube that quantifies historical contribution margin by customer, product, and end market. Establish the customer profitability cube as a new embedded process within the company.
- Link current customer profitability realization to impending customer renewals to ensure pricing is appropriate.
- Develop a long-term solution for tracking and reporting customer profitability and accurate job costing with a link back to the pricing and estimating process.

End-Market Analysis and Go-to-Market Strategy

- Further analyze existing customer end markets to understand projected growth rates, anticipated demand by product or service offering, market share opportunities for both existing and prospective customers, profitability profiles, and investment required to execute future growth strategies.

- Strategically identify and select new customers' targets and end markets to pursue.
- Determine future offering strategy and investment required.
- Identify and implement solution for improved front-end customer-facing technology.

Acquisitions or Mergers with other companies, brands, technologies, systems, and the like

- Build business development office plan and develop M&A strategy.
- Increase business development capabilities.
- Create M&A strategy plan including outreach to select targets identified through lender group.
- Identify investment banks and others specializing in industry for potential transactions.
- Build out state of company capabilities and verticals to analyze key areas to target M&A.
- Build out competitive positioning for company.

2. **Make operational improvements, operational engineering, and product and service innovation.**
   - Elimination of redundancies
   - Operational jump-shifts, perhaps fueled by new technologies or systems, where scope is a function of resources (including levers) and time
   - Lean, continuous, and incremental improvements
     - Develop a comprehensive, end-to-end production strategy that appropriately links forecasted customer demand with procurement efforts, labor and equipment management, inventory management, freight, and production scheduling. In the interim, remediate immediate staffing, procurement, production scheduling, and freight challenges.
     - Chart end-to-end process flow from customer order to delivery and setup. Identify performance gaps and remediation actions.
     - Assess current volume forecasting methodology and link to production capacity to develop a near-term, modified approach.

- Conduct fulsome supplier review to identify improvements with regards to pricing, potential consolidation of duplicate suppliers, terms, payment methods, lead time, and so forth.
- Assess overall production reporting including use of metrics and automation. As required, develop production metrics and daily, weekly, and monthly key performance indicators (KPIs) to monitor performance and improve production efficiency.
- Assess structural engineering capabilities and potential needs.
- Assess potential product and service innovations.

3. **Invest in top-line and bottom-line enablers.**
   - Putting in place a full management team capable of managing another doubling of revenue for the next owner
     - Recruit for open C-suite, board, and business development positions.
     - Establish delegation of authority protocol, decision-making, and governance structure.
     - Provide executive onboarding support and training.
     - Monitor employee safety, customer demand changes, and other changes.
   - Strengthening governance
     - Form board, audit, compensation, and technology committees.
   - Instilling financial engineering or cash management
     - Finalize operating plan, 5-year reforecast, and capital plan.
     - Create capital planning function to include IT investments, equipment, and other capabilities.
     - Set management equity, debt/leverage, board participation.
     - Set compensation structures.
   - Establishing the required infrastructure
     - For organizations focused on *design*, this might look like a new product development factory;
     - For organizations focused on production, this might look like efficient procurement and manufacturing machines;
     - For organizations focused on delivery, this might look like a distribution network or ecosystem;

- For organizations focused on service, this might look like service-delivery and experience differentiators;
- All supported by IT systems including enterprise management and business intelligence, CRM.
- Identify vendor to conduct a cybersecurity full review—critical in today's age; implement recommended security changes.
- Review cloud disaster recovery and business continuity planning remediation.
- Conduct Microsoft and other relevant license audits to ensure compliance and optimize or lower license count where feasible.
- Commence IT organization leadership assessment and search in conjunction with executive team.
- Build data warehouse to use as workflow management tool within the sales organization.

Financial Reporting Systems

Financial Planning and Analysis (FP&A) and Accounting

- Review and potentially supplement monthly and quarterly operating review packages to ensure reporting framework is consistent across locations.
- Review daily and weekly financial and operational KPI tracking and reporting and discuss other items to include.
- Review existing internal control environment and discuss process to address deficiencies identified by external auditors.
- Finalize the opening balance sheet and purchase accounting.
- Stand up forecasting capabilities and establish rigorous 5-year forecast.
- Review future organizational staffing plan.
- Review current working capital management and assess for possible improvements (to include customer credit review).
- Build robust month-end close process and calendar to ensure timely and efficient month-end reporting.

Treasury

- Review daily cash reporting process, output, and overall cash management setup and strategy.
- Review 13-week cash flow reporting process and output.
- Review and potentially enhance existing lender reporting process.
- Explore setting up new revolver loan and asset-based lending (ABL) to provide additional liquidity.
- Review disbursement process for potential improvements and efficiencies.

Tax

- Conduct tax and structure planning for the new company.
- Create quarterly shareholder reporting distribution cadence and audience.
- Update payroll reporting.
- Review purchase price allocation as related to fund management and the go-forward balance sheet.

Insurance

- Review all insurance programs with the company and its broker to determine if there are any updates or changes needed after the transaction has closed. This review will include re-benchmarking all limits and coverages under all current insurance policies.
- Provide any information required to complete the underwriting and issuance of the insurance policies to have in place at the closing.

Compliance

- Create compliance program.

Human Resources (HR) Management Systems

- Create and roll out management equity incentive plan including documentation and communication.
- Continue work on retention strategies and organizational design.
- Support recruiting and placement of senior leadership.
- Assess and support general HR function, as needed.

- Review company organizational structure and chart and assess for future needs.
- Set up new employee agreements.
- Review current employee benefits package.

The most up-to-date, full, editable versions of all tools are downloadable at primegenesis.com/tools.

TOOL 3.1

Situation Analysis Checklist

1. **Customers** (First-line, customer chain, end users, influencers)

   Needs, hopes, preferences, commitments, strategies, price/value perspectives by segment.

   First-line/direct customers

   - Universe of opportunity—total market, volume by segment.
   - Current situation—volume by customer; profit by customer.

   Customer chain

   - Customers' customers—total market, volume by segment.
   - Current customers' strategies, volume and profitability by segment.

   End users

   - Preference, consumption, usage, loyalty, and price value data and perceptions for our products and competitors' products.

   Influencers

   - Key influencers of customer and end user purchase and usage decisions.

2. **Collaborators** (suppliers, allies, partners, government and community leaders in ecosystem)
   - Strategies, profit/value models for external and internal stakeholders (up, across, down).
3. **Culture** (behaviors, relationships, attitudes, values, environment)
4. **Capabilities**

   Human (includes style and quality of management, strategy dissemination, culture)

   Operational (includes integrity of business processes, effectiveness of organization structure, links between measures and rewards, and corporate governance)

   Financial (includes capital and asset utilization and investor management)

   Technical (includes core processes, IT systems, supporting skills)

   Key assets (includes brands and intellectual property)

5. **Competitors** (direct, indirect, potential)
   - Strategies, profit/value models, profit pools by segment, source of pride
6. **Conditions**
   - Political, government, regulatory, legal trends
   - Economic (macro and micro) trends
   - Social, demographic, health trends
   - Technological trends and disruptions
   - Environment and climate change impact on your organization
   - Market definition, inflows, outflows, substitutes trends including consolidation and cross-vertical expansion

Pulling it together:
SWOT analysis and thinking about:

- Sources, drivers, hinderers of revenue, profits, and value.
- Current strategy and resource deployment: Coherent? Adequate? De facto strategy?
- Insights and scenarios (To set up: What, so what, now what?)
- How to leverage internal strengths to take advantage of external opportunities
- How to shore up internal weaknesses to deal with external threats

TOOL 3.2
SWOT

View in context of mission, vision, and nature of business (develop, produce, distribute, service)

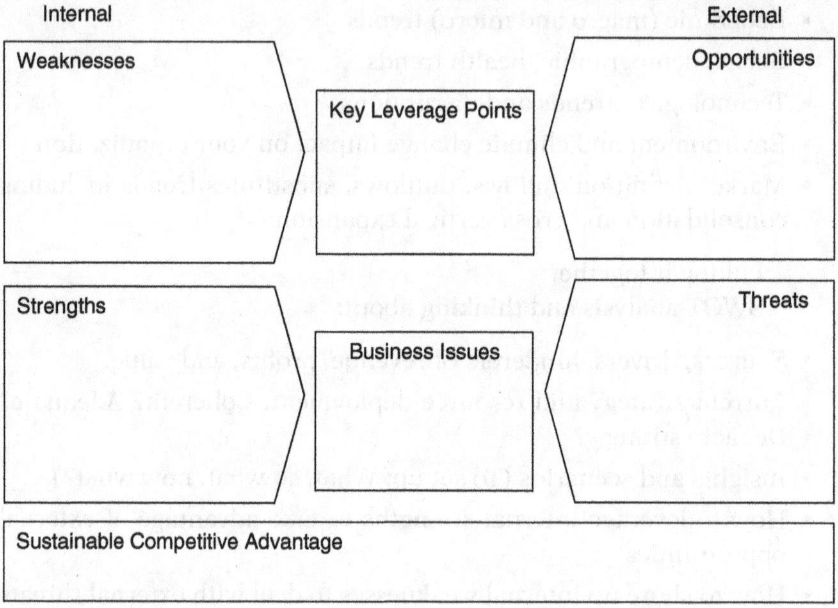

Strengths	Internal to organization—things we do better
Weaknesses	Internal to organization—things we do worse
Opportunities	External to organization—things to capitalize on
Threats	External to organization—things to worry about

Key Leverage Points

Opportunities against which we can leverage our strengths (where play to win)

Business Implications

Threats to which our weaknesses make us vulnerable (where play not to lose)

Sustainable Competitive Advantages

Key leverage points that can be sustained over extended period of time

TOOL 3.3

Business Planning

Core focus of enterprise
Design, produce, deliver, or service:
Overarching strategy and posture:

Strategic priorities:
To drive customer impact and profitable commercial growth organically:
Inorganic growth—further acquisitions, mergers or joint ventures:
To enhance operational rigor and accountability across supply chain, production, distribution, service optimization:
Operations strategy:
Operational jump-shifts:

Strategic enablers and core competency and capabilities:

Organizational and operating priorities to help deliver the strategic enablers, competency, and capabilities:
People:
Infrastructure:
All supported by:

- Governance engineering (management equity, debt and leverage, board participation, license to operate legally, ethically, socially):
- Brand positioning and marketing materials, collateral, tools (including websites)—strengthen brand differentiation with prospective and current employees, customers, suppliers, allies, influencers, and the communities in which we operate:
- Strengthen go-to-market capabilities through the sales pipeline: generating awareness, fueling interest, and then activating desire.
- Financial reporting, tax, accounting, compliance infrastructure—financial engineering, arbitrage, or balance sheet and cash management including foreign exchange opportunities and risks:
- IT systems including enterprise management and business intelligence, CRM:
- HR management systems:
- Data, technology, IT, security infrastructure:
- Operational infrastructure including procurement and supply chain:

(Continued)

TOOL 3.3 Business Planning (continued)

- Innovation and technology:
- Systems and processes:
- Balance sheet and cash flows:
- Mergers and acquisitions:

CHAPTER 4

Innovation: A Fundamental Strategic Choice

	The Strategic Playbook	The Commercial Playbook	The Operational Playbook	The Financial Playbook	The Governance Playbook	The Organizational Playbook	The Change Management Playbook
Concept Research Investment Case	The Investment Case	Organic Revenue Growth	Cost Optimization	Deal/ Due Diligence	Regulatory	Culture Incentives	Integration Leader Change Management
Negotiation Deal/Due Diligence	Focus		Operational Excellence: Supply Chain, Distribution, Continual Improvement	Financing	Financial	Leadership	Communication
Contract		Customers					
Close	Plans			M&A	Board	People	Announcement
Integration Acceleration Next Normal	Innovation	Marketing & Sales	Technology			Politics	Adjustments

The fourth component of the strategic playbook is innovation. The choice to innovate and how you innovate are strategic choices.

Choose whether your innovation will drive new products, next version of existing products, or higher prices—most likely in design- or service-focused organizations or drive down your production or delivery costs.

Full disclosure: This chapter is not like the others. Neither it nor innovation travels in a straight line. It's a curation of several of George's articles on innovation and creativity. Some will love this. Some will hate it. If you find yourself hating it, feel free to move on to the next chapter.

With that said, the flow of this chapter moves from overall tips to innovation strategies to creativity to systems. Take these innovation tips and strategies into consideration as you build out your strategic, commercial, operational, and financial plans and drive success with your mergers and acquisitions (M&A) or private equity (PE) deal.

Innovation Tips

The holy grail of innovation is the moment of sudden breakthrough. But those moments don't happen in vacuums. As suggested by some of the top names in business at the 2013 C2-MTL conference in Montreal, you must (1) prepare in advance, (2) focus on solving problems, and (3) follow through to turn ideas into reality and stay ahead of your competition.[1]

At the conference, George had the chance to interview Neri Oxman, John Mackey, Bobbi Brown, Diane Von Furstenberg, and Richard Branson after their presentations. Here are some tips from what they told George that can help spark your next flash of innovation.

Look at the World with a Child-Like Innocence.

Oxman and her MIT Mediated Matter group have moved beyond "bio-mimicry" to actually designing with nature: bio-inspired fabrication. Their new silk pavilion was actually created by 6,500 silk worms. She told George that she envisions scaling this idea with a swarm of 3-D printers to expand beyond any one printer's gantry as part of her search for "variations in kind" moving well beyond "better, faster, cheaper, bigger."

In George's interview with Oxman at the C2 Conference in Montreal, Oxman told George about her "fork in the road." She's a trained architect and designer. The choice she faced was whether to focus on design or go into research. She chose research because it gave her the opportunity to design her own technology. It allowed her to influence both products and processes—both influenced by nature.

She's a big proponent of variations in kind—true innovations. She's convinced these come from "being vulnerable," not so much from solving a problem as from innocence and different worldview. It's that different worldview that allows the innovator to come up with solutions new to the world when problems do come.

[1]Bradt, George, 2013, "Innovation Tips from Richard Branson, John Mackey, Bobbi Brown and Others," *Forbes* (May 29).

Invite Others in on the Innovation Process.

Mackey is certain that Whole Foods must continue to innovate to stay ahead of its competition and that its conscious culture is its only competitive advantage. As Whole Foods adds stores, he insists on "No me-too new stores." He told George he holds his division presidents accountable for innovation. "We value it and encourage it."

One of Mackey's tenets is to "decentralize as much as possible." This goes well beyond region, well beyond store level, to the teams within the stores. He pushes experimentation, knowing full well that "most fail." He's fine with that because the "successful ones spread."

He uses loose innovation guidelines, if any at all. Suggesting instead that if people go too far his leadership can always "tug" them back in. He's convinced it's easier to do this than to get people to innovate in the first place.

He told the story of walking a new store in San Antonio 22 years before. His wife pointed out that the few people in the store were not likely to buy Whole Foods' value proposition over the long-term. She was right. The store closed. But then 22 years later, Whole Foods opened a new store in almost the identical spot. When Mackey and his wife walked this new, booming store, he told her, "You know all those people that were never going to shop here. They're all dead. These are their children." Some ideas are right, just not at the time.

Focus on Unsolved Problems.

Brown told George how she was on a TV shoot and had forgotten her eyeliner. To make do, she grabbed a Q-Tip and used it to brush some mascara on her eyelids, solving her immediate problem. The next morning, she was surprised to see the mascara still in place. The gel in the mascara had made it last. She called her design team and had them mock up the first gel liner, which is now her most copied product.

Many of Brown's innovations have come from thinking, "It would make so much sense if. . ." She describes these as "random ideas mixed with common sense."

This was just one of the examples Brown shared with George. She also related how using a clean baby wipe to remove her makeup prompted her to create a baby wipe–like makeup remover. And she told George about wanting to wear cowboy boots with jeans she had.

When they wouldn't fit, she cut them off—the boots, not the jeans. These stories all go to her philosophy of having a clear vision but then being open to change direction as needed. She's good at this because she seems to be able to understand what's needed next. Definitely a big idea to change direction before anyone else knows you need to.

George admits this was a difficult interview for him. He's still not sure he understands what the difference is between mascara and eyeliner. But Brown made it easy for him. She seemed to genuinely enjoy teaching a complete ignoramus (George) about what she did. George thinks that's part of what enables her to innovate and connect.

After Initial Success, Follow Through.

Von Furstenberg told George her wrap dress happened "by accident." Her original T-shirts morphed into wrap tops and then into wrap dresses, catching on because they were "easy, proper, decent, flattering, and sexy." They may have happened by accident originally, but their ongoing (then 40-year) success is directly related to Von Furstenberg's follow through.

It's often difficult to separate the brand from the personality. On one hand, while a major attribute of the Virgin brand is Richard Branson, and a major attribute of Apple was Steve Jobs, and a major attribute of Walmart was Sam Walton, in each of these cases the brand name and the personality were different. Those brands survive their founders. It's harder when the founder's name and brand name match as they do with von Furstenberg.

Of course, there are examples of success. The Disney brand is thriving—perhaps because its sub-brands are anything but Mickey Mouse. McDonald's is a golden arch, and maybe a clown. Very, very few people think of Richard and Maurice.

Von Furstenberg has spent time thinking about the difference between the brand and herself. A big part of her follow through is setting up the brand as her legacy: celebrating freedom, empowering women, color, print, bold, effortless, sexy, on the go. Of course, she's a living example of the brand now. Over time, others need to step up as that example.

Aim Higher Than Your Competitors.

Branson has achieved remarkable success taking the Virgin brand into industries "out of frustration" with existing record, airline, and telecommunication companies and the like. He looks for "obvious gaps in the market" and launches products or services that are "heads above everyone else." He told George that keeping them above everyone else is the key to ongoing success.

When pushed, Branson described the Virgin Cola example:

> Virgin Cola was our greatest success in that we were so successful in the UK that we absolutely terrified Coke. They sent a 747 with bag loads of money and 20 SWAT teams to the UK and we suddenly found it disappearing from all the shelves. They decided just to stop the company completely before we could get going out around the world. Because you've got two cans of soft drink, although people at the time preferred the Virgin brand of cola—we were outselling them and Pepsi at 3:1—we didn't have a fundamentally better product. When British Airways tried to do that to us in the aviation business, we were able to beat them. We were not in soft drinks.

It's one of Branson's main themes. As he said in a 2013 graduation speech:

> We always enter markets where the leaders are not doing a great job, so we can go in and disrupt them by offering better quality services.

He grew so tired of waiting for NASA that he launched his own space travel program. This is definitely a man who reaches for the stars over and over again, as he did when he traveled into space himself in 2021.

At the same time, anyone in the main conference room when Branson spoke at C2-MTL had to have been struck by how he and the audience engaged. His Q&A time with the audience turned into a series of extraordinarily inspiring conversations as he wanted to understand the questioners' context, hopes, and ideas. He was genuinely curious and offered genuinely helpful advice to each individual. We all walked out thinking he deserved all the success he has had and looking forward to the contributions we know he's going to continue to make to the world through "The Elders" and all the other great programs he's enabling.

Race to the Top.

The fundamental choice is whether to compete on price or on differentiation. Competing on price is a race to the bottom with no winners. Competing on differentiation requires engagement with each of three phases of innovation.

Unfortunately, more and more are racing to the bottom in the face of a long-term decline in creative skills. Conference attendee Kraner told George how he had founded the Hatch Experience a decade ago to combat this, gathering diverse groups of next generation influencers, global thought leaders, and community builders annually to mentor each other in a veritable petri dish of creativity and interdisciplinary idea generation.

Make the right choice. Race to the top. And help others race to the top. Then we'll all win.

Innovation Strategies

Evolutionary Versus Revolutionary Innovation

A Procter & Gamble (P&G) alumni reunion years ago included a chief executive officer (CEO) panel on innovation facilitated by Tim Brown, president and CEO of the innovation consultancy IDEO. Panelists included P&G's then chair and CEO A. G. Lafley, Steelcase's then CEO Jim Hackett, and Meg Whitman, who at that time was heading up eBay. At the heart of this panel was a discussion of the difference between evolutionary innovation and revolutionary innovation.[2]

The panelists generally agreed that large organizations like P&G, Steelcase, and eBay could be very good at evolutionary innovation. Their scientists, researchers, and developers were more than capable of building on their organizations' existing strengths and making step-by-step incremental improvements. This is a valuable capability that helps these organizations continue to evolve.

However, larger organizations often struggle with revolutionary innovations because they require different capabilities, mindsets, and cultures than the ones that made them successful. Unlike smaller companies, large, successful corporations have much more to lose.

---

[2]Bradt, George, 2012, "Evolutionary, Revolutionary or Blended Innovation: Which Is Right for Your Organization?" *Forbes* (April 3).

New and different projects that don't serve current customers and are not in line with current product or service offerings are often viewed as distractions and thus downplayed. It's less tempting to bet the ranch on a new idea when the ranch is big.

eBay and PayPal

During the panel discussion, Whitman discussed how eBay had looked at buying PayPal early on in its existence. She told the group that she had decided not to buy it because she didn't think it could have survived inside of eBay. Instead, Whitman waited until it was a big enough company to make a meaningful impact. It was better for eBay to pay more for a stronger PayPal later, than to pay less for a weaker, unsustainable PayPal earlier.

What goes around comes around. As part of its explanation for why eBay's then CEO John Donahue was putting 38-year-old Zong founder David Marcus in charge of PayPal, the *Wall Street Journal* noted it was so that Marcus could "use his entrepreneurial background to operate PayPal 'like a smaller company.'"

Procter & Gamble

P&G faced the same issues. At that time, only about 15 percent of its innovations were meeting revenue and profit targets. Lafley decided it could do better by looking for a blend of evolutionary and revolutionary innovations. He tasked Bob McDonald, then chief operating officer (COO) and later CEO, and chief technology officer (CTO) Bruce Brown with the task.

Brown described their progress, discussed why P&G has been able to triple its innovation success rate, and offered some thoughts for others thinking about innovation. Looking at P&G's strategy through the lens of its behaviors, relationships, attitudes, values, and environment (BRAVE), we can get a sense of why they have been so successful. Let's look at these components in reverse.

Environment P&G remains committed to innovation. As Brown told George, "Innovation is the primary driver of our organic growth." When he took over as CTO in 2008, one of the first calls he got was from former CEO Smale, who reinforced the importance of innovation and went through each of P&G's $1B brands, laying out the technological innovation that had produced a point of inflection in its growth.

Values P&G is all about "touching and improving lives." You can't improve peoples' lives with the same solutions to the same problems. Thus, innovation matters a lot to P&G's ability to fulfill its purpose.

Attitude Brown knew that P&G's "culture would default to evolutionary" innovation if left on its own. Indeed, between 2003 and 2008 the size of P&G's initiatives declined by 50 percent. To counteract this trend, P&G's senior leadership adopted a more assertive attitude and pushed each category toward blended innovation, which layered revolutionary innovations on top of its commercial and sustaining innovations, looking for ways to innovate within its categories (like new detergent delivery systems) and beyond its categories (like dry cleaners).

Relationships P&G innovates to improve lives through its business groups. While it invests in breakthrough technologies that can work across categories, the rubber meets the road at each category's annual innovation review where they determine which category needs to grow. That focus serves to strengthen the relationships between the 8,000 scientists and researchers (1,000+ PhDs), in 26 innovation centers on five continents, and the business units.

Behaviors This organization's innovation program is inspired by its consumers. All behaviors around strategic thinking and implementation drive to the consumer whether it's a new-to-the-world technology, a new application of a technology, or an evolution of a technology.

Which Innovation Approach Is Right?

They all work. Each is right—for different organizations and different contexts.

- If you are a startup on the cutting edge with not much ranch to bet, go for it. Revolutionize the world. If you don't, you won't get noticed.
- If you are Apple and your ranch is built on revolutionary innovations, keep going. Stick with the attitude that made you successful in the first place.
- If you are a large, successful company with a big ranch and a culture not prone to revolutionary innovation, stick with

evolutionary innovation—especially if you're in commodity category where you have to manage costs.

- If you can blend evolution and revolution and are prepared to invest to do so at a level comparable to P&G, the blended approach may work for you.

They all work, but not at the same time. Pick the one that's right for your situation, business model, and organization.

The Innovation Versus Scale Trade-Off

The most effective senior leaders are master delegators. Before doing anything themselves, they ask "Who can do this task instead of me?" Then Minority Business Development Agency head Henry Childs said that was now the wrong question. Instead, they should ask, "What can do this task instead of any of us?" They should do this in areas they can scale while investing in their areas of competitive advantage.[3]

Childs said this as part of the interactive state of the market conversation at a CEO Connection Mid-Market Convention. One of the recurring themes there was how artificial intelligence is fueling the new industrial revolution. It's all about leveraging technology to scale through points of inflection.

In a different session, Wharton Professor Gad Allon explained the difference between growth and scale. He suggested growth generally involves increasing revenues and costs together. Scaling involves growing revenues faster than costs.

Assume you're in the business of carrying boxes down a flight of stairs. You can grow your business by hiring another person to help you. Your revenues and costs increase. Or you can leverage a ramp and move more boxes yourself. Your revenues increase, but your operating costs do not. That's leverage.

There's an obvious trade-off between efficiency and differentiation. If you're leveraging a tool or technology to scale up, your competitors can do the same. Since the price of everything tends to get competed down to its marginal cost over time, you could end up in a race to the bottom before you blink.

---

[3]Bradt, George, 2019, "The Innovation Versus Scale Tradeoff—Not Who, What," *Forbes* (October 1).

Professor Allon suggested leaders should ask four questions: "Are we propelled to scale? Are we willing? Are we able? And are we ready?" He suggests not everyone needs, wants, and can scale. "Scaling up often means giving something up." If that "something" is the competitive advantage that justifies your superior margins, scaling up may be exactly the wrong thing to do.

Another speaker suggested a middle way. Instead of making a people versus technology trade-off, that speaker proposed thinking in terms of both and "using technology, outsourcing or managed services to complement or augment" your people.

Implications for You

Thinking this way adds an important dimension to your strategic resource choices. As discussed, all companies design, produce, sell, deliver, and service. A fundamental premise is that you're better off picking one primary area of focus, investing to be best in class in that and efficiently managing everything else to fuel investment in that area.

Asking what instead of who changes your approach to this. More efficient design, production, delivery, or service could come from outsourcing part or all of those functions, employing lower-paid people, or leveraging technology to make fewer high-caliber and highly paid people more efficient. Of course, this applies to your primary area of focus as well. There's no reason not to leverage technology to make things easier for all your high-caliber and highly paid people.

The moment you outsource something core to your competitive advantage, you give up your competitive advantage. But there should be no downside to leveraging technology to complement or augment the efforts of the people giving you a competitive advantage.

Where Innovation Meets Scale

The mid-market is where innovation meets scale. Mid-market companies are generally too big to be as nimble as startups and too small to have the scale of huge corporations. This is why the speaker's thinking about using technology, outsourcing, or managed services to complement or augment people should be generally appealing to the mid-market.

While it's generally appealing, it's specifically wrong in some circumstances. Where you have a competitive advantage, you have to invest in talent and knowledge to fuel predominant or superior innovation. Ask who, and leverage technology here carefully. On the other hand, in areas where it's good enough for you to be strong or merely acceptable, ask what and outsource, deploy managed services, or leverage technology liberally to free up funds to invest in your areas of competitive advantage.

Creativity

The Three Keys to Bringing Out the Best in Extraordinarily Creative People

Managing extraordinarily creative people is challenging if not impossible. But you can bring out their best if you give them leverage, inspire, enable, and empower them. Their leverage comes from understanding and taking full advantage of their own natural talent, temperament, and inclinations. Inspiring them is about protecting them, pointing the way forward and encouraging them. Enabling and empowering them is about giving them the resources, time, and space they need to imagine, play, practice, and create.[4]

By anyone's definition, Salient Technologies' David Yakos is extraordinarily creative. *Origins* magazine describes him as one of its 45 top creatives and an "inventor, maker, designer, painter, adventurer, and engineer. From aerospace to toys, he blurs the lines between art and engineering."[5] (This last piece sounds a lot like what sparked the magic at Disney's creative oasis—Imagineering.)

Leverage

The world needs three types of leaders: artistic, scientific, and interpersonal. They need to be creative themselves and bring out creativity in others. For example, Yakos likes to "confuse the world of art and engineering." Just as he is part artist and part mechanical engineer, his product development process blends creativity and practicality "from ideation to production":

1. Conceptual design, where you explore the look and function of the concept
2. The prototype process, where you physically and digitally test the feel and function

[4]"The Three Keys to Bringing Out the Best in Extraordinarily Creative People," *Forbes* (November 2, 2016).
[5]Per *Chicago Toy Fair* magazine September 26, 2016.

3. The production design, where you communicate with the factory the design intent using manufacturing files and engineering drawings

Yakos's mother saw this innate talent and nurtured it. In an interview with Tanya Thompson, he described how

> my mother cut down an empty drier box, filled it with supplies including empty shampoo bottles, egg cartons, string and everything else I would need to build my first spaceship, first homemade pair of paper shoes and a cardboard robot suit. It was David's Creative Corner. I could visit that world and come back with something new, an invention that was unique and never before seen.

Yakos has a natural curiosity, intellectual playfulness, and a keen sense of humor and is aware of his own impulses.

Inspire

Extraordinarily creative people need to be protected, directed, and encouraged. At the same time, Wilson suggests they need to be uninhibited and willing to take risks given their heightened emotional sensitivity and being perceived as nonconforming.

Yakos knows that "all great businesses begin with an idea, but it takes engineering and product development to turn an idea into a reality." That's his focus and his firm's focus. And they've done well through the years, winning *Popular Science*'s Best Prototype of 2013 and then the Chicago Toy & Game Group's Toy & Game Innovation (TAGIE) award for excellence in toy design for David's Mega Tracks for Lionel Trains.

Enable and Empower

Enabling and empowering extraordinarily creative people is about tools and time. They need resources, connections, and basic tools. And they need time to play and learn in line with Wilson's premise that the most creative go through a large number of ideas, often thriving in disorder and chaos.

Yakos told George that

> people are almost embarrassed with their own creativity. We need to give people permission to stop being adults and engage in

> child-like imaginative play. It's not about learning how to be imaginative or creative. It's about never growing out of it. . .. I live in a safe place where it is okay to have silly ideas and safe to fail as part of taking "a broad sweep of ideas, (and) polishing the best ones."

And they need people around them with complementary strengths that can sometimes serve as the adults in the room.

Implications

1. Don't try to fix extraordinarily creative peoples' "opportunities for improvement." Help them be even better at what they are already good at.
2. Encourage them by protecting them, pointing the way forward and recognizing the cool things they come up with and do.
3. Give them the time and space they need to imagine, play, practice, and—wait for it—create.

Inspiring, Enabling, and Empowering Evolutionary Innovation—from Middle Managers

Inspiring, enabling, and empowering evolutionary innovation is one of the fundamental jobs of leaders. This is because evolutionary innovation is essential to an organization's survival and won't happen on its own.[6]

Having figured out how to determine whether evolutionary or revolutionary innovation is right for your organization, the problem to be solved here is how leaders can inspire, enable, and empower that evolutionary innovation. Fortunately, Tim Ogilvie, CEO of Peer Insight and coauthor of the book *Designing for Growth*, has a point of view on how to do this, which he recently shared in *Time*:

> Innovation depends on the three P's: Passion, Permission, and Protocols. (Natural innovators) run on Passion, get the little Permission they need from their VP, and. . .make their way without much in the way of formal innovation Protocols.[7]

---

[6]Bradt, George, 2013, "Inspiring, and Enabling Evolutionary Innovation—From Middle Managers," *Forbes* (February 14).

[7]*Time* online version: https://business.time.com/2012/08/17/how-to-get-innovation-from-the-big-middle/#ixzz2ALIo5qzx

Ogilvie went on to talk about the need to flip the formula with middle management, leading with permissions and protocols before adding passion. He then took George on a deeper journey through this approach.

Permission

Evolutionary innovation is generally prompted by solving a known problem where many creative solutions are possible. Permission involves asking people to solve that problem and giving them resources with which to do so. A lot of people in organizations who may be reluctant to step up as "innovators" are happy to help solve a problem when asked. So set the expectation by asking for help.

Then give them the physical and emotional space they need to innovate. 3M does this by explicitly calling on all its employees to spend 15 percent of their time working on something new. Google requires 20 percent. Problem solvers need relief from their day jobs to work on your problem. They also need a space in which to innovate. This could be a project room, their own web room, or an empty drier box, or tree house, but they need time and space that makes them feel safe and a deadline to produce their best answers.

Protocols

By definition, asking people to innovate is asking them to step out of their comfort zone. There will be a natural fear of failure. You need protocols to shift the frame away from success or failure and focus instead on learning. One of Ogilvie's main suggestions is to borrow from the scientific method: Ask people up to come up with hypotheses and design experiments to test them. A good experiment succeeds when it either proves or disproves the hypotheses. Teams treat experiments differently from tests. Conducting experiments taps into our natural curiosity, whereas performing tests can trigger a fear of failure.

Passion

Once they have been given permission and are supported by the right Protocols, these evolutionary innovators will naturally discover their Passion for creative problem-solving. Encourage these people. Give them permission to play and their enthusiasm will often infect others.

Some team members may not be at all excited about innovation. That's OK. Don't push them to innovate. Instead, invite them to contribute in some small way. Everyone likes to be thought of as a contributor.

The bottom line is that innovation is not an optional exercise. Darwin's lesson is that survival of the fittest is about those best able to adapt. Adapting requires innovation. You can't stand still. If you're not adapting and innovating, you are falling behind your innovating competitors. If you fall too far behind, your very survival comes into question.

So give your people permission to innovate by asking them to solve known problems. Put in place protocols that make it as easy as possible for people to innovate, and inspire a passion for innovation, problem-solving, or at least contributing.

Why Adding Constraints Increases Innovation

It is counterintuitive. You would think the more scope, time, and resources you have, the easier it would be to innovate. Chris Denson, director of Ignition Factory at Omnicom Media Group, says you would be wrong. He suggests, "The more limited you are, the more creative you have to be. Time constraints eliminate second guesses. Constraint is a unifier." This may explain why larger, resource-rich organizations struggle with revolutionary innovation.[8]

Let's look at Denson's points one by one.

Mission Constraint Is a Unifier.

HATCH's Yarrow Kraner described the constraints adventure hostel Selina's cofounder Rafi Museri has had to deal with

> to reimagine a new vertical, catering to a quickly evolving digital nomad audience, this group needed to move quickly, efficiently, and responsibly to scale at a pace that would put them on the map quickly, without breaking the bank. All of the furniture and fixtures are hand-crafted by up-cycling found trash, rubble, and debris and giving second life to previously consumed resources.

To accomplish scaling at this rate with such artisan craftsmanship, Selina's creative director Oz Zechovoy had been training ex-gang members to be carpenters, builders, and welders. They were quickly growing from 3 locations and then to 10 by the end of 2016 and to over

---

[8]Bradt, George, 2016, "Why Adding Constraints Increases Innovation," *Forbes* (March 9).

90 locations within the next 4 years, creating hundreds of new jobs and positively impacting Panama's economy.

In this case, the constraint forcing innovation was the overlapping missions: to build adventure hostels catering to the evolving digital nomad audience and, at the same time, to give products and people in Panama a second chance.

Time Constraints Eliminate Second Guesses.

An example of time constraints forcing innovation is found in the way NASA team members came together during the Apollo 13 crisis. Right from *"Houston, we've had a problem,"* the team reacted flexibly and fluidly to a dramatic and unwelcome new reality—a crippling explosion en route, in space.

The team went beyond its standard operating procedures and what its equipment was "designed to do" to exploring what it "could do." Through tight, on-the-fly collaboration, the team did in minutes what normally took hours, in hours what normally took days, and in days what normally took months. This innovation was critical to getting the crew home safely.

The constraint here was all about time. Not only was failure not an option, but success also had to come fast. Very fast. This imperative broke down all sorts of petty barriers, and got everyone rallied around what really mattered, leading to innovation out of necessity.

The More Resource Limited You Are, the More Creative You Have to Be.

Kraner described Kalu Yala as an example of just this:

> The world's most sustainable community—that started as a conscious real estate play, but the founder realized that it would take millions of dollars to build out a destination before attracting buyers, and flipped into an institution as its first priority, teaching while learning about sustainable best practices.

Can civilization and nature coexist? Can our diverse cultures coexist with each other?

The first phase and the foundation of the plan was the institute: an educational platform for students from around the world who are collecting, implementing, and documenting best practices in sustainable living. The work-study program had hosted students from all over the world from 25 countries and 150 colleges.

Kalu Yala's Jimmy Stice didn't set out to build an institute. But as he put it, "Constraints are what give a design its focus and ultimately, its true shape."

Implications

Innovation requires one of the only three types of creativity: connective, component, or blank page. The surprise is that these thrive on less resources rather than more. Don't overwater your plants, and don't over-resource your innovation:

- Narrow and focus the mission.
- Give tight deadlines.
- Limit resources.

If you need innovation, put people in a box with limited resources and a tight deadline. The real innovators will thrive on the challenge and find surprising, new, and perhaps revolutionary ways out of the box.

Why the Route to Creativity Runs Through Distress

Want to prompt creativity? Make someone unhappy. If people are happy, there's no need to change. But if people are faced with others or their own distress, they will work to find creative ways to bridge the gap from bad to good and unhappiness to happiness.[9]

Happiness is good—three goods: good for others, good at it, good for me. This means there are three opportunities to create distress: others' distress, distress from strengths mismatch, or personal distress.

Others' Distress

Many of society's advances were born out of someone's finding new, creative ways to solve others' problems. Fire was born out of the need for a better way to keep warm. Vaccinations were born out of the

[9]Bradt, George, 2017, "Why the Route to Creativity Runs Through Distress," *Forbes* (April 19).

need to protect people from diseases. Pet rocks were born out of the existential need for more meaningful holiday gifts. The list goes on and on.

Albert Einstein told us that we couldn't solve problems with the same level of thinking that created them. When some people's level of distress with others' unhappiness reaches a breaking point, they move to new levels of thinking and create new ways to solve the underlying problems.

Prompt creativity by helping people see others' needs.

Distress from Strengths Mismatch

The world needs different types of leaders: artistic, scientific, and interpersonal. Those leaders have different strengths and different ways of thinking. Some of the most creative ideas have come when those leaders are forced to think in different ways.

Doug Hall has been forcing people to do this for decades. Hall was trained as a chemical engineer and as a circus clown. He was a brand manager at Procter & Gamble, eventually becoming "master marketing inventor" there before starting his company Eureka Ranch. In its early days, Eureka Ranch drove creativity, stimulus, and fun and helped all sorts of business executives play outside of their comfort zone by deploying things like Nerf guns, water cannons, and whoopee cushions. (More on Hall later in this chapter.)

Howard Gardner suggests there are nine different types of intelligence:

1. Naturalist intelligence (nature smart)
2. Musical intelligence
3. Logical-mathematical intelligence (number/reasoning smart)
4. Existential intelligence (getting at the meaning of life)
5. Interpersonal intelligence (people smart)
6. Bodily-kinesthetic intelligence
7. Linguistic intelligence (word smart)
8. Intrapersonal intelligence (self smart)
9. Spatial intelligence (visual/picture smart)

Thus, stimulate different leaders' creativity by getting them to access different types of intelligence than they normally do.

- Stimulate artistic leaders outside of their visual, kinesthetic, musical, linguistic comfort zones.
- Stimulate scientific leaders outside of their naturalistic, logical-mathematical, existential comfort zones (though I'm not sure anyone is ever really comfortable pondering the meaning of life).
- Stimulate interpersonal outside of their intrapersonal and interpersonal comfort zones, getting them to think like artistic or scientific leaders.

This all comes down to prompting creativity by making people think or act in new ways.

Personal Distress

Brand communication agency Sid Lee's Will Travis will tell you that if the road to creativity runs through distress, the road to extreme creativity runs through extreme distress. Travis has climbed several of the world's highest summits, including Vinson Massif in Antarctica in the most brutal –45 °C conditions imaginable, motorbiked with the Paris Dakar, and traversed the 18,000 Khardung La pass in the Himalayas and generally put himself in extremely stressful situations.

These experiences have helped Travis both see things in different ways and keep things in perspective. As he put it,

> Facing situations of life and death implications elevates one's vision way above the severity of the business landscape, resulting in both centered and humanistic decision making, that business school nor mentors can never teach.

Travis uses this perspective to help the people he leads face and manage their own fears. It's painful when a client coldheartedly rejects a creative team's heart-invested work, but we have to keep it in perspective that it's not a life-threatening situation. Travis suggests, "You have to fail. Failure puts you in a friction zone, puts you in a zone where you have to make a decision, you have to change and do something different to survive and move on."

Systems

How to Lead the Change from Haphazard to Systematic Innovation

Almost everyone accepts the importance of innovation. Why then do most organizations do it so poorly? That's because innovation is generally random, haphazard, one-off, and outside the norm. Instead, make it systematic and part of your everyday culture.[10]

Hall is a master innovator, always innovating himself and helping others innovate. His book *Driving Eureka: Problem-Solving with Data-Driven Methods and the Innovation Engineering System* has easy-to-understand frameworks, processes, and ideas. Additionally, it also contains valuable tools, along with some of Hall's best stories.

The book's fundamental framework deploys:

- Blue cards to focus your efforts
- Starting with the customer problem as what matters and why
- A meaningfully unique framework
- Diversity of ideas to multiply your impact
- A systemic process

Blue Cards

Hall suggests using one set of cards—blue cards—to charter teams. These lay out your purpose, what you see as the very important opportunity or system improvement, clarity on whether you're looking for "LEAP" or "core" innovation on a long-term strategic or project-specific basis, whether this applies to the entire organization or a specific division or department, your name for the effort, a narrative describing how you got here, the strategic mission, strategic exclusions (barriers), tactical constraints (e.g., design, time, resources, investment, regulation), and areas for project exploration or long-term innovation.

Customer Problem

Hall has taken a classic positioning statement and repurposed it to help frame innovation efforts. The elements include:

---

[10]Bradt, George, 2018, "How to Lead the Change from Haphazard to Systematic Innovation," *Forbes* (November 13).

- Customer and problem (think target)
- Customer promise (think benefit)
- Product, service, system proof (think reason to believe)
- Meaningfully unique (dramatic difference)

Meaningfully Unique Framework

This is an evolution of the framework Hall has been using for literally decades.

> Meaningfully Unique = [Stimulus mining / Drive out fear] raised by diversity of thinking

His definition of meaningfully unique is that people will pay more for something.

Hall has been against pure brainstorming forever. He sees it as just sucking the useless stuff out of tired people. Instead, he suggests providing people stimuli to prompt new thinking through exploring, experiencing, and experimenting, building off his early days of creativity, stimulus, and fun. None of this works unless you can give people permission to innovate and remove their fear of failure, embarrassment, and punishment.

And the value of diverse perspectives, people, and ideas multiplies the impact of everything.

Diversity

One of Hall's favorite quotes through the years has been "In God we trust. All others must bring data." Data is an equalizer. Doing things like using Fermi estimating (breaking an estimate into discrete, bite-sized parts) help remove fear and make it easier for diverse people to participate. There's much more to be said about the value of diversity. Lack of diversity is one of the main reasons the highest-performing teams always fail over time.

Process

A core tenet of Hall's innovation engineering system is an easy-to-follow process: define, discover, develop, and deliver with plan–do–study–act cycles within it and a healthy dose of mind mapping to keep things moving. Blue cards charter groups that come up with ideas. Another set—yellow cards—helps groups track those ideas.

Yellow cards include idea headlines, customer–stakeholder, problem, promise, proof, price–cost, raw math, death threats (to the idea), and passion (why we care). They clarify whether the idea addresses a LEAP or core opportunity or system in line with the blue card used to charter the group.

In closing, Hall reminded George about the importance of

> leadership's role in the process of enabling the system of development. Recall 50+ percent of value is lost during development. Simply telling people what to do is not enough. Leadership needs to embrace a new mindset where they take responsibility for the systems of development. Command and control and leadership by numbers needs to be replaced with "Commanders Intent" and systems that enable innovation by everyone. Only the leadership can do this, as only the leadership has the responsibility and authority for the whole.

How Directed Iteration Brings Order to Creative Idea Generation

On one hand, you want to inspire and enable people to come up with the most outlandish, wonderful new ideas. On the other hand, you need to move forward in a way that all can follow. Break the trade-off with directed iteration around a *double l'enfant*. Innovation requires the mind of l'enfant (child). A great model for orderly progress was Pierre L'Enfant's long-term vision for a new Federal City, now Washington, D.C., and how to get there in steps. Marry the two with directed iteration, continually building on your current best thinking on the way to your long-term vision.[11]

Neri Oxman and the Mind of L'Enfant

Oxman suggests the beginner's mind is filled with innocence. "As a child you think you are shrinking when you see an airplane take off."

She's a big proponent of variations in kind—true innovations. She's convinced these come from "being vulnerable," not so much from solving a problem as from innocence and different worldviews. It's those different worldviews that allow innovators to come up with new-to-the-world solutions when problems do come.

---

[11]Bradt, George, 2018, "How Directed Iteration Brings Order to Creative Idea Generation," *Forbes* (May 1).

Preserving that innocence and wonder is essential in inspiring and enabling innovation. It's hard to do when constrained by the need to deliver reliable revenue and profit streams. This is why larger organizations tend to be better at evolutionary innovation and entrepreneurs tend to be better at revolutionary innovation.

Pierre L'Enfant

Washington, D.C., is relatively easy to navigate geographically. Planned in the late eighteenth century, lettered streets run east to west, and numbered streets run north to south. Avenues cut across in diagonals with large traffic circles, parks, malls, and public buildings placed appropriately. Contrast that to London, where taxi drivers have to study for 2 years to earn the knowledge to do their jobs, or Tokyo, where buildings in each 1 square mile zone are numbered in the order in which they were built and most streets do not have names. The difference is L'Enfant's long-term vision and plan.

After Thomas Jefferson agreed to support Alexander Hamilton's national finance plan in return for Hamilton's support for moving the capital to the banks of the Potomac River, Jefferson worked with L'Enfant on a plan for the city. Whereas Jefferson envisioned a relatively small grouping of government buildings, L'Enfant envisioned the people, organizations, and businesses that would inevitably be attracted to the new nation's capital. He began with a long-term vision for what the District of Columbia could be and then figured out how to get there in steps.

Directed Iteration

A critical step in the Battersea Arts Centre's (BAC's) scratch process is iteration. Their only objective is to come up with more interesting works of art. Given that, it doesn't really matter which road they take. (More on the scratch process in the next section.)

> Alice asked the Cheshire Cat, who was sitting in a tree, "What road do I take?"
>
> The cat asked, "Where do you want to go?"
>
> "I don't know," Alice answered.
>
> "Then," said the cat, "it really doesn't matter, does it?"
>
> **—Lewis Carroll, *Alice's Adventures in Wonderland***

When it does matter, use your long-term vision to direct those innovative iterations, continually improving current best thinking as iterative steps along the way to that destination. This is as much an attitude as an approach. Creative ideas are fragile things. They don't survive criticism well.

1. Start with long-term vision or the problem to be solved.
2. Unleash your minds to create ideas.
3. Take your current best thinking and ask, "What else would move us toward the long-term vision?"
4. Create more ideas.

How to Create and Assess Ideas Better: Merge IDEO's Human-Centered Design and BAC's Scratch

Going into more depth on the BAC's scratch process, the path to better ideas runs through creating, assessing, pausing, and then doing it again as appropriate. This is based on a few premises:

1. Beginnings are magic.
2. None of us is smart enough to make it perfect the first time.
3. All of us together are stronger than any one of us.
4. Breaks are good.[12]

The steps combine IDEO's human-centered design and the Battersea Arts Center's (BAC) Scratch.

Create

- Prepare by learning, listening, and observing patterns of behavior and points of pain and inconvenience.
- Generate ideas—with champions to carry them through.
- Develop a minimum viable products and rapid prototypes.

Assess

- Get responses from different users, peers, others.
- Analyze, filter, and decipher those responses.

[12]Bradt, George, 2017, "How to Create and Assess Ideas Better: Merge IDEO's Human-Centered Design and BAC's Scratch," *Forbes* (May 18).

Pause

- Take a break to think about something else and refresh your perspective.

Again?

- Modify what you had to evolve your best current thinking.
- Iterate until you're ready to.
- Implement.

The steps of IDEO's human-centered design process include:

1. Observation—patterns of behavior and points of pain and inconvenience
2. Ideation
3. Rapid prototyping (minimum viable product)
4. User feedback
5. Iteration
6. Implementation

The BAC's artistic director David Jubb explains their scratch process as a "structured framework for artists developing work in partnership with audience." Its steps include:

- *Idea:* Begin with a story, vision, challenge—with a champion to carry them through
- *Planning:* Develop an idea to a point where it can be tested.
- *Test:* Experiment, taking creative risks in public.
- *Feedback:* Listen and gather responses.
- *Analysis:* Filter and decipher feedback.
- *Time:* Take up space to think about something else.

Then, iterate back to a new improved idea.

In many ways, these are more detailed versions of the old total quality process of planning, doing, checking results, acting on the process, and returning to plan the next cycle.

Beginnings Are Magic.

Scratch and human-centered design both pivot off the *idea*. Whether you're an artistic leader trying to impact perceptions and feelings or a scientific leader who cares about solutions and knowledge, the spark is an idea, an inspiration, a testable hypothesis. These need to be championed, cared for, and nurtured throughout the process. They are the secret sauce, the magic.

Jubb agrees with that and goes on to say, "Part of Scratch is having the opportunity to feel like you're beginning, again and again, even when you've finished."

None of Us Is Smart Enough to Make It Perfect the First Time.

Webster defines *iteration* as "a procedure in which repetition of a sequence of operations yields results successively closer to a desired result." It defines *rework* as "to work again or anew." Iteration is planned, progressive, and positive. Rework is unanticipated, wasteful, and demoralizing.

A new analyst joined the U.S. State Department when Henry Kissinger was secretary of state. He worked for weeks on a paper and gave it to his boss, who passed it on to Kissinger. It came back with one note on the cover: "Not nearly good enough. Do it again."

The analyst worked all weekend and resubmitted. This time the note said, "Still not good enough. Do it again." The analyst worked all night. When his boss arrived, he asked permission to give the report to Kissinger himself.

Kissinger said, "This is the third time you've submitted this report. Is it absolutely, positively the best you can do?"

"Yes sir."

"In that case, I'll read it."

That's rework. Had Kissinger set clear expectations and provided helpful, progressive comments along the way, the analyst would have been able to do better, faster.

All of Us Together Are Stronger Than Any One of Us.

This goes to the value of getting feedback along the way from people with diverse perspectives and ideas. This is about co-creating in mutually productive discussions as opposed to selling the single best way to do something

Breaks Are Good.

There's value in walking away from something for a period of time and then coming back to it. Thomas Jefferson made a habit of putting letters aside overnight and relooking at them in the light of day. Give yourself mental and physical breaks to create space and see things anew. Start by taking a break before you reread this particular section.

Why You Should Eliminate Your Chief Innovation Officer

The whole premise behind a chief innovation officer goes beyond useless to completely and utterly counterproductive. If one person is in charge of innovation, everyone else is not—and they must be. Anyone not innovating is falling behind those that are. Charles Darwin taught us that that is a bad thing. So: no chief innovative officers. No distinctions between scientific, artistic, and interpersonal leaders. Everyone is responsible for innovating, creating, and leading.[13]

From STEM to STEAM

At HATCH Latin America, Creative Coalition president actor Tim Daly explained to George why this is so important. He was one of the innovators and communicators at a session with President Barack Obama in early 2009. As they discussed the science, technology, engineering, and mathematics (STEM) education initiative to boost these subjects, Daly asked, "Where's the A? It's the arts that put engineering and technology in the human context. Arts are the emissaries and custodians of our culture." Thus, STEM became STEAM (science, technology, engineering, arts, and mathematics).

The argument for including arts in education is compelling. Daly shared some data:

- 70–80 percent of young people who get out of jail in Los Angeles go back. That drops to 6 percent for young people who take part in the Inside Out creative writing workshop.
- 30 percent of U.S. high school students drop out, but students who have taken arts programs through middle school are three times more likely to graduate than the norm.

[13]Bradt, George, 2016, "Why You Should Eliminate Your Chief Innovation Officer," *Forbes* (March 16).

- When you factor in the costs of recidivism and failure, an investment in youth arts programs returns $7 for every $1 spent.

This is why Daly "became radicalized about the importance of arts and art education." As he puts it, science is "meaningless" without arts. Artists make people feel.

Daly led a breakout group at HATCH on arts and education. One of its ideas was how to move people's view of art from dangerous to irrelevant to being part of the answer. The idea was to involve all three of the different types of leaders the world needs: tapping the scientific leaders for the rational, data, value, and brain science arguments; the artistic leaders for the emotional connection and stories, and interpersonal leaders to deal with the politics and business of getting funding and support.

No False Trade-Offs

Innovation is too important to be left to the chief innovation officer. Everyone must innovate. Everyone must create whether they prefer connective, component, or blank page creativity. Science is too important to be left to the scientists. Everyone needs to understand science, technology, engineering, and math. And everyone needs to leverage their own artistic side to communicate facts in a way that taps into emotions and sparks value-creating behaviors.

However, as one chief innovation officer explained to George, when making a cultural shift (like following a merger or acquisition), a chief innovation officer "*can* be an effective catalyst for change, as long as that person's charter is to create the right conversations and underlying business processes that connect the appropriate functions in a powerful and integrated way."

Break the trade-offs with some good old-fashioned gap bridging:

1. *Get everyone aligned around a shared purpose*. Without a shared picture of your mission, vision, and values, nothing else is going to work. Determine where you are going to play and what matters and why.
2. *Build a common understanding of the current reality*. Take a cold, hard, dispassionate view of the facts around where you stand with regard to your customers, collaborators, capabilities, competitors, and conditions in which you operate. Remember that adding constraints actually increases innovation.

3. *Bridge the gaps*. Work through and implement choices around how you are going to win, how you're going to connect, and the impact you are going to have. This is where you mash up your scientific, artistic, and interpersonal leaders so they can leverage their individual strengths and preferences to innovate, create, and communicate together.

Words matter. So do eliminate chief innovation officer titles to help inspire and enable everyone to do their absolute best together to realize a meaningful and rewarding shared purpose.

Three Imperatives for Service Innovation

Innovating in a service-focused business works best if the innovations are (1) aligned with your core purpose, (2) meet a future consumer need, and (3) can be executed by your organization.[14]

Noodles CEO Kevin Reddy explained this model to George and how it works at his organization. Since dining out is a truly discretionary expense for every one of Noodles' customers, it must deliver a superior experience every time every customer comes through its doors. Ultimately, we're all in service businesses, so this applies to all of us.

Align Around a Shared Purpose

People in the organization must understand, believe, and act on its core purpose. Reddy knows that any innovation and change must flow from, and contribute to, that core purpose, connecting with both current and new guests.

In Noodles' case this is about how it defines the dining experience, which Reddy summarized as "really good food, served by genuinely nice people, in a friendly, welcoming place."

Noodles differentiates itself by providing quicker service and a finer dining experience than other casual restaurants (though not as quick as quick serve or as fine as fine dining). It is about delivering a superior dining experience at a great value in terms of financial and time costs.

---

[14]Bradt, George, 2013, "Three Imperatives for Service Innovation," *Forbes* (February 20).

Understand Future Consumer Needs

Innovation is forward-looking. Solving yesterday's problems is important but not innovative. Copying what others do well is often a good approach, but it is not innovative. Reddy suggests that innovation starts with knowing and believing in where consumer needs are going, then creating a picture of what's important, followed by "inspiring and motivating people to embrace that vision."

Thus, "true innovation is about taking risk." Reddy's steps are:

1. Choose the future consumer needs you are going to focus on.
2. Create a picture of what success is.
3. Get clear on the behaviors required to get there.

Do the Doable

Armed with possible ideas, Reddy suggests the next step is "really understanding what our system can execute." It's a truism that a good idea poorly executed is not worth anything. Reddy and his team make sure the ideas build on their core purpose, move the organization toward where consumers are heading, and then make sure the whole organization:

1. Believes in and is passionate about the innovation
2. Is clear about how to bring the innovation to life
3. Has the training and tools required to execute

Reddy gave George a good example of a Noodles' innovation. Surprise. Much of the "really good food" Noodles serves is noodle-based. (Who would have thunk?) Consumers are valuing more and more ethnic variety in their food options. So Noodles is serving an increasing array of global flavors.

One option is Japanese Pan Noodles. It's a consumer-driven idea in line with Noodles' core purpose. But execution is key as there's a "dramatic difference between getting it right and getting it almost right—with the consumer being really pleased and not happy." Exactly 3 minutes is required to get the right caramelization; 15 seconds too little or too much doesn't work. Since Noodles is committed to going from order to delivery in 5 minutes, these 15 seconds count.

Japanese Pan Noodles work because they are in line with Noodles' purpose, meet an emerging consumer need, and can be delivered well—as must your innovations.

Take these innovation tips and strategies into consideration as you build out your strategic, commercial, operational, and financial plans and drive success with your M&A or PE deal.

The most up-to-date, full, editable versions of all tools are downloadable at primegenesis.com/tools.

TOOL 4.1

BRAVE Innovation

Environment: Where to play? (Context)

Start with a shared understanding of your organization's innovation needs.

Values: What matters and why? (Purpose)

Reconfirm organization's mission, vision, and guiding principles to guide everything else you do.

Attitudes: How to win? (Choices)

Aim your efforts at business concepts and models and not just product and service inventions and improvements.

Relationships: How to connect? (Communication)

Behaviors: What impact? (Implementation)

DEFINE *(Purpose—team charter)*

DISCOVER/CREATE *(Creative abrasion and collaborative problem-solving)*—leverage diverse strengths

DEVELOP AND ITERATE *(Creative agility and discovery-driven learning)*—"Current Best Thinking"

ASSESS *(Creative resolution and integrated decision-making)*—drowning ugly ducklings

DELIVER, IMPLEMENT, AND SCALE

PART II

The Commercial Playbook

CHAPTER 5

Organic Revenue Growth: So Valuable

	The Strategic Playbook	The Commercial Playbook	The Operational Playbook	The Financial Playbook	The Governance Playbook	The Organizational Playbook	The Change Management Playbook
Concept Research Investment Case Negotiation Deal/Due Diligence Contract Close Integration Acceleration Next Normal	The Investment Case Focus Plans Innovation	Organic Revenue Growth Customers Marketing & Sales	Cost Optimization Operational Excellence: Supply Chain, Distribution, Continual Improvement Technology	Deal/ Due Diligence Financing M&A	Regulatory Financial Board	Culture Incentives Leadership People Politics	Integration Leader Change Management Communication Announcement Adjustments

The first component of the commercial playbook is organic revenue growth because the commercial playbook focuses on revenue. The next two components—customers and marketing and sales—go into more depth. Costs get picked up in the operational playbook, and inorganic growth through further mergers and acquisitions (M&A) gets picked up in the financial playbook.

Growing organic revenue requires marketing and sales efforts. Let's use Philip Kotler's definition of marketing: "the science and art of exploring, creating, and delivering value to satisfy the needs of a target market at a profit."[1] Sales then converts that value into transactions.

Every sales funnel that ever was is a variation of awareness–interest–desire–action.

[1]Per https://kotlermarketing.com/phil_questions.shtml.

Awareness

⇨ Interest

⇨ Desire

⇨ Action

The pivot is desire. If you don't have a product or service that others are going to value, nothing else matters.

Generally, marketing owns the top of the funnel, generating awareness, and fueling interest. Again, generally, sales turns that desire into action. With that in mind, growing the top-line has to involve new customers or current customers buying more or paying more.

Mergers enable this with cross-selling, new ways, new products, new geographies, end markets and new technologies.

Cross-selling is the art and science of getting the customers of one of the formerly separate entities to buy the products or services of the other entity or entities either in existing or new markets (geographies or end markets).

Awareness: Making them aware of the other products or services

⇨ Interest: Making it easier for them to learn about or access the other products or services

⇨ Desire: Focusing on the products or services that best meet unmet needs

⇨ Action: Sales shepherding conversion, perhaps with bundled sales

Getting existing customers to use current products or services in new ways is the art and science of moving those new ways through the funnel.

Awareness: Making them aware of the other uses

⇨ Interest: Helping them understand and enabling the new uses

⇨ Desire: Focusing on the new uses that meet unmet needs

⇨ Action: Sales shepherding conversion, leading with information

New products in this case means the new products or services enabled by the merger or acquisition. These could come from:

- New innovation, technologies, and design capabilities enabling the invention of products and services that the separate entities could not have invented themselves
- New production capabilities enabling the actual production of new products and services that could not have been produced before
- New distribution capabilities enabling the distribution of new products and services that could not have been distributed before
- New service capabilities enabling the service of new products and services that could not have been serviced before

The common thread is the elimination of constraints.

Each approach will require its own go-to-market and end customer market pursuit strategies driving trial, repeat, continuity, or stocking as appropriate.

Marketing, Communications, and Customer Interface

Some basics almost always apply around mission, marketing objectives, and overarching marketing approach:

- Discuss the current mission and go-forward strategy.
- Agree on internal and external communication preferences and strategy.
- Enhance website for use as both a marketing tool and current customer tool.
- Assess and build out digital marketing presence.
- Consider establishing marketing point people based on the organization's core focus:
  - Someone to obtain, assess, and channel consumer and customer insights in a design-focused organization
  - A business-to-business marketing expert in a production-focused organization

- A partnership or alliance lead in a distribution-focused organization
- A marketing experience lead in a service-focused organization

Sales Model and Organization

Similarly, the sales organization will be different in different organizations, targeting primarily new users (design,) other businesses (production), a broad ecosystem (delivery), or customer experience (service). In almost all cases, you'll need to:

- Build out customer relationship management (CRM) focused on pipeline, forecast, customer profitability, and estimates.
- Assess existing sales models and determine if a strategy focused on specific industry verticals or a regional or geographically focused model would be more appropriate.
- Determine the go-forward customer growth strategy and balance of focus between new customer pursuits and upselling existing customers.
- Determine incremental sales resources required to pursue new customers, expand point of sale and point of purchase service offering, and execute the go-to-market strategy.
- Assess current sales commission and incentive plan and align with sales targets, organizational strategy, and industry standards.

On this last, understand that sales people are different animals from others in the organization. In general, long-term incentives help align leadership and owners around value-creation goals. Sales people work line of sight. The more you can make their incentive plan look like a commission on sales they make, the better. This will be discussed more in the later playbooks since incentives are critical to the success of the merger or private equity (PE) deal.

Customer Profitability

Dissect customer profitability with a profitability cube. Then link to renewals and develop a tracking and reporting system:

- Prepare a customer profitability cube that quantifies historical contribution margin by customer, product, and end market. Establish the customer profitability cube as a new embedded process within the company to help make marketing and pricing decisions, translating this into the most motivating terms you can for sales people.
- Link current customer profitability realization to impending customer renewals to ensure pricing is appropriate.
- Develop a long-term solution for tracking and reporting customer profitability and accurate job costing with a link back to the pricing and estimating process.
- Develop a cash flow view for each customer, end market, and geography as many costs and investments are not covered in the profit and loss (P&L), such as capital and working capital.

End Market Analysis and Go-to-Market Strategy

Think through markets and customer needs to focus your solutions:

- Further analyze existing customer end markets to understand projected growth rates, anticipated demand by product or service offering, market share opportunities for both existing and prospective customers, and profitability and cash flow profiles and investment required to execute future growth strategies. This helps target your marketing and sales efforts.
- Strategically identify and select new customers targets and end markets to pursue. The flip side of this is being clear which customers and markets you choose not to serve.
- Determine future offering strategy and investment required.
- Identify and implement solution for improved front-end customer-facing technology.
- Acquisitions or mergers with other companies, brands, technologies, and systems.

Here, we're referencing the impact of these on organic growth. We'll deal with the inorganic growth in Chapter 6.

- Build business development office or increase your business development capabilities to plan, develop, and implement an M&A strategy to build the capabilities you need to drive organic growth.
- Create that M&A strategic plan and then outreach to selected targets identified through lender groups or others.
- Identify investment banks and others specializing in industry for potential transactions—especially if not private equity owned.
- Build out state-of-company capabilities and verticals to analyze key areas to target M&A.
- Build out competitive positioning for the company in terms of M&A.

CHAPTER 6

Customers: From Which All New Value Flows

	The Strategic Playbook	The Commercial Playbook	The Operational Playbook	The Financial Playbook	The Governance Playbook	The Organizational Playbook	The Change Management Playbook
Concept	The Investment Case					Culture	Integration Leader
Research Investment Case		Organic Revenue Growth	Cost Optimization	Deal/ Due Diligence	Regulatory	Incentives	Change Management
Negotiation Deal/Due Diligence	Focus		Operational Excellence: Supply Chain, Distribution, Continual Improvement	Financing	Financial	Leadership	Communication
Contract Close	Plans	Customers		M&A	Board	People	Announcement
Integration Acceleration Next Normal	Innovation	Marketing & Sales	Technology			Politics	Adjustments

The customers component of the commercial playbook goes into more depth on this aspect of organic revenue growth. A key focus of a mergers and acquisitions (M&A) deal or private equity (PE) investment is around incremental organic revenue growth.

The most important point in this chapter is to reinforce the approach of working through customers, people, capabilities, and costs—in that order. First, figure out how you're going to win with customers. This chapter is all about customers.

Customers are the people your organization sells to or serves or could sell to. These comprise direct customers who actually give you money, along with their customers, their customers' customers, and so on down the line. Eventually, there are end users or consumers of whatever the output of that chain is. Additionally, there are the people who influence your various customers' purchase decisions. Take all of these into account from the consumer back.

Consumers are the people that actually ingest, wear, use, or experience your product or service. They are the ultimate C in a chain of SIPOCs (supplier–input–process–output–customer). They add no value to your product or service, no further design, no further production, no further distribution, no further service. When they are done, your product or service is consumed.

Start with them. Figure out their needs, hopes, and desires. Figure out what other product or services they might consume instead of yours. Figure out the value you add to their lives or businesses and what they would be willing to pay for that—the value equation. It is important to think through technology disruption and how to stay ahead of the competition (even those competitors who don't exist today), discussed more in other chapters.

$$\text{VALUE (relative, perceived)} = f\,\frac{\text{BENEFITS (relative, perceived)}}{\text{COSTS (relative, perceived)}\ \text{(money, time, stress, etc.)}}$$

Relative perceived *value* = function of relative perceived *benefits* / relative perceived *costs*

The ultimate benefits are emotional feelings derived from positive features. Costs include money, time, and stress.

Who or what would you say are Coca-Cola and Walt Disney World's main competitors? (Hint: it's not Pepsi and Universal Studios.) We're oversimplifying a little to make a point. But when a Coca-Cola–drinking 12-year-old walks into a convenience store with a pocket full of change, their real decision is not Coke versus Pepsi but, rather, Coke versus a bar of chocolate or an ice cream popsicle.

Actually, Coke has different competitors in different situations. The 12-year-old is looking for a treat. Someone getting off a soccer pitch after a hard workout is looking for liquid replenishment. A worker trying to stay awake in the middle of the afternoon is looking for energy. And so on.

Disney World's main competitor is college educations. It turns out many middle-income families put aside money each year to pay for their children's college education. Some of them will take 1 year and use that year's savings to pay for a once-in-a-lifetime trip to Disney World.

Of course, in that example, the parents are partly consumers and, even more importantly, the purchasers.

Purchasers

Purchasers pay money. Dogs consume dog food, but they don't purchase it. Of course, in some cases like the Disney trip, purchasers are consumers as well. But it's often helpful to think about them differently.

Strategic Sales

One of the key steps in the Miller Heiman methodology of the strategic selling process is identifying the buying influences involved (economic, user, technical, coach):

- Economic buyers give final approval as the single person or group who can say yes when others say no and can veto other buyers' approval.
- User buyers use the product and, as their success is tied to it, make judgments about impact. There may be several.
- Technical buyers screen out options. They focus on the product and service, can't give final yes, but often give a final no. There may be several technical buyers at the same time.
- Coaches help you navigate the buying organization and identify other buying influences. They may work for the buying organization, your organization, or neither.

We could go into more detail on this—but you know enough to go on to the next chapter.

CHAPTER 7

Marketing and Sales: Which Every Organization Must Do

	The Strategic Playbook	The Commercial Playbook	The Operational Playbook	The Financial Playbook	The Governance Playbook	The Organizational Playbook	The Change Management Playbook
Concept	The Investment Case					Culture	Integration Leader
Research		Organic Revenue Growth	Cost Optimization	Deal/ Due Diligence			
Investment Case					Regulatory	Incentives	Change Management
Negotiation			Operational Excellence: Supply Chain, Distribution, Continual Improvement				
Deal/Due Diligence	Focus			Financing	Financial	Leadership	Communication
Contract		Customers					
Close	Plans			M&A	Board	People	Announcement
Integration		Marketing & Sales					
Acceleration	Innovation		Technology			Politics	Adjustments
Next Normal							

The marketing and sales component of the commercial playbook gets at how to drive organic revenue growth with customers. With a new merger and acquisition (M&A) or private equity (PE) deal, this is the lifeblood of driving incremental value and coupled with the other playbooks driving success for your deal.

As noted before, every marketing and sales funnel there ever was is a variation of AIDA: awareness, interest, desire, action. It's all about helping prospects move through the funnel. This chapter lays out the basic steps of AIDA to do that by working through four tools:

Tool 7.1 Purchase and Sales Funnel Management—essentially an overview

Tool 7.2 Marketing Planning

Tool 7.3 Creative Brief

Tool 7.4 Strategic Selling—elaborating on more complex sales

Note the most up-to-date, full, editable versions of all tools are downloadable at primegenesis.com/tools

Tool 7.1: Purchase and Sales Funnel Management

Awareness: Step 1 Is Making People Aware of Your Offering—You to Them

This is going to be different depending on the size of your target audience. If it's a small set, you can reach out to them and those influencing them directly. If it's a broader set, you'll likely need some sort of mass media like TV, radio, print, online, and streaming. In any case, remember the objective is awareness—broad and shallow. So don't invest too much in any one person. This is generally a marketing function, with sales less involved.

Interest: Step 2 Is Fueling Interest in Your Offering—You and Them Together

Some of those aware of your offering will express an interest. This is where you start a conversation either live or virtually. By definition, conversations are two-way. You want to learn more about them as they are learning more about you and your offerings. Note some of these conversations may go on for extended periods of time.

If it's a more sophisticated, complex business-to-business (B2B) sale, this is where sales gets involved:

- Identify *buying influences*: economic, user, technical buyers, coaches—their response modes (growth, trouble, even-keeled, overconfident,) and their win-results and red flags.
- Develop a *sales strategy* to get the right people in front of the right buyers with the right messages at the right places at the right time over time.
- Think through and deploy *components of conceptual selling*: understand the customers' concept[1] of what they want to happen, generate ideas to help with that, and select the best option.

---

[1]"We are not here to sell a parcel of boilers and vats, but the potentiality of growing rich beyond the dreams of avarice." Samuel Johnson

- Implement with *single sales objectives* for each sales call moving people from unaware to aware to understanding and interested to believing and desiring to action step by step—outline proposition, presell proposition, propose solution, close, follow up.

Desire: Step 3 Is Responding to Their Desire for Your Offering—Them to You

In general, what triggers the jump from interest to desire is a change in their situation or ambition. At this point, your job is to help them understand how your offering can meet their needs better than any other option. If it doesn't, point them to an offering that does. If it does, help them move to action.

Action: Step 4 Is Closing the Sale and Moving the Prospect to Action—You to Them

If your offering meets their needs better than any other option, consider the momentum close. Make it as easy as possible for them to say yes at every step. Often this involves a trial offering to let them get a taste of what your full offering can do for them on the way to making ever larger and larger commitments.

Notes on Building Up Your Sales Team

- Recruit with the right *strengths,* including hunters, innovators, and strategists (to bring in new accounts); farmers (to nurture and develop existing accounts); managers (to direct efforts of salespeople); and an operational team to recruit, train, coordinate, track, support sales, and serve customers.
- Build the right *tracking* systems to understand activities, the impact of those activities, and the effect of those impacts as prospects move through the funnel.

Awareness building

Awareness-building activities (costs)

Leads generated by activities (cost and prospect)

Attempts to connect with leads

Connections with leads or opt out

Interest
Agreement to receive further information (opportunities) or opt out

Agreement to meet or opt out

Desire
Proposal

Action
Purchase (cost and order) or opt out

- *Train* your sales team on potential prospects' hopes and needs, on your offering and how it meets those hopes and needs, and on your tracking systems.
- *Leverage* your tracking systems to understand what's working well and less well so managers can redirect sales efforts and training as appropriate.

Tool 7.2: Marketing Planning

Environment: Where to Play?

Context

Start with a 6Cs analysis:

- *Customers:* Revisit your thinking on customers from Chapter 6 and lay out first-line customers, the customer chain, end users and consumers, influencers. Look across geographic, demographic, behavioral, and market segments. Dig into growth rates, trends, preferences, needs, hopes, commitment, strategies, price–value perspective by segment.
- *Collaborators:* Look at suppliers, business allies, outsource opportunities, government and community leaders, allies—needs, hopes, preferences, commitment, strategies, price–value perspective by group.
- *Culture:* Behaviors, relationships, attitudes, values, and environment.
- *Capabilities:* Core human, operational, financial, technical, and key asset capabilities.
- *Competition:* Look at your direct, indirect, and potential competitors. Look at the different types of competitors, in different

locations, for different products. Understand your competitors strategies, profit-value models and their profit pools by segment, as well as their source of pride.

- *Conditions:* Social, cultural, demographic, political, governmental, regulatory, economic and technological, market definition—inflows, outflows, and substitutes; health; climate trends.

Then look at your:

- *Current position:* Markets, market share, buyers, why buy, life cycle (introduction, growth, maturity, decline, exiting).

Bring it together with a SWOT analysis if not already in the plans section: => Insights regarding leverage points and business issues

Values: What Matters and Why?

Purpose, including the organization's overall mission (Why?) vision (What?) and values:

- *How marketing fits* within that and helps move things in that direction.

Attitude: How to Win?

Overall organizational or commercial strategy including value proposition:

- *Marketing strategy:* Broad choices (How?). Be clear on what aspects of marketing need to be predominant (top 1 percent), superior (top 10 percent), strong (top 25 percent), competitive (above average), good enough or not do (outsource or not do at all).
- *Positioning:* This may be the most important marketing tool. Get this right:
  - *Target:* Customer and problem the customer needs solved.
  - *Frame of reference:* Other choices the customer could or should consider.
  - *Benefit:* Promise—meaningfully unique. All benefits are ultimately emotional.

- *Support and attributes:* Permission to believe (product, service, system proof).
- *Brand character, attitude, and voice:* Who we are.

Why It's Crucial to Align Brand Positioning with the Essence of Your Organization

Everything communicates—everything you do and say and don't do and don't say internally and externally. Given that, aligning what you say about your brand with what you do and what you are as an organization has to make sense. Do that by connecting every aspect of your brand positioning with the essence of your organization.[2] Apple and the Four Seasons do this particularly well.

This happens at the intersection of three frameworks:

Brand positioning: Target; frame of reference; benefit; support and attributes; brand character, attitude, and voice.

Core focus: Design, produce, deliver, service.

BRAVE leadership: Where play? What matters and why? How win? How connect? What impact?

Positioning is all about setting yourself apart from your competition in the mind of your customer. There is an old Procter & Gamble list of ways to be competitive. In descending order of impact, that list is:

1. *Superiority* on some benefit or attribute that meets customer needs significantly better than competition or than an enlarged or reduced set of competition, perhaps going all the way to focusing on one competitor's point of weakness—claims, comparisons, side-by-side demos.
2. *Distinctive* product benefit, emotional benefit, attribute, or character that no one else is offering or talking about.
3. *Communicating* your offering better than your competition through a distinctive selling idea, claim versus a standard of excellence, leveraging loyal customers, portraying before and

[2]Bradt, George, 2022, "Why It's Crucial to Align Brand Positioning with the Essence of Your Organization," *Forbes* (January 18).

after situations, torture tests, setting up a special problem only your brand can solve, expert endorsement.

Aligning Brand Positioning

Now, let's cross the three frameworks:

- *Target* is another way of asking where to play.
- *Frame of reference* sets up whom you need to beat to win with your target.
- *Benefit* must, must, must match up with what matters and why and your design, produce, deliver, or service focus. This is the heart of be–do–say integrity and exactly what Simon Sinek gets at in his why–how–what golden circle *TED Talk*.[3]
- *Support* or permission to believe is all about how to win.
- *Character* is to your brand what culture is to your organization. People care what they buy and whom they buy from. Make your external brand character match your internal brand culture or pay the price when you get found out.

So, as you think through your brand positioning, make sure:

- Your *target* matches the set of customers and problems the organization chooses to serve.
- Your organization is actually competing against those called out in your *frame of reference*.
- Your organization delivers the *benefit* you're promising. Promises of new or innovative require design focus. Promises of reliability or confidence require production focus. Speed promises require delivery focus. Experience promises require service focus.
- Your organization is investing to win by being predominant (top 1 percent), superior (top 10 percent), or, at least, strong (top 25 percent) in the areas *supporting* your promised benefit while being above average or competitive, good enough or scaled, or outsourcing or not doing other things.
- Your brand *character* fits the organization culture.

---

[3]Sinek, Simon, 2010, "How Great Leaders Inspire Action," *TED Talk* (May 4).

Aspirations

This is, of course, harder for organizations at points of inflection. In these cases, there may be a gap between the aspirational and current organization and culture. It's tempting to jump to an aspirational brand positioning at the same time. Be careful not to get too far ahead of your truth. It's better to underpromise and overdeliver than the alternative:

- *Product/services:* Features and benefits like quality, scope, warranty, packaging, and service.
- *Packaging:* Which serves both as a primary container, secondary container, and communication channel or display. Witness how much time children spend looking at cereal boxes.
- *Pricing:* Premium, penetration, economy, bundling, promotional, list, discount, bundling, payment terms, leasing, and so forth.
- *Place:* Distribution channels, channel margins, locations, logistics—transport, warehouse, order fulfill.
- *Promotion and advertising or communication:* Networking, direct marketing, advertising, training programs, writing and articles, publicity and press releases, trade shows, fairs, events, website, newsletters and e-zines, e-books, affiliate programs, search engine optimization, sampling (i.e., charity auctions), sponsorships, contests, online auction, merchandising—collateral you'll need.
- *Promotion strategy:* Trial, repeat, continuity, stocking.

The creative brief, Tool 7.3, can help here.

Sales strategy: Who's going to contact whom, when, how frequently, and so forth.

Sales team training: Keep reading, and also see Tool 7.4 on strategic selling.

Strategic relationships: Who's going to help you.

New business development: Either selling more to existing customers (farming) or bringing in new customers (hunting).

Launch plan approach: Pulling together all the aspects of the work effort.

Ongoing research, insights: To keep learning and evolving.

Marketing budget and allocation across efforts: Because strategies are theoretically elegant and practically useless until they are resourced.

Relationships: How to Connect

There are choices to make about how to spark relationships to (1) build awareness, (2) deepen relationships at interest level, and (3) turn prospects desire into action.

- *Sales approach:* What getting done by when by whom with what resources?
- *Buyers:* Build relationships with the different types of buyers: economic, user, technical, and coaches. Understanding the business results and personal wins each seeks.

Behaviors: What Impact

- *Specific plans* to move people through AIDA funnel with checklists, milestones, and timing.
- *Expected competitive reaction:* Because you can't gain share without someone losing share. Think through how others may react and what you're going to do then.
- *Other risks:* Think through the things you can't control, the unintended consequences of your actions, and contingency plans.

Tool 7.3: Creative Brief

Begin with a *project description*. This is much more than a summary. Each part may be important:

- *Opportunity:* The problem to be solved or the opportunity to be captured, leading with *why* this work needs to be done in the first place.
- *Approach:* The general approach to solving the problem or capturing the opportunity. Is this advertising, public relations, external or internal communications, or something else?
- *Output:* The specific creative expected to be delivered whether it's a page, poster, complete program, or something else.
- *Timing:* When the output should be delivered.
- *Logistics:* How the person or organization being briefed should work with the person or organization briefing them.

- *Decision-making:* Clarity around who will make key decisions. A RACI (Responsible, Accountable, Consulted, Informed) can help here:
  - Commissioning authority or customer
  - Accountable: The person called to account. Overall ownership of results. Drives decisions. Ensures implementation.
  - Responsible: Does work defined and delegated by accountable person.
  - Consulted: Provides expertise-based input (to be considered) and/or direction/concurrence (to be followed)—Two-way conversations.
  - Informed: In advance or after the fact—One-way communication.
  - Support: Assist in completing the work.

Resources

The people that will be involved full-time, part-time, or as part of the RACI

Budget for the work itself

Operational tools to assist the person being briefed

- *Accountabilities:* Specific accountabilities of the person being briefed including milestones and their timing on the way to the overall deliverable.
- *Consequences:* Expected impact on the universe, world, customers, the organization, and the person being briefed.
- *How to leverage the win:* What will happen after the work is completed.

Environment: Where to Play—Context (with More Rather Than Less Detail to Spark Ideas)

1. *Customers:* First-line, customer chain, end users, influencers—needs, hopes, preference, commitment, strategies, price and value perspective by segment.
2. *Collaborators:* Suppliers, business allies, partners, government and community leaders—needs, hopes, preferences, commitment, strategies, price, and value perspective by group.
3. *Culture:* Behaviors, relationships, attitudes, values, environment.

4. *Capabilities:* Core human, operational, financial, technical, and key asset capabilities.
5. *Competitors:* Direct, indirect, potential—strategies, profit–value models, profit pools by segment, source of pride.
6. *Conditions:* Social and demographic; political, government, and regulatory; economic; market definition; inflows, outflows, and substitutes; health, climate trends, and implications.

=> Insights drawn from these (So what?):
Maybe the most important part of the brief

Values: What Matters and Why

Purpose including the organization's overall mission (Why?), vision (What?), and values as well as how this project fits within that and helps move things in that direction. Summarize this as "To [do some mission] so that [some vision is achieved]."

- *Objective:* General statement of what trying to accomplish.
- *Organization's overall purpose:* Write down so those being briefed have it in front of them so they understand *why* they need to do what they are doing.
- *Fit:* Be explicit about how this work will move the organization toward its purpose.

Attitude: How to Win

- *Strategy:* Broad choices (How?). Be clear on what aspects of the work need to be superior, parity with the best, strong or above average, good enough or minimum viable, or out of scope and avoided. If this is advertising, this is where you would capture the copy strategy. If this is communication, this is where you would capture the communication strategy. And so on.
- *Overall organizational or commercial strategy, including value proposition:* Write this down so the person, team, or organization being briefed has it in front of them so they understand how the strategy for this work fits into the overall organization's strategy.

- *Positioning:* Target, frame of reference, benefit, support and attributes—permission to believe; brand character, attitude, and voice.
  - *Target:* Customer and problem the customer needs solved.
  - *Frame of reference:* Other choices the customer could or should consider.
  - *Benefit:* Promise—meaningfully unique. All benefits are ultimately emotional.
  - *Support and attributes:* Permission to believe—product, service, system proof.
  - *Brand character, attitude, and voice:* Who we are.
- *Posture* goes hand in hand with strategy and adds richness to the strategy choices. Get at the organization's bias to be proactive: either fast follower, prepared or responsive.

Relationships: How to Connect

Mandatory elements focused on the few critical elements that will drive the connection with the target audience. These could include components like visuals, selling idea, look, voice, communication points, information, and media and channels. Be clear on mandatory brand equities and mandatory execution equities like the mandated inclusion of a "psssss" sound when the Folger's coffee can was opened and we see the steaming coffee pour. Tell the people doing the work where they have freedom and where they don't:

- *Visuals (or sounds):* Be specific about logos and images that must be included.
- *Selling idea:* If this is a piece of an already existing campaign, be specific about the selling idea.
- *Look:* Be clear on any guidelines, preconceptions, or biases around the overall look and feel of the creative.
- *Voice:* Be clear on any guidelines, preconceptions, or biases around the overall voice of the creative.
- *Communication points:* Be clear on any guidelines, preconceptions, or biases around specific communication points that should be included.

- *Information:* Be clear on any guidelines, preconceptions, or biases around specific information that should be included.
- *Media and channels:* Be clear on any guidelines, preconceptions, or biases around specific media or channels in which the creative will be deployed.

Behaviors: What Impact

- *Desired response:* How the target will move through AIDA (aware–interest–desire–action) after experiencing the creative.
- *AIDA progress:* Lay out the "from–to" progress this creative should accomplish, such as:
  - This creative will make the target aware.
  - This creative will spark interest in those already aware.
  - This creative will fuel desire in those interested.
  - This creative will cause the target audience to act in this way.

Tool 7.4: Strategic Selling

This is a cheat sheet for Miller and Heiman's strategic selling steps.

1. Set the single sales objective:
   a. Make it specific, measurable, timelined, outcome focused
   b. You'll want one single objective for each sales call, moving people from unaware to aware to understanding and interested to believing and desiring to action step by step.
   c. For each sales call or step, set a specific objective, know how you're going to measure success, set a time target, and drive toward an outcome.
2. Identify the buying influences involved (economic, user, technical, coach):
   a. Economic buyers give final approval as the single person or group who can say yes when others say no and can veto other buyers' approval.
   b. User buyers use the product and their success is tied to it, make judgments about impact. There may be several.

c. Technical buyers screen out options. They focus on the product and service, can't give final yes, but often give a final no. May be several.
d. Coaches help you navigate the buying organization and identify other buying influences. May work for buying organization, your organization, or neither.
e. Response mode of each buyer (growth, trouble, even-keeled, overconfident) and their needs and wants:
    i. Growth buyers are motivated by making things even better.
    ii. Buyers in trouble have problems they think must be solved to survive.
    iii. Those with an even-keel think things are fine as is (and hard to sell).
    iv. Overconfident buyers think things are fine (and hard to sell now).
f. Win results for each buyer:
    i. You'll need both business results (impact and effect that are good for the organization) and personal wins (good for the buyers personally) to make the sale.
g. Red flags
    i. Missing pieces of information, uncertainty about information, any uncontacted buying influence, buying influences new to the job, reorganizations

3. Develop a sales strategy:
    a. Strategy is about creating and allocating the right resources in the right way to the right places at the right time over time. When it comes to a sales strategy, this is about getting the right people in front of the right buyers with the right message and the right places at the right time over time.
    b. Start with the right prospects, allocating your time to those who need and know they need your product or service and will be good, valuable customers for you over time.
    c. Then get the right people from your side connected with the right people from their side at the right time in the right way.
    d. Think through components of conceptual selling:
        i. Understand/get > generate/give > select best/commit

   ii. Customer's concept: Their image of what they want to happen as a result
   iii. Sales call plan
4. Outline the proposition:
   a. This is about positioning and communication and the framework for your offer.
   b. Positioning:
      i. To specific buyer (economic, user, technical, coach)
      ii. X is the brand of *frame of reference*
      iii. That *benefit* (Result for organization, win for buyer)—matching their concept
      iv. Because of *support* (attributes)
5. Presell the proposition:
   a. Testing and consulting with buyers and influencers.
6. Propose the solution:
   a. Marrying the framework with the customers' concept and win–win solution ideas.
7. Close and follow up:
   a. Get to yes and implement with excellence.

As a reminder, the marketing and sales component of the commercial playbook gets at how to drive organic revenue growth with customers. With a new M&A or PE deal, this is the lifeblood of driving incremental value, and coupled with the other playbooks driving success for your deal, the following tools will help you lay out your thinking and help build your commercial plan.

PART III

The Operational Playbook

CHAPTER 8

Cost Optimization: To Free Up Resources to Fuel Commercial Growth

	The Strategic Playbook	The Commercial Playbook	The Operational Playbook	The Financial Playbook	The Governance Playbook	The Organizational Playbook	The Change Management Playbook
Concept	The Investment Case					Culture	Integration Leader
Research		Organic Revenue Growth	Cost Optimization	Deal/ Due Diligence			
Investment					Regulatory	Incentives	Change Management
Case							
Negotiation							
Deal/Due	Focus		Operational Excellence: Supply Chain, Distribution, Continual Improvement	Financing	Financial	Leadership	Communication
Diligence							
Contract		Customers					
Close	Plans			M&A	Board	People	Announcement
Integration		Marketing & Sales					
Acceleration	Innovation		Technology			Politics	Adjustments
Next Normal							

The operational playbook has three components: cost optimization, operational excellence, and technology. This chapter gets at cost optimization to free up resources to fuel commercial growth.

As the French philosopher and mathematician Blaise Pascal taught us a few centuries ago, while in theory there's no difference between theory and practice, in practice, there's a great deal of difference. Don't underestimate the importance of your operational, executional, and financial practices in terms of putting all your value-creating theories into practice and in freeing up the resources you need to fuel them.

You'll need:

- Resource allocation practices

- Rules of engagement
- Action plans and processes
- Performance management plans and processes: operating and financial performance standards and measures

Resource Allocation

In theory, strategy is about the creation and allocation of resources to the right place in the right way at the right time over time. You thought that through or will think that through per the guidance in Chapter 3.

Now drop the other shoe. If there's a right place and a right way and a right time, there's a wrong place, a wrong way, and a wrong time when it comes to allocating resources. To allocate resources to something, you have to pull resources away from something.

A simple example: Employee raises for the next year. You decide raises should average 4 percent. Your first idea is to give below-average performers 3 percent raises, average performers 4 percent, and above-average performers 5 percent. This works mathematically, but then you decide to give outstanding performers 10 percent raises. That throws the math out the window. You cannot allocate more resources to outstanding performers without taking them away from someone else. Mathematically, you're going to have to give others less of a raise, reduce what you're paying people in some positions, or eliminate positions to fund this.

This is the heart of what comes to the minds of most people when they hear the word *synergy* in a merger or acquisition. It matters—a lot. It's the way to free up resources to fund the most important value creators. As we said in Chapter 3, the critical resource allocation choice is to

- *Win* by being predominant or top 1 percent, superior or top 10 percent, and strong or top 25 percent; or
- *Not lose* by being above average or competitive and good enough or scaled; or
- *Not do* by outsourcing or not doing at all.

Now's the time to turn that theoretical framework into practical reality.

- *Predominance* is a bold, expensive choice. You're going to have to outspend everyone else and give these areas a tremendous amount of your attention and time.

- *Superiority* is one click below predominant—almost a shared predominance in which there is no one better than you. You're going to have to outspend 90 percent of your competitors and give these areas a huge amount of your attention and time.
- *Strong* is a winning position. You may not be *the* market leader. You may not be able to attract *the* absolute best people. But you will be *a* market leader and will attract strong people. Outspending 75 percent of your competitors and devoting your best attention and time is a material choice.
- *Competitive* is another word for average. "We pay competitive salaries" is playing for a tie. Expect to be in the middle of the pack. Expect to devote an average amount of attention and time to these areas.
- *Good enough* is code for "minimum viable." Your objective here is to devote as little money, attention, and time as you can to get by. This is the first place to cut resources by systematizing, automating, and scaling processes.
- *Not do* is as bold a choice as predominance. Michael Porter taught us that strategy is choosing what not to do. Former PrimeGenesis partner Harry Kangis took it one step further, suggesting that choosing not to do something that's a bad idea is easy. The hard choice is choosing not to do something that's a good idea—for someone else.

Good Enough Example

The Power Information Network collected retail data from automotive dealers, turned it into reports, and used it to model the impact of marketing programs. The real value creation was in the models. We overinvested in model makers, bringing in PhDs from all over the world. Then we sat down with the people collecting and managing the data and had this conversation:

> "We're dividing the organization in two. There will be an A team and a B team.
>
> "The A team are the model makers. They are our competitive advantage. They are going to get paid more, get faster, bigger raises and faster, bigger promotions. We're going to push them hard.
>
> "You are the B team, collecting and managing data. You need to be just good enough. Expect to get paid less, get slower raises and slower promotions. But expect to have lives outside of work.

"You have three choices:

1. You can say, "This is fine. It's a job. I'll be here from 8:30-4:30, earn my pay, and then go play golf or tennis with my friends and family."
2. You say you want to be on the A team. If you've got the required strengths, we'll move you and push you and pay you.
3. You can leave. Not right now. Stay as long as you want and then leave for another organization in which what you do puts you on their A team.

"Note that was three choices, not four. You don't get to complain."

Then we made it clear to the chief operating officer that his job was to manage this group so that the rest of the senior management team never had to talk to them again. We couldn't focus more time on our customers and A team model makers without spending less time with the B team.

So leap into this with both feet. Get granular on the specific human, financial, technical, and operational resources required by your strategic priorities, programs, projects, and tasks. Identify the sources of those resources over the short, mid-, and long term. Put in place processes to create and apply those resources.

Where to Start

Create a list of high value-creating processes to look at while layering in the new required processes on top to deliver the needed cost reductions, leverage capital synergies across assets and capital and working capital, and fuel revenue growth.

Marketing and Sales

Go-to-Market Process, Driving Commercial Success

- Market definition and frame of reference to understand the universe of opportunity
- Market segmentation to sharpen your "where to play" choice
- Target market insights to help you win

- Brand positioning and competitive differentiators, the bedrock of all your communication (and everything communicates)
- Lead generation to fill the top of the marketing and sales pipeline: awareness–interest. Advertising, PR, referrals are critical tools for lead generation

Sales Process

- Lead nurturing to move prospects through the marketing and sales pipeline: interest–desire
- Customer relationship management (CRM) system and process to enable a disciplined approach to managing the marketing and sales pipeline
- Lead conversion, moving prospects through the final parts of the marketing and sales pipeline: desire–action
- Demand management to ensure you can deliver on your commitments

Design

- Follow through with last-mile commercialization of innovations to make them real.
- Strengthen the innovation pipeline with evolutionary and revolutionary innovations, each of which play their own role per the discussion in Chapter 4.

Production

- Reduce inefficiencies and waste in current processes: safety, quality, delivery, and cost, focusing resources on the few highest value-adding production activities, and automating, outsourcing, or eliminating the rest.
- Institute goal deployment process.
- Make rapid-cycle execution improvements.
- Deploy Lean daily management.
- Leverage improvement events.

Delivery

- Apply SIPOC to the ecosystem: supplier–input–process–output–customer focusing resources on the few highest value-adding delivery activities, and automating, outsourcing, or eliminating the rest.

Service

- Refine focus on highest-value customers.
- Inspire, enable, empower those serving them with stronger delegation to those serving customers, with everyone else in supporting roles.

CHAPTER 9

Operational Excellence: Supply Chain, Distribution, Continual Improvement

	The Strategic Playbook	The Commercial Playbook	The Operational Playbook	The Financial Playbook	The Governance Playbook	The Organizational Playbook	The Change Management Playbook
Concept Research Investment Case	The Investment Case	Organic Revenue Growth	Cost Optimization	Deal/ Due Diligence	Regulatory	Culture Incentives	Integration Leader Change Management
Negotiation Deal/Due Diligence	Focus		Operational Excellence: Supply Chain, Distribution, Continual Improvement	Financing	Financial	Leadership	Communication
Contract Close	Plans	Customers		M&A	Board	People	Announcement
Integration Acceleration Next Normal	Innovation	Marketing & Sales	Technology			Politics	Adjustments

Operational excellence: supply chain, distribution, and continual improvement comprise the second component of the operational playbook. The heart of operational excellence is turning your cultural choices into guiding principles and then continually improving how you implement them.

What do these have in common?

1. Communication. Respect. Integrity. Excellence.
2. Social responsibility. Sustainability. A spirit of partnership. Pro Ehrenamt volunteering initiative.

Each of these is a nice set of corporate values set in stone and ignored by the organization's leaders. The first set belonged to Enron, which got brought down by a complete lack of integrity. The second set is directly from the website of Volkswagen, whose chief executive officer (CEO) resigned because the company was lying about emission tests.[1]

Specifically, as described by Elaine Shannon of the nonprofit Environmental Working Group,

> The company had deliberately installed a "defeat device" in diesel vehicles sold worldwide from 2009 to this year. The device was really a bit of software coding expressly engineered to spoof standard emissions testing instruments and evade the federal Clean Air Act and related state rules.

Whether Volkswagen CEO Martin Winterkorn knew about this or not, he was the leader of an organization in which people blatantly contradicted one of its four core values. As Shannon explained in a brief interview,

> At the end of the day a company or nonprofit group, all it has to sell is its values and reputation." VW was about being "humble, iconic (and then added) greenness." But "they lied." And now, "VW is all about dishonest cars."

The emissions scandal could not have happened if VW's leadership actually believed in its stated values.[2]

The good news was that those values were relatively straightforward, easy to understand and remember. The bad news was that they weren't real. As part of their effort to recover, the company created a new set: Values from us, values for us. Staff from all over the world were involved in developing the brand's new corporate values—an important step forward on the journey to improving the corporate culture.

This was a complete abrogation of leadership. Instead of inspiring, enabling, and empowering others to do their absolute best together

---

[1]Bradt, George, 2015, "What VW's Next CEO Must Do to Save the Organization," *Forbes* (September 23).

[2]Bradt, George, 2018, "Executive Onboarding Note: What VW's New CEO Must Do to Get the Company Back on Track," *Forbes* (April 12).

to realize a meaningful and rewarding shared purpose, VW's leaders essentially let everybody come up with whatever they thought was useful. Involving? Yes. Democratic? Yes. Practical? You tell us. Here's what they came up with:

Values from Us, Values for Us

Genuine

Speak out | No fear of hierarchies | Honest | Across hierarchies | Open | Transparent | Focus on the real issue | Take a stand—less politics

Courageous

Be an inventor | Examine habits | State my opinion | Challenge | Try out new things | Decide, decide, decide

Customer-Oriented

Listen | Understanding customers around the globe | For the best product | High quality | For customer mobility | What our customers want, not what we want

Efficient

Less discussion | Economical | Fast | Effective | Concentrated | Cost-conscious | Take responsibility | Do things

Mindful

Empathy | Respectful | Less focus on status | Thoughtful | Issue, not status

If people can't understand, remember, and follow five words—*social responsibility, sustainability, partnership, volunteering*—how are they going to understand, remember, and follow 111 words? To be fair, VW would tell you their new values from us, values for us are about *genuine, courageous, customer oriented, efficient,* and *mindful,* and the other words just elaborate on them. Let's test that. Without looking back, how many of these six key words can you remember? (Most won't remember most.)

The tragedy is that Volkswagen's name is a core message, mantra, and guiding principle all rolled into one. At its best, VW owned "the people's car." The VW Beetle and VW Bus were iconic parts of everyday folks' lives. Few companies have it this easy. Everyone at Novo Nordisk knows they're all about defeating diabetes. People at Coca-Cola focus on refreshing the world's consumers. NASA in the 1960s was completely focused on putting a man on the moon.

VW's leadership message has to fit with VW's roots and help the organization get back to those roots. They should make "people's car" their mantra. They should believe in the value of the right cars for ordinary folks, talk about that, and drive that one idea in everything they do. VW forgot its five core values. No one is going to remember their new 111 words, but if the core guiding principle is "volks wagen," no one at VW will ever forget it.

At PrimeGenesis, we had five values:

- *Inspiring:* Committed to excellence and the pursuit of mastery
- *Results-oriented* over short-term with urgency; sustainably with long-term view
- *Integrity* beyond reproach
- *Lasting relationships:* Doing what's right for clients over the long run
- *Team:* Committed to each other, supportive, collaborative

Nice—but not as proscriptive as they could be. We turned them into guiding principles with verbs and have followed these ever since. Same ideas—with verbs.

- Inspiring: Commit to excellence and the pursuit of mastery.
- Results-oriented: Drive results with urgency over the short term and sustainably with a long-term view.
- Integrity: Be, do, say beyond reproach.
- Lasting relationships: Be, do, say what's right for clients over the long run.
- Team: Commit to support and collaborate with each other.

Do this for all your cultural choices. Turn them into guiding principles—with verbs. For example:

Behaviors: What Impact

Working units: One organization, interdependent teams => Think and act as one organization made up of interdependent teams.

Relationships: How Connect

Power, decision-making: Diffused/debated – confront issues => Confront issues in debate at all levels.

Attitude: How Win

Strategy: Premium price, service, innovation => Innovate to deliver superior products and services worthy of premium prices.

Values: What matters and why

Risk appetite: Risk more and gain more (confidence) => Risk more to gain more with confidence.

Environment: Where play

Work–life balance: Health and wellness first => Put health and wellness ahead of short-term productivity.

Action Plans

On the surface, this one is relatively straightforward. Solve for what's getting done by whom, by laying out the actions, measures, milestones and timing, accountabilities, and linkages to make things happen.

In a merger, you want to maintain and evolve the best of the current processes while adding new processes as required. You do not have to change everything. And you certainly do not have to change everything all at once. Start with the processes around the core focus of the newly combined organization (design, produce, deliver, service). Then move on to strategic enablers.

Identify the processes that are working well—in either organization.

Fold the other organization's process into that.

- Make a hard shift where possible.
- Adopt the new process completely as is first, with no changes.
- Then, once the combined process is running smoothly, improve.

What to Do If You're Being Swallowed

This is opposite sides of the same coin. Whether your process is swallowing another or being swallowed, make it about the process, not you. Give the work your best thinking and effort and things will go well.

We'd grown Procter & Gamble's Puritan cooking oil business +50 percent in 2 years by positioning it as a healthier alternative because it was made from canola. The trouble was that we were taking market share from Procter & Gamble's Crisco oil as well as others. In an annual category review, the CEO said, "I don't want to end up with the #2 and #3 brands in the category. Merge Puritan into Crisco as "Crisco Canola Oil."

We did, first thinking through the strategy and approach, then mapping out a plan, then implementing the plan, then moving the brand people to other brands. That's the right order. Whichever side you're on, if you do what's right for the business, the people in charge will do what's right for you.

There are some important steps to getting teams off to the best start on programs, projects, tasks—including merging process. (See Tool 9.1. Team Charter.)

Purpose and Direction (Why)

- Define the mission, vision, and objective
- Use the specific, measurable (including return on investment [ROI] where applicable), achievable, realistic, and time bound (SMART) format to define the goal and the required components along the way.

Context: Why are we doing this?

- Explain the intent behind the mission, vision, and objective to ensure that team members understand the collective purpose of their individual tasks.
- Provide sufficient information to help the team visualize the desired output. (For example, include customer requirements if they exist.)
- Clarify what happens next. Make sure that the team understands the follow-on actions to ensure that momentum is sustained after the objective is delivered.

Approach (How)

Resources: What help do we need?

- Ensure that the team has and can access all the human, financial, data, and operational resources needed to deliver the objective.
- Clarify what other teams, groups, and units are involved and what their roles are.
- Allocate resources in a timely manner to ensure delivery.

Guidelines: How are we empowered to do this?

- Clarify what the team can and cannot do with regard to roles and decisions including mandatory executional elements and enterprise-wide standards, procedures, and practices.
- Lay out the interdependencies between the team being chartered and the other teams involved.

Accountability: How will we track and monitor?

- Clarify what is going to get done by when, by whom, and how the team and you are going to track milestones so that you can know about risks in advance and can intervene well before milestones are missed.
- Clarify command, communication, and support arrangements so that all know how they are going to work together.
- Schedule regular updates.
- Know the signs when course corrections or reevaluations are necessary.

Performance Management

Put in place weekly demand management; daily, weekly, and monthly business operations management; and semiannual performance management systems with a focus on

1. Pricing and margin stabilization
2. Liquidity
3. Demand management and customer experience via application of technology tools
4. Supply chain resiliency
5. Market share expansion

The pivot point is milestones.

Let's start with some definitions:[3]

Objectives: Broadly defined, qualitative performance requirements

[3]Bradt, George, et al., 2022, *The New Leader's 100-Day Action Plan* (Hoboken, NJ: Wiley).

Goals: The quantitative measures of the objectives that define success

Strategies: Broad choices around how the team will achieve its objectives

Now add:

Milestones: Checkpoints along the way to achieving objectives and goals

Milestones are the building blocks of tactical capacity[4] that turn a burning imperative into a manageable action plan. Your new combined team's milestone management practice, if done right, will be a powerful team reinforcer. Milestone management is about identifying accountability, monitoring progress, and taking action to stay on track.

Burning imperative meetings tend to produce many ideas and choices on flip charts. They are all completely useless unless someone takes action to make them happen. As Steve Jobs once said, "Ideas are worth nothing unless executed. They are just a multiplier. Execution is worth millions." This chapter is about execution. In brief, to help ensure that the team delivers the desired results, in the time frame specified, you must delegate well. That involves:

- *Direction:* Clearly defined objectives, goals, strategies, and desired results.
- *Resources:* Make available the human, financial, technical, and operational resources needed to deliver.
- *Bounded authority:* Empower the team to make tactical decisions within strategic guidelines and defined boundaries.
- *Accountability and consequences:* Clearly define standards of performance, time expectations, and positive and negative consequences of success and failure.

Along the way, strive for absolute clarity around:

- *Interdependencies:* Be aware of critical interdependencies that exist within the team, with other teams and projects, and with outside resources.

[4]Bradt, George, 2021, "How Tactical Capacity Bridges the Gap Between Strategy and Execution," *Forbes* (March 30).

- *Information flows:* Know what information needs to be shared when and with whom. Ensure there is a method to share that information in a timely manner.
- *Collaboration:* Know what negotiations and joint efforts are needed to ensure alignment and adherence.

Rarely is the delivery of a milestone reliant on one person. More often than not, a milestone requires contributions from several members of the team across many functions. Despite the complexity of delivery, each milestone should be assigned one "captain" who is ultimately accountable for the delivery of that milestone.

The captain is not the person required to do all the work, but rather, the key spokesperson for the communication of issues regarding the timely delivery of that milestone. The captain should be the final decision-maker, responsible for communicating across groups, ensuring needed information flows, collaboration, and delivery of the desired result. Avoid co-captains. They never work. There needs to be a single point of accountability.

Practices are the systems that enable people to implement the plans. They need to be coupled with systems of metrics and rewards that reinforce the desired behaviors. There is an old saying: "Show me how they are paid, and I'll tell you what they really do."

John Michael Loh, U.S. Air Force Air Combat Command, during the first Gulf War, said, "I used to believe that if it doesn't get measured, it doesn't get done. Now I say if it doesn't get measured it doesn't get approved. . . .You need to manage by facts, not gut feel." As former senator Daniel Patrick Moynihan put it, "You're entitled to your own opinions, but not your own facts."

Specific performance measurements, accountabilities, and decision rights free people and teams to do their jobs without undue interference and provide the basis for nonjudgmental discussion of performance versus expectations and how to make improvements. It is essential that people know what is expected of them. When the expectations are clear, people also must have the time and resources needed to deliver against those expectations. The milestone management process is focused on clarifying decision rights and making sure that information and resources flow to where they need to go.

Milestones Enable Quicker Adjustments Along the Way

NASA and the Apollo 13 ground team provide a useful example of this. The objective of getting the astronauts back home alive after the explosion in space was compelling but overwhelming. It was easier to work through milestones one by one:

1. Turn the ship around so it could get back to Earth.
2. Manage the remaining power so it would last until the astronauts were back.
3. Fix the carbon monoxide problem so the air remained breathable.
4. Manage reentry into the atmosphere so the ship didn't burn up.

The power of milestones is that they let you know how you're doing along the way and give you the opportunity to adjust. They also give you the comfort to let your team run toward the goal without your involvement, as long as the milestones are being reached as planned.

You might evaluate your team's journey to a goal like this:

Worst case: The team misses a goal and doesn't know why.

Bad: The team misses a goal and does know why.

Okay: The team misses a milestone but adjusts to make the overall goal.

Good: The team anticipates a risk and adjusts along the way to key milestones.

Best: The team hits all its milestones on the way to delivering its goals. (In your dreams.)

Imagine that you set a goal of getting from London to Paris in 5 1/2 hours. Now imagine that you choose to drive. Imagine further that it takes you 45 minutes to get from central London to the outskirts of London. You wonder: "How's the trip going so far?"

You have no clue. You might be on track. You might be behind schedule. But it's early in the trip, so you might think that you can make up time later if you need to. So you're not worried.

If, on the other hand, you had set the following milestones, you would be thinking differently:

- Central London to outskirts of London: 30 minutes
- Outskirts of London to Folkestone: 70 minutes

- Channel crossing: load: 20 minutes; cross: 20 minutes; unload: 20 minutes
- Calais to Paris: 3 hours

If you had set a milestone of getting to the outskirts of London in 30 minutes and it took you 45 minutes, you would know you were behind schedule. Knowing that you were behind schedule, you could then take action on alternative options. The milestone would make you immediately aware of the need to adjust to still reach your overall goal.

You and your team are going to miss milestones. It is not necessary to hit all your milestones. What is essential is that you have put in place a mechanism to identify reasonable milestones so that you have checkpoints that allow you to anticipate and adjust along the way to reaching your destination on time.

Milestone management for your team is the same process but will require more complexity and different time horizons depending on the work:

- For multiyear efforts, you may want to set and manage annual or quarterly milestones.
- For major programs you may want to set and manage monthly milestones.
- Programs tend to be made up of projects generally managed with weekly milestones.
- Projects involve tasks, generally managed with daily milestones. The exception is in a crisis, when milestones may need to be managed even more frequently.

Manage Milestone Updates

Deploying a mutually supportive, team-based follow-up system helps everyone deliver results. Organizations that have deployed this process in their team meetings have seen dramatic improvements in team performance. Teams that don't, almost always fail to meet expectations. Yes, your milestone management process is that crucial. Follow these steps as well as the prep and post instructions laid out in Tool 9.2, and you'll be well on your way to ensuring that the team achieves its desired results on time.

The most up-to-date, full, editable versions of all tools are downloadable at primegenesis.com/tools.

TOOL 9.1

Team Charter

Use this tool for getting teams off to the best start on programs, projects, and tasks—including merging process.

1. Purpose and Direction (Why)
   - Define the mission, vision, and objective
2. Approach (How)
   - Resources: What help do we need?
   - Guidelines: How are we empowered to do this?
3. Accountability: How will we track and monitor?

TOOL 9.2

Milestone Management

Use this tool to manage milestone management meetings and to follow up on progress as a team.

Milestone Management Process

1. *Set Up:* Track what is being done, by whom, when

   Leader conducts a weekly or biweekly milestones management meeting with their team.

Prior to Milestones Management Meetings

1. *Update:* Each team member submits their updates to their milestones and their most recent wins, learning, and areas in which they need help.
2. *Review:* Each person reads and reviews updates before the meeting.

   If help is requested, relevant data, reading, analysis, and so forth is submitted in advance.

At Milestones Management Meetings

1. *Part 1, Reporting:* Each team member gives a 5-minute update in the following format: most important wins, most important learnings, areas where they need help. Reporting only. No discussion. Or go even further and skip the reporting part of the meeting, assuming everyone has read the updates so you can go straight to problem-solving.
2. *Part 2, Pause and Prioritize:* After reporting, the leader pauses to order topics for discussion by priority.
3. *Part 3, Problem-Solving by Priority:* Group discusses priority topics in order, spending as much time as necessary on each topic.
4. The remaining topics are deferred to the next milestones management meeting or a separate meeting. Key items are updated and communicated.

This is depicted in Figure 9.1.

FIGURE 9.1 Milestone Tracking

Milestone Tracking				
Wins:				
Learning:				
Need help with:				
Priorities	**When**	**Who**	**Status**	**Discussion**
			Complete	Done
			On-track	All under control to hit milestone. No help needed.
			At risk	Need help to hit milestone. (+sign of interdependent team)
			Will miss	Need help to get back on track or change timing.

CHAPTER 10

Technology: Because All Companies Are Technology Companies Today

	The Strategic Playbook	The Commercial Playbook	The Operational Playbook	The Financial Playbook	The Governance Playbook	The Organizational Playbook	The Change Management Playbook
Concept Research Investment Case	The Investment Case	Organic Revenue Growth	Cost Optimization	Deal/ Due Diligence	Regulatory	Culture Incentives	Integration Leader Change Management
Negotiation Deal/Due Diligence	Focus		Operational Excellence: Supply Chain, Distribution, Continual Improvement	Financing	Financial	Leadership	Communication
Contract Close	Plans	Customers		M&A	Board	People	Announcement
Integration Acceleration Next Normal	Innovation	Marketing & Sales	Technology			Politics	Adjustments

The third component of the operational playbook is technology. While it's an important, stand-alone component on its own, it's even more important as a critical enabler of the first two components.

> The machines rose from the ashes of the nuclear fire. Their war to exterminate mankind had raged for decades, but the final battle would not be fought in the future. It would be fought here, in our present.
>
> **James Cameron and Gail Hurd, *The Terminator***

The machines are winning.

Don't believe me? Then believe harmon.ie chief executive officer (CEO) Yaacov Cohen. He watches teenagers at birthday parties texting each other (on machines) instead of talking to each other. He notices his breakfast table where each family member is hiding behind their own device, enslaved by their machines. Movie theaters used to ask us not to smoke or talk. Now they ask us to turn off our machines.[1]

The machines are winning.

Today's technology is adding addictions, disrupting the workflow and making many of us less efficient and eff—(Sorry. Had to respond to a text message. But I'm back now.)—making us less efficient and effective.

This was not the hope. This was not the promise. This was not what we set out to do. It's time to make the technology work for us instead of letting the machines win.

Cohen has a different vision of what technology should do. His vision is one of technology augmenting relationships instead of reducing them, one of technology enabling collaboration instead of cementing silos. In his world, it acts as an intuitive aide instead of as a relentless disruptor. How?

His answer has three parts. Enable:

1. Document sharing so everyone can work on the same document and see all the versions.
2. Interaction via instant messages, text, voice over Internet, videoconference, and so forth.
3. Sharing and interaction within whatever platform each individual user chooses.

Cohen and his harmon.ie team have designed a suite of connected apps to do just this while maintaining the right attitude to technology and machines.

Machine Strategy

Make sure you are leveraging technology to further your strategy. Your technology choices must help you win where it matters. Having the

[1]Bradt, George, 2013, "Make Technology Work for You or Else," *Forbes* (January 16).

most advanced knowledge is merely a fleeting advantage. Technological superiority is not in itself a strategy; it's part of enabling a greater vision.

Machine Posture

Think through how technology aids you along the proactive-responsive scale. Do you need your technology to help you innovate and get ahead of your customers' needs? Or, do you need your technology to help you keep in touch with your customers so you can be responsive to needs they identify?

Machine Culture

Be conscious of how technology influences your behavior and relationships with others. If the technology is enabling your relationships, great. If the technology is allowing you to have a bigger impact than you would without it, great. If not, the machines are winning. And that's not acceptable.

BRAVE Technology

Apply the five BRAVE (behaviors, relationships, attitudes, values, environment) questions to your technology.

Where Play

As we've said, technology is an enabler. Leverage across your priority choices to improve effectiveness or efficiency in different situations.

- Look first at where you choose to *win* by being predominant or top 1 percent, superior or top 10 percent, or strong or top 25 percent. In these places, invest in technology to improve effectiveness. These should be your most leverageable technology investments with the return on investment (ROI) based on revenue acceleration.
- Then look at where you choose *not to lose* by being above average and competitive, or good enough and scaled. In these places,

the technology investments should drive efficiencies with the ROI based on total cost reductions across the organization.

- Finally, look at where you choose *not to do* by outsourcing or not doing at all. In these places, you should not make any direct technology investments at all.

What Matters and Why

Scope is a function of resources and time:

If I need to move 10 boxes up a flight of stairs (scope) and there's one person capable of moving one box every 5 minutes (resources), it's going to take 50 minutes to move the boxes (time).

If I need them moved in a half an hour, I need two people.

Or a fancy technological solution called an elevator to enable one person to move all the boxes in 10 minutes themself.

What matters is technology's impact on effectiveness or efficiency.

How to Win

This is the pivot, figuring out the right technology. In the moving example, other technologies might have been pullies or ramps or magnets or giants.

How Connect

The technological solution never stands alone. Think SIPOC (supplier–input–process–output–customer) and the suppliers of inputs into the process so the outputs meet the needs of the next person in the customer chain. Don't guess at other capabilities, needs, and barriers. Ask them.

What Impact

And we're right back to the beginning. No one cares about the technology. They care about what the technology enables them to do.

PART IV

The Financial Playbook

CHAPTER 11

The Deal and Due Diligence: Iteratively

	The Strategic Playbook	The Commercial Playbook	The Operational Playbook	The Financial Playbook	The Governance Playbook	The Organizational Playbook	The Change Management Playbook
Concept	The Investment Case					Culture	Integration Leader
Research		Organic Revenue Growth	Cost Optimization	Deal/ Due Diligence			
Investment Case					Regulatory	Incentives	Change Management
Negotiation			Operational Excellence: Supply Chain, Distribution, Continual Improvement				
Deal/Due Diligence	Focus			Financing	Financial	Leadership	Communication
Contract		Customers					
Close	Plans			M&A	Board	People	Announcement
Integration		Marketing & Sales					
Acceleration	Innovation		Technology			Politics	Adjustments
Next Normal							

The financial playbook has three components: (1) the deal and due diligence, which need to happen iteratively; (2) financing the deal; and (3) further mergers and acquisitions (M&A).

When it comes to the deal, the first of the many investments you need to get a return on is the purchase price. As we've seen, only 17 percent of deals add value. Thus, it is better not to pay enough and lose than to over pay and *win* one of the 30 percent of deals that require a lot of work for no gain or, even worse, one of the 53 percent of deals that actually destroy value.

We've combined our thinking on doing the deal and due diligence into one chapter as you may need to go back and forth.

Let's start with doing the deal, the expected transaction price for your investment case from Chapter 1, most likely a number somewhere between *fair value* and *must have at any price*. These might inform your opening, expected, and maximum prices.

Your target may have gone through the same thinking, yielding, for example, something like this:

You:	$30MM Opening Walkaway	$40MM Expected Minimum	$50MM Maximum Expected	$60MM+ Walkaway Opening
Target	$25MM	$35MM	$45MM	$55MM

You
In this case, you think the fair value of the company is $35MM and know how to invest $10MM to add value and then sell it for $55MM. This, of course, assumes perfect knowledge, perfect plans, perfect execution, and everyone else and every force on the planet doing exactly what you expect. Given the unlikelihood of all those assumptions being true, you hedge your opening and maximum positions by $5MM each.

You plan to:

Open with a $30MM bid.

Expect to do a deal at $40MM.

Pay as much as $50MM.

Walk away from the conversation if the target is looking for anything more than $60MM.

Target
In this case, you expect the target to know the fair value of the company is $35MM and also how to invest $10MM to add value and then sell it for $55MM.

You think they might:

Open with a $55MM ask.

Expect to do a deal at $45MM.

Accept as little as $35MM.

Walk away from the conversation if you offer anything less than $25MM.

The Deal to Be Done

In this case, there's a win–win deal to be done. Depending on whom else joins the bidding and your relative negotiating strengths, the purchase price should be somewhere between their $35MM minimum and your $50MM maximum and most likely somewhere between your $40MM and their $45MM expected prices.

Negotiating

The only negotiating result that can stand the test of time is win–win. BRAVE negotiating can get you there, working through behaviors, relationships, attitudes, values, and the environment from the outside in as you prepare in advance, manage the moment, and follow through.[1]

Prelude

Environment

Start with context, history, recent results, and the needs of others that won't be directly involved in the negotiations.

In particular, look for shadow boards: family members in a family-owned business, other partners in a private equity–owned business, government officials in businesses in some countries, and the like.

Values

Next, think through your own needs and concerns—and the other party's needs and concerns.

Attitude

Think through your strategy and plan for the negotiation as well as your posture and general approach. The expected deal price is an important component of that.

But it's far from the only component. Different factors will come into play in different types of mergers and acquisitions.

---

[1]Bradt, George, 2014, "Brave Negotiating: A Better Path to Win–Win," *Forbes* (September 16).

Types of M&A

Cash Acquisition

In a *cash acquisition*, things can be relatively straightforward. You give the target cash. They buy a yacht and sail off into the sunset without ever looking back. This situation, and only this situation, may be just about the deal price.

Acquisition over Time

In an *acquisition over time*, there are deal points to be negotiated around when payments are earned (or not) and when and how they are paid.

Acquisition in Which Some of the Key People Stay

In an *acquisition in which some of the key people stay*, things get trickier as there may be deal points around those key people's roles, responsibilities, compensation, termination agreements, and the like.

People can be less than perfectly rational at times. They may care about things like their own sense of self-worth, reputations, and even impact on others in their lives. One leader sold his residential clinic to a private equity firm as part of a roll-up. They thought they could create value with cross-marketing and cross-referrals between clinics as well as improved training and best practice sharing fueled by cost-savings from economies of scale. The leader stayed on to run the day-to-day operations of the clinic.

At a strategic planning with the overall enterprise's CEO later, this leader disagreed with part of the new direction. He said, "When we agreed to partner with you all, this was not what we had in mind." Do you see the issue? He had not "agreed to partner." He had sold his business. He wasn't even a minority owner. He was an employee.

This is an example of why you need to consider everyone's sense of self-worth, sense of reputation, and thinking about how things impact others in their lives up-front, as you're negotiating the deal.

Merger in Which You'll Have Control

In a *merger in which you'll have control*, the negotiation will involve the items in an acquisition in which some of the key people stay as well as resolving how decisions are going to be made—essentially, minority rights.

Merger of Equals

In a *merger of equals*, the big issues are going to be about roles, responsibilities, and decision rights. These are particularly tricky as co-CEOs often get into trouble.

Attention to detail and planning out as many scenarios as you can imagine is critically important to noncontrol and even majority control deals. Even if you have done deals with the other parties in the past, plan for the downsides and remote scenarios and ensure those are documented as issues will arise and differences of opinion will raise their heads over the coming months and years. Think about the shareholder agreements, board governance rights, drag-along-and-tag-along rights, and so forth and so on.

For example, Away company founder Steph Korey broke all three key tenets of effective leadership communication when she came back as co-CEO.[2] This was never going to end well. The basic mantra is *be–do–say*, lining up what you do with what you say with what you believe. The way she led before she relinquished the CEO role the first time was most likely her default way of leading. She tried to step aside as CEO and then changed her mind, leaving a whole lot of people confused. And confusion is not the goal of effective communication.

Korey got caught. She stepped aside and then stepped back. But who she was had not changed. Her underlying beliefs had not changed.

This is why *be–do–say* is such an important thing to keep in mind in any leadership position and especially during crucibles of leadership like onboarding into new jobs or restarting things. Start with who you are, what you believe. Then act that way. Finally, communicate both in your words.

Let's back up. Korey took her learnings from Kate Spade, Bloomingdales, and Warby Parker and partnered with Jennifer Rubio to co-found Away in 2015. Their business success was indisputable. *Adweek* called them a "Breakthrough Brand with Ingenious Marketing." They primarily sold luggage direct-to-consumer while also having a couple of physical stores and their own travel-focused podcasts and magazines. The company was valued at $1.4 billion in 2019.

---

[2]Bradt, George, 2020, "Why Steph Korey's Return to Away as Co-CEO Is Doomed to Fail," *Forbes* (January 13).

Yet that success came at a cost. People described Korey as someone with a "fanatical work ethic." She was all in with this venture, willing to do whatever it took to satisfy customers, build the brand, and build the business. The trouble was that she required everyone else to be just as fanatical and pushed at least some of them way too far. However, "the result is a brand consumers love, a company culture people fear, and a cadre of former employees who feel burned out and coerced into silence." That is not sustainable.

So Korey brought Lululemon alum Stuart Haselden in as CEO and took the title of executive chair in December 2019. Then, just 35 days later, she reversed course and jumped back in as co-CEO.

This gets us to the fundamental problem. Her actions did not match her words and underlying beliefs. She couldn't help herself. She said, "Her behavior and comments were 'wrong, plain and simple.'" That read like she believed Zoe Schiffer's *Verge* article allegations[3] and needed to step away to change the culture. But then she came back. Actually, she never left. She just changed her title temporarily. She'd always been running the company. She was still running the company.

When she came back it was fair to expect the culture to stay toxic as she still believed that everyone should share her fanatical work ethic.

She was out within 6 months—this time for good.

Lessons for You Take *be–do–say* seriously. Everything communicates. Everything you say and do and don't say and don't do sends a message.

Say Your words are your first level of communication. People hear or see what you say and they form an impression. Words matter. Context matters. Think things through in advance so you're choosing the right words in the right context for the people you're trying to communicate with so they hear what you wanted them to hear and feel the way you intended them to feel.

Early on, Steph Korey certainly said all the right things. People partnered with her. People invested in her. People worked for her. People appreciated what she said.

---

[3]Schiffer, Zoe, 2019, "Emotional Baggage," *Verge* (December 5).

Do Words matter. But actions matter more. In the end, people are going to believe what you do more than they will believe what you say. If you're walking the talk, it's fine. If your actions reinforce your words, people will believe both over time.

This is where Korey diverged. She said Away's values were "thoughtful, customer-obsessed, iterative, empowered, accessible, in it together." There's nothing wrong with these. But, as Shiffer pointed out, Korey actions and expectations were different.

- *Empowered* employees didn't schedule time off when things were busy, regardless of how much they'd been working.
- *Customer-obsessed* employees did whatever it took to make consumers happy, even if it came at the cost of their own well-being.

Be Even if your words match your actions, if they don't match your underlying fundamental beliefs, you're going to get caught—like Korey did.

Be especially cautious in a merger of equals. Shy away from co-CEOs if you can. When Harris and L3 communications merged, they agreed the former CEO of Harris, Bill Brown, would be CEO of the combined L3Harris for 2 years, and then former CEO of L3 Chris Kubasik would take over as CEO. There was always someone in charge and never co-CEOs.

If you must have co-CEOs, make sure their approach to behaviors, relationships, attitudes, values, and the environment are compatible.

Merger in Which You Won't Have Control

In a *merger in which you won't have control*, you'll be on other side of some of the previous points. Eldonna Lewis-Fernandez, author of *Think Like a Negotiator*, suggests two of the seven most common negotiating mistakes come into play here:

Mistake 1: Lacking confidence; born of preparation, anticipating objections, and discerning hot-button triggers—"Think about these things in advance, including what you will do if they hit one of your emotional triggers."

Mistake 2: Thinking something is nonnegotiable—"Everything is negotiable! It's a mindset."

Manage the Moment

Relationships are at the heart of successful negotiating. If you can't connect with someone, you can't get to a win–win result. So get started; clarify issues, positions, interests; find and create alternatives; build agreement.

Get Started

Start by connecting as human beings. Pay attention to how you show up to help others to be open to you. Eldonna suggests this includes the way you dress and the colors you wear. If they're wearing suits, wear a suit. If they're wearing jeans, wear jeans. Fit in.

Eldonna also suggested that if someone says, "I see your point," they may have a bias to visual communication. Draw them pictures. If they say, "That sounds like. . .," they may have an auditory bias. Explain things. If they say, "That feels good to me," pay attention to kinesthetics. Net, bias your communication mode to what will best connect with them.

Then fix any outstanding issues before trying to move on. Make sure you follow up on anything you committed to do and tackle unanswered questions. Doing so builds credibility. Not doing so destroys it.

Focus on areas of agreement: common interests, shared values. Start with the things that get heads nodding in the right direction. You're aiming to make everyone feel good. Why not start there.

Mistake 3: Not building relationships first.

As Eldonna puts it, "Get personal." Clarify issues, positions, interests.

Once you've connected, you can move to the substance of the conversation. The advice is to state, support, listen, probe (staying rationally focused on issues being negotiated). Then summarize new areas of agreement and differences to resolve.

Mistake 4: Not asking for what you want. Do so.

Find and Create Alternatives

Problem-solving requires a healthy dose of listening. Ask about needs and priorities. Share information about your own needs and priorities. Solicit ideas. Suggest alternatives.

PrimeGenesis partner Roger Neill suggests the vast majority of disagreements are rooted in misunderstanding. Understanding is born of listening. Don't fall into what Eldonna calls:

Mistake 5: *Talking too much*. Have enough confidence and presence to let someone else fill the silence.

Build Agreement

Armed with understanding you're ready to build an agreement. This will involve proposals, concessions, summarizing, and testing for agreement. Don't hesitate to bring back in personal connections. And make sure you lock in next steps and timetables.

The last two mistakes rear their ugly heads here.

Mistake 6: Not documenting.
Mistake 7: Signing without reading. Get it down in writing. Make sure everyone reads it. Then sign it.

Follow Through

Behaviors are what actually happen after the agreement—the implementation. Make sure you deliver your part. Keep communicating. Monitor progress and revise together as conditions change. This way you'll enter the next negotiation with a context of mutual respect and trust. It's only win–win if it looks, sounds, and feels like win–win to all involved over time.

Due Diligence

Due diligence is your chance to check the accuracy of the information provided and your own assumptions between making an agreement in principal and closing a deal. The critical thing to keep in mind is that due diligence is successful either if it leads to a satisfactory merger or acquisition or if it prevents one that would have been unsatisfactory.

The due diligence checklist (Tool 11.3) or in the M&A Leader folder at www.primegenesis.com/tools digs into eight areas: (1) financials, (2) business structure and operations, (3) contracts, (4) product and intellectual property, (5) customers, (6) employees, (7) infrastructure, physical assets, and real estate, and (8) legal and compliance. Digging into all those is essential.

Another approach is to dig into the information and assumptions on synergy value creators, cost reductions, and cultural compatibility.

Value Creators

Look back at and check the value creators in your investment case.

Strategic Priorities

Strategic priorities are things directly increasing customer impact, revenue, and profitability (e.g., medical practice deciding to add ankle surgery to portfolio).

Product and Service Development Does the target company really have the product and service development strengths they said they did or you thought they did?

Look at their pipeline and track record over time. For something like each of the past 5 years, look at what they said they were going to develop and look at what happened to the items in their pipeline. Did they move forward? Did they get into the market? What was the new product or service's impact on customers, revenues, and profits?

Then dig into why things did or did not work to get at what the organization did well and less well. This is particularly important when the core focus of the organization is design. The organization will need to include people with design-oriented innate talent for design, learned knowledge about design principles, practiced skills in the elements of design, hard-won experience actually designing things that worked and did not work, and apprenticed craft-level artistic caring and sensibilities.

On one hand, you'll know the organization's design strengths through their results. On the other hand, you'll benefit from digging into how they recruit and develop their design people and how their apprenticeship program works—if they have one.

Pricing Does the target company really get and deserve the pricing they said they did or you thought they did?

For example, during the early months of Covid, there was an exodus of people from cities to "safer," less-congested areas. To attract or keep tenants, landlords gave them incentives of free rent for a period of months. While a person renting a $1,000 a month apartment would pay only $10,000 for the year, the landlord could still say the apartment rented for $1,000 a month. Your due diligence should uncover the real price they are getting, not posting.

Marketing and Business Development Are the company's relationships with its customers really as strong as they suggested or you thought?

One of the big things to look at here is customer concentration. The higher a percentage of the organization's business with any one customer, the greater that customer's leverage with the organization.

For example, this is part of how Walmart gained so much leverage with so many of its suppliers. They agreed to buy ever more and more product from suppliers for ever more and more price breaks, reducing those suppliers' marginal contribution on sales to Walmart ever more and more.

Understand the difference between ongoing relationships and serial transactions. There's a huge difference between the security of a supplier that's part of a 20-year aerospace program and a supplier to Costco that fills its stores with the best current deal and reevaluates after each and every shipment.

Enhance Operational Rigor and Accountability

Supply chain due diligence is the flip side of the marketing due diligence. On the procurement side, the higher a percentage of the organization's business with any one supplier, the greater the organization's leverage with the supplier. But the higher a percentage of the organization's supply with any one supplier, the greater that supplier's leverage with the organization.

As noted earlier, at one point United Sporting Goods was the largest distributor of sporting guns in the United States, connecting multiple suppliers with multiple retailers. They had no single supplier and no single customer that represented more than 5 percent of their business. This gave them enough market power to be market makers, effectively telling their suppliers what to make and their customers what to sell. They made outrageous profits in the process.

Look at supply chain history, the current situation, contracts in place, and relative position with suppliers per the previous explanation. On the supply chain management side, look at the supply chain managers' strengths in terms of knowledge, skills, experience, and relationships. Look at the steps in the organization's supply chain process to see what they do well across supply chain planning and purchasing. Dig into the numbers over time.

Production Success

Production success requires the discipline to do the same thing over and over the same way with the same results while continuing improving things at the same time on a consistent basis.

Dig into the production process, its systems, tools, and track record of success and improvement across effectiveness and efficiency measures to see what they do well and less well. Look at things like production costs, waste, inventory, and working capital management. Look at the organization's talent, knowledge, skills, experience, and production craft and how they recruit and develop their production-oriented people.

Distribution Success

Distribution success requires an ecosystem. By definition, you have to distribute things from one party to another, often through a third party. Start here by understanding what the organization does itself when it comes to distribution and what they manage through third parties. Then look at the effectiveness and efficiency measures and drivers of those measures.

At UPS, the critical cog in the wheel is the drivers. In an effort to reduce driver turnover, the organization dug into what they liked and disliked about their jobs. They liked driving and interacting with customers. They did not like physically loading the trucks in the morning.

So the organization hired a bunch of minimum-wage people to load the trucks, gave them minimal training and a lot of close supervision, and put them to work. The new loaders had about 300 percent turnover per year as this was not a self-fulfilling job and had no career progression with UPS. The company was fine with this because it reduced driver turnover.

Service Optimization

Service optimization is ultimately about the customer experience—especially in service-oriented organizations. Look at how the organization views service and measures success. For some organizations, service is merely a necessary cost. Look at how these organizations are moving service delivery to others, including self-service. Dig into their efficiency measures over time.

Other organizations differentiate based on their service. For these organizations, pay more attention to effectiveness measures and their track record over time compared to the broadest possible competitive set. Restaurants, for example, consciously competed with supermarkets and caterers even before the pandemic. Not every service-oriented organization needs to deliver the experience of a lifetime. But dig into what level of service they are trying to provide and how their customers think they're doing.

Strategic enablers and core competencies and capabilities drive things directly increasing customer impact, revenue, and profitability (e.g., X-ray machines and radiologists to diagnose ankle surgical needs).

Organizational and operating priorities help deliver the strategic enablers, competencies, and capabilities.

People

Look deeply into the organization's people at all different levels. Look at senior leadership (commercial, operations, tech and information technology [IT], finance, human resources [HR], legal, research and development [R&D], mergers and acquisitions [M&A]), middle management, and individual and team strengths, including project management and transformation.

Dig deeply into the core individuals with the same rigor you would if you were hiring them—because you are. Do the background checks. Understand what they've done in the past and their strengths, motivation, and fit with the culture you're building.

Look across the ADEPT components—acquiring, developing, encouraging, planning, and transitioning—to understand the organization's capabilities in hiring talent. Start with planning to get at the organization's

- Future capability planning (Do they do future capability planning? How well has it worked?)
- Succession planning (Do they have succession plans in place to replace their key leaders and individual performers over time?)
- Contingency planning strength (Do they have contingency plans in place to be ready to replace those same people with short notice if necessary?)

Then look at the organization's talent acquisition program. How well have they done recruiting new talent and why? Look at their talent development program and results—particularly in their core area per the previous explanation.

Look at their encouragement program and results. A big part of this is compensation and benefits and how it lines up with competitors given their strategy.

In areas where the organization chooses to be	Compensation should be in the
Predominant	Top 1% of the market
Strong	Top 25%
Above average	"Competitive" or above average
Good enough	Average

But encouragement is much broader than compensation and benefits. Look at recognition and reward systems all adding up to employee satisfaction. Look at how the organization transitions talent, moving people out, across or up as appropriate. Infrastructure, systems, and processes and balance sheet and cash flows are often enablers of growth or sources of cash to fuel grown.

Cultural Due Diligence

By the time most organizations start thinking about corporate culture, they already have one. Rick Rudman, cofounder and CEO of cloud marketing software provider Vocus, is unashamedly open that he and his cofounders did not plan their culture. It emerged. But as it emerged, they made conscious choices about what to keep and what to evolve.[4]

Over a 6-year period, Vocus acquired seven companies, and the cultures of those companies it acquired did not combine to form an entirely new culture. Rather, Vocus carefully selected organizations that fit into its already established culture. Rudman was convinced that corporate culture is the only truly sustainable competitive advantage. But it's rarely the first advantage of a startup.

Vocus' founders set out to "write incredible software." They chose to "take the business seriously, but not ourselves seriously." From the start, they worked hard and took time during the day to have some fun, like stopping by Toys 'R Us to bring some toys back to the office. Even their first official planning session consisted of the company's eight employees working on the train on the way to an evening in Atlantic City. (Think Las Vegas meets the Jersey Shore.)

That "became a culture that worked," said Rudman. People were attracted by that culture and "became a part of us." Vocus' culture became one of their sources of pride. In terms of the components that make up the Vocus culture, let's break it down in terms of BRAVE (behaviors, relationships, attitudes, values, and environment).

Vocus' *environment* speaks volumes. They laid out their 93,000 square foot corporate office to have the look and feel of a town (Seaside, Florida, to be specific). As Rudman explained, it had a main street for people to stroll on, a coffee shop for people to escape to, an oasis for food, a fitness center, and a "bored" room for formal meetings. (Yes, "bored" is spelled right.)

Their *values* didn't change much. They still drive "open communication and teamwork while allowing opportunity for individual achievements," "integrity," "customer focus," and working and playing hard. Vocus' employees share the same *attitude* of taking work seriously without taking themselves too seriously. The environment, values, and attitude inform their *relationships,* guiding, if not defining, the way they work together.

All this led to a set of *behaviors* that made it a fun place to work but where employees were able to make a large impact on their

[4]Bradt, George, 2013, "Managing the Evolution of Your Startup's Corporate Culture," *Forbes* (March 20).

customers. To support the Vocus way of life, the company had several internal committees dedicated to cultivating its culture. The "it's all about you" committee enhanced employee work lives by introducing programs like on-site basketball tournaments and group yoga classes, and the "It's not all about you" committee pushed employees out into the community to volunteer.

Rudman works very hard to sustain and improve the Vocus culture. He chose to acquire smaller companies and fold them into the Vocus culture. One example was iContact, which was a larger acquisition than normal. Rudman shared that folding iContact in took "a lot of proactive work," which included building a new environment for them similar to Vocus' headquarters, changing their language and acronyms, and helping them become part of the Vocus family.

In many ways, culture is a shared set of BRAVE preferences. People joining a startup need to buy in to the founders' preferences. Of course, culture evolves—but it rarely shifts quickly. And above all else, the right fit is what matters most. (See Tool 11.1, Culture.)

Then go on and complete your assessment of infrastructure, systems, and processes and the balance sheet and cash flows.

Infrastructure

- Data, technology, IT, and security infrastructure is an enabler.
- Operational infrastructure including procurement and supply chain is both an enabler and source of cash.
- Organizational and HR infrastructure is an enabler.
- Financial reporting, tax, accounting, and compliance infrastructure is an enabler.
- New product development infrastructure is an enabler.

Systems and Processes

- Enabling commercial growth and operational rigor

Balance Sheet and Cash Flows

- Deferred maintenance and modernization investments are sources of cash.
- Growth-oriented capital spending is an enabler.
- Back office finance and tax are enablers.

Ongoing Due Diligence

Jim Donald's first day as the CEO of Pathmark began early, at 1:30 a.m., when he stopped by one of the supermarket chain's 24/7 stores to strike up a conversation with an associate. By 8 a.m., he was at the head office, getting briefed by his exec team. But he'd already learned something from the associate responsible for managing $75 million in inventory in one of the highest-crime areas of the country.[5]

"When you go where you've never been before, you're going to see things you didn't expect to see. You can't necessarily rely on your executive team to be so candid to tell you about what's behind the scenes," says Donald.

That associate never expected to see Donald again—and he told Donald that on his way out. But Donald was back the next week and the following week. The word spread. Donald's hands-on approach showed front-line team members that their opinions and experience were valued at the highest levels of the company.

The importance of hearing feedback directly from your front-line people is something Donald learned from working with another retail legend, Sam Walton of Walmart. When they visited stores, Walton would get on the microphone and invite employees and customers to come ask him questions.

"Great leaders always perform on their employees' or their customers' home courts. There is no way that doing right by your frontline can happen from your office, from your home or from your computer in your home. Whether it's a personal or virtual reach-out, go where you've never gone before, see and learn things on the frontline that you might be learning for the very first time."

The late former chair of the Joint Chiefs of Staff and U.S. Secretary of State Colin Powell called this getting at the "ground truth." The Powell Doctrine lays out five keys to using all the force necessary to achieve a decisive and successful ongoing result:[6]

---

[5]*Axonify*, 2021, "'The Turnaround King' on Why Frontline Employee Engagement Is a Business Imperative" (June 4).

[6]Bradt, George, 2021, "Five Keys to the Decisive Action You Need to Accelerate Out of COVID-19," *Forbes* (April 20).

1. Get to the ground truth.
2. Set a decisive objective.
3. Concentrate decisive force at the decisive place and time.
4. Prepare your troops for success.
5. Be personally present at the point of decisions.

Get to the Ground Truth

Powell described the need for leaders to know ground truth. This is unvarnished, unfiltered truth about the harsh reality. Powell got his from chaplains, sergeants major, inspectors general, and normal soldiers.

Get your ground truth from data, facts, and first-line supervisors. They are close enough to the front lines to know the truth, one step back so they can see the forest and not just the trees, and far enough away from you not to be afraid of you.

Set a Decisive Objective

A decisive objective at a decisive place and time is one that, if you gain it, you win—what Carl Clausewitz, a nineteenth-century Prussian general, called the strategic center of gravity. Ask the first two BRAVE questions, "What matters and why?" and "Where to play?" to inform your objective and first strategy choice, respectively. Research by Marakon confirmed, yet again, that, "The path to superior performance is determined by management's decisions about where to focus the firm's strategic resources (time, people, and capital)."

Concentrate Decisive Force at the Decisive Place and Time

Powell said, "Concentrate combat power at the decisive place and time," directing "every military operation towards a clearly defined, decisive, and obtainable objective"—mass, objective, offensive, surprise, economy of force, maneuver, unity of command, security, simplicity.

In the first Gulf War, U.S. General Norman Schwarzkopf asked for one aircraft carrier battle group. Powell gave him two because he felt it "added to the insurance policy that would give us ultimate victory."

Former U.S. President Jimmy Carter failed to rescue the U.S. hostages in Iran and later said, "If I'd sent two helicopters, I would have been reelected president."

Ask "How to win?" The essence of strategy is the creation and allocation of resources to the right place at the right time over time. This is about concentrating your efforts to create a decisive advantage over your opponent—whether it's a business competitor or virus. Identify your key resources and deploy more than you think you need when and where it really matters.

Prepare Your Troops for Success

"Soldiers given a task they haven't been prepared for lose confidence in themselves and, fatally, in their leaders," said Powell. Prepare them and take the necessary time to get them ready to win. This is about clear direction, bounded authority, resources, and accountability. Make sure your people:

- Know what's expected of them—the clearly defined, decisive, and obtainable objective.
- Understand what tactical decisions they can make on the way to achieving that objective.
- Have the financial, technical, operational, and human resources they need to succeed.
- Accept their accountability to achieve that objective with those resources.

Be Personally Present at the Point of Decision

The point of decision is the place where key decisions can make the difference between success and failure. Following through and being personally present there will allow you to adjust your plans in real time as "no plan survives first contact with an enemy." Strategy and planning are useless intellectual exercises until they are turned into decisive impact.

Darwin told us it's not the strongest that survive, but those best able to adapt. This is why, even if you've delegated accountability, you must follow through and be fully engaged at the critical moments. Ideally, you'll ask your subordinates, "How can I help?" You've put them in charge of achieving their objectives—until you need to change. When you do, don't hesitate to take back control and redirect resources.

Guest Contributor Karl Bailliez

As a potential acquirer, the financial due diligence process gives me an opportunity to form a view as to what a fair value of the target company might be. Meaning that any financial information that has been made available during the due diligence process is broken down and analyzed to try to understand what the underlying business really looks like.

Each company and each deal is different; therefore, the analysis undertaken will also need to be tailored. Financial due diligence is a generic term that can actually be applied to a vast range of processes and analyses, with the goal of giving comfort to an initial valuation, which in turn will support the ultimate purchase price offered.

More recently, sellers and buyers have become extremely sophisticated in their approach to transactions, with sellers increasingly coming to market with a team of advisors who have prepared and presented the business in the light they want the market to see—which in turn has removed some of the opportunity for buyers to chip price.

Buyers therefore need to really understand the value drivers of the target business and get into the details driving the financials to be able to formulate decent arguments that will hold up in a pricing negotiation.

I typically see four distinct but highly intertwined components to the financial due diligence process as follows:

1. Quality of earnings analysis (QofE)
2. Debt and debt-like items analysis
3. Net working capital analysis
4. Review of the purchase agreement

These components are critical to help reaffirm the valuation of the company and therefore the price that you are willing to pay for the business to be acquired given each focuses on a key aspect of the pricing bridge (Table 11.1).

Quality of Earnings Analysis

The quality of earnings analysis does just that—it tests the quality of the underlying operating performance of the target business. Often

Table 11.1
The Purchase Price Components

Headline Price / Enterprise Value *Commonly calculated as a multiple of EBITDA*	**$xxm**	**Quality of earnings analysis**
(+) Cash	$xxm	Debt and debt-like items analysis
(–) Net Debt	$xxm	
(+/–) Diff. between Closing Working Capital and Target Working Capital	$xxm	Net working capital analysis
Equity Value	**$xxm**	
(+/–) Other purchase price adjustments		Purchase agreement
Net Purchase Price	**$xxm**	

EBITDA is used as the operating performance metric and is defined as earnings before interest, tax, depreciation, and amortization. This is effectively a proxy for the cash flow of the business to be acquired, or in other words, the amount of recurring cash flow available for debt service.

To understand the underlying performance of the business, any one-time, unusual, or nonrecurring items should be normalized out of the reported financials. Clearly any adjustment identified in diligence that reduces these underlying earnings will have an impact (at the multiple) to net purchase price. These quality of earning adjustments are often based on a difference of opinion between the selling and buying parties on how something should be accounted for, for the purposes of pricing a deal—and hence are judgmental.

Debt and Debt-Like Analysis

As laid out in the previous pricing bridge, any item of debt reduces (and cash increases) net purchase price on a dollar one basis—therefore, it is critical to ensure that all debt and debt-like items are identified during the financial due diligence process so that they can be included in price.

Working Capital Analysis

A certain amount of working capital is required to generate the underlying operating performance of the business. If the seller delivers the business with an insufficient amount of working capital, the net price should be adjusted accordingly.

The working capital analysis will identify what the normal level should be through looking at a series of historical and future trends. This analysis is key for pricing but also, for a buyer, it is needed to identify if any form of short-term financing (e.g., revolver) is required on day 1.

Review of the Purchase Agreement

The purchase agreement summarizes what the seller is selling and what the buyer is buying. It sets out how net purchase price will be arrived at and how risk will be allocated between the parties upon closure of the deal. Therefore, the components of the negotiated pricing bridge (Table 11.1) should be clearly laid out in the agreement—and the final part of due diligence is to ensure that the purchase agreement sets out properly the negotiated and agreed upon terms.

The most up-to-date, full, editable versions of all tools are downloadable at primegenesis.com/tools

TOOL 11.1

Culture

First, understand your own culture and the culture of your target company. A form like this can help. Mark your culture with Us for *us*. Mark their culture with Ts for *them*. You can get there with surveys, observations, or both. The gaps are issues.

Environment—Where Play

Workplace		
Remote, virtual, open, informal	1 – 2 – 3 – 4 – 5	In-person, closed, formal
Work-Life Balance		
Health and wellness first	1 – 2 – 3 – 4 – 5	Near-term productivity first
Enablers		
Human, interpersonal, societal	1 – 2 – 3 – 4 – 5	Technical, mechanical, scientific

Values—What matters and why

Focus		
Do good for others/ESG	1 – 2 – 3 – 4 – 5	Do good for selves, what good at
Risk Appetite		
Risk more, gain more (confidence)	1 – 2 – 3 – 4 – 5	Protect what have, minimize mistakes
Learning		
Open, shared, value diversity	1 – 2 – 3 – 4 – 5	Directed, individual, single-minded

Attitude—How Win

Strategy		
Premium price, service, innovation	1 – 2 – 3 – 4 – 5	Low-cost, low-service, minimum viable
Focus		
Divergence from competitors	1 – 2 – 3 – 4 – 5	Convergence on market leader
Posture		
Proactive, breakthrough innovation	1 – 2 – 3 – 4 – 5	Responsive, reliable steady progress

(Continued)

TOOL 11.1 Culture (continued)

Relationships—How Connect

Power, Decision-Making		
Diffused, debated—confront issues	1 – 2 – 3 – 4 – 5	Controlled, monarchical
Diversity, Equity, Inclusion		
All welcome, valued, respected	1 – 2 – 3 – 4 – 5	Bias to work with people just like us
Communication, Controls		
Informal, verbal, face-to-face	1 – 2 – 3 – 4 – 5	Formal, directed, written

Behaviors – What Impact

Working Units		
One organization, interdependent teams	1 – 2 – 3 – 4 – 5	Independent individuals, units
Discipline		
Fluid, flexible (guidelines)	1 – 2 – 3 – 4 – 5	Structured, disciplined (policies)
Delegation		
Inspire, enable, empower, trust	1 – 2 – 3 – 4 – 5	Narrow, task-focused direction

TOOL 11.2

Negotiating

Make a Plan

Map out their needs and concerns and map out your needs and concerns. Both should be done across all the critical dimensions of the negotiation:

Their walkaway:

Their maximum or minimum:

Their expected:

Their opening:

My opening:

My expected:

My minimum or maximum:

My walkaway:

Get Started

Somehow negotiations are always easier if you can start by agreeing. Find the areas that you agree on and discuss those first.

Areas of Agreement:

Areas for Debate:

1. Listen to the other person's position and probe for understanding. Don't challenge at this point. Just seek to understand.
2. State your position.
3. Support your position with other information.

Clarify Positions

(Listen to their position. State your position. Support with other information.)

(Continued)

TOOL 11.2 Negotiating (continued)

Find Alternatives

Look for ways to meet everyone's needs. Often, this involves bringing another dimension into the picture.

Gain Agreement

Again, there's a process for managing this:

1. Receive and make proposals.
2. Receive and make concessions on different dimensions.
3. Summarize the situation.
4. Test agreements.
5. Circle back to concessions until there's a complete agreement.

Implement

TOOL 11.3

Due Diligence Checklist

Think in terms of commercial, operational, and value creation due diligence

1. Review and verify all financial information.

The quality of the financial information provided will be affected by different factors, such as:

- The complexity of the target company: its legal form, its footprint (domestic vs. global), the number and nature of material tax jurisdictions, whether the company is freestanding vs. carve-out, whether it has grown organically or from acquisitions
- The nature of the transaction—public company vs. private deal, joint venture/less-than-controlling investment, taxable vs. tax free, asset vs. stock deal, carve-out of a division, and so forth.
- The existence or not of audited financial statements—if the target is a small business, keep in mind that most small business financials have been compiled by the seller with the goal of minimizing taxes, so they will need to explain everything in detail, including the owner's benefit (seller's discretionary income) and cash flow.
- The timing and stage of the transaction—competitive auction vs. exclusivity, preliminary phase vs. fully committed bid process.
- The extent of seller's readiness.

Though not exhaustive, the following list provides a good framework of what information needs to be reviewed as part of the financial due diligence procedures:

- Financials (audited or not): income statements, cash flow statements, balance sheets, trial balances, and any underlying financial information available (If the financial statements are audited, it is customary to request access to the audit and tax work papers prepared by the company's external auditors and tax advisors.)
- Transaction documentation: confidential information memorandum and management presentation, sell-side due diligence report (if applicable)

(Continued)

TOOL 11.3 Due Diligence Checklist (continued)

- Due diligence reports related to previous transactions (acquisitions, divestitures)
- Internal management reports (including monthly operating reviews and presentations prepared for the board of directors or shareholders)
- Key performance indicators used by the management team to monitor their business
- List of any off-balance-sheet liabilities and commitments
- Credit report
- Tax returns for at least the past 3 years—federal, state, foreign
- General accounting policies (e.g., revenue recognition)
- Risks attendant to foreign operations (e.g., exchange rate fluctuation, government instability)
- All debts, their terms, and any contingent liabilities
- Analysis of revenue and gross profit margins by geography, segment, range of product, SKU
- Analysis of fixed and variable expenses
- Inventory of all products, equipment, and real estate, including book and market value
- Accounts receivable, inventory, and accounts payable reports (including aging, calculation of related reserves)
- Financial projections (budgets for the last 3 years, forecast for the current year)
- Industry and company pricing policies
- Economic assumptions underlying projections (different scenarios based on price and market fluctuations)
- Explanation of projected capital expenditures, depreciation, and working capital arrangements
- External financing arrangement assumption
- Draft purchase agreement

2. Review and verify the business structure and operations.

Take a closer look at how the business is structured and how it makes its money. Any information about competitors, market penetration, or trends in the industry could be useful in determining the company's future earnings potential. This is your opportunity to review and verify the business model, customer base, products and services, as well as labor, materials, and operational costs.

- Company's articles of incorporation and amendments
- Company's bylaws and amendments
- Summary of current investors and shareholders—shares outstanding, owners, options, warrants, rights, notes, any other potentially dilutive securities with exercise prices and vesting provisions
- All company names and trademark brand names
- All states where the company is authorized to do business
- All products and services, including production cost and margins (Follow the product through the key steps to understand strengths and gaps.)
- Design and innovation—especially if the company is design led, or how they acquire ideas from others
- Production—looking at the whole supply chain from sourcing materials to handling materials to physically producing and managing inventory
- Delivery and distribution—looking at the whole ecosystem of partners, allies, and contractors to understand how products and services move through the system
- Service—looking at the guided accountability of the front-line service providers
- Supplier database, purchases by supplier
- Share of their business
- Purchasing agreements

3. Review and verify all material contracts.

Does the business have any partnerships or joint ventures with other companies? Does the business have any existing loan agreements, lines of credit, equipment leases, or other indentures? Find out what obligations or agreements are in place that you may be expected to comply with or respond to that are part of doing business.

- All nondisclosure or noncompete agreements, any guarantees
- Company purchase orders, quotes, invoices, or warranties

(Continued)

TOOL 11.3 Due Diligence Checklist (continued)

- Security agreements, mortgages, collateral pledges
- Letters of intent, contracts, closing transcripts from mergers or acquisitions
- Distribution agreements, sales agreements, subscription agreements
- All loan agreements, material leases, lines of credit or promissory notes
- Contracts between officers, directors, or principals of the company
- Stock purchase agreements or other options

4. Dig into Product and Intellectual Property Information

Understand what you're getting in terms of product and intellectual property:

- Services and products: customers and application
- Past and predicted growth rates
- Market share
- New product development—strategy, people, activities, pipeline status and timing, costs, technology enablers, risks
- All company's patents, trademarks, and copyrights
- Product inventions, formulas, recipes, or technical know-how
- All rights owned data and digital information
- All work-for-hire or consulting agreements
- Who owns or controls the rights to the intellectual property?
- Has the IP been patented?

5. Review and verify all customer information.

Review all customer lists and databases. Find out who are the largest customers in terms of sales as well as what they've purchased over the last 2–3 years. How are these customers acquired and retained? Are they on renewable subscription agreements?

- All customer databases, subscriber lists, and sales records, revenue by customer
- Purchase agreements
- Customer communication

- Refund policies
- Status and trends of main relationships
- Description of the competitive landscape within each market segment including:
  - Market position and related strengths and weaknesses as perceived in the marketplace
  - Basis of competition (e.g., price, service, technology, distribution)
- Brand and product positioning, marketing strategies
- Marketing plan, customer analysis, competitors, industry trends
  - If the company is #1 in its market, understand how it differentiates itself from its competition and what you're going to have to do to keep it differentiated.
  - If the company is not #1 in its market, understand what is required to converge on the #1 player and what you expect their response to be.
  - Understand how people move through the sales funnel from being unaware to aware to interested to desirous to purchase. Look at influencers, purchasers, users.
- Company's brand identity, including logo, website, and domain
- All advertising programs, marketing programs, and events
- Distribution channels
- Sales force and sales pipeline: Sales role in building awareness, interest, desire, action, sales cycle, and sales force compensation.
- Copies of standard communications and correspondence
- Any customer research data, white papers, or research
- All attorneys and law firms representing the company, area of practice
- Pending litigation or threats of litigation
- Any unsatisfied judgments
- All insurance coverage and policies
- All professional licenses and permits

6. Review and verify all employee information.

Ask for the company's employee roster and an organizational chart. Find out who the key employees are and what their

(Continued)

TOOL 11.3 Due Diligence Checklist (continued)

responsibilities entail. This may be an important opportunity to find out if any employees plan to leave the company after it's sold and if you should offer them some sort of incentive to stay.

- Employee roster, organizational chart, and job descriptions
- Employee contracts and independent contractor agreements—including noncompete, nondisclosure, severance agreements, and outsourced work to freelancers, consultants
- Payroll information and employee tax forms. Look for:
  - Owners either not paying themselves a fair salary or overpaying themselves to increase or decrease profits
  - Leaders' and managers' compensation as a data point on the strength and expected retention of leaders and managers
  - Human resources policies and procedures
  - Employee benefits, retirement plan, and insurance

Get a read on the company culture looking at key BRAVE dimensions of its environment, values, attitudes, relationships, and how they behave. Look at these from different perspectives and compare to reference organizations.

7. Review and verify all infrastructure, physical assets, and real estate.

Get a full inventory of all the company's property and its current market value, including automobiles, equipment, real estate, and inventory.

- Real estate, including office locations, warehouses, current leases, and titles
- A schedule of all fixed assets, including product inventory, furniture, fixtures, and equipment
- Information technology infrastructure: data centers

8. Check for any legal or compliance issues.

Are there any outstanding legal issues or ongoing litigation that you need to know about? Who represents the company? Does the company have proper insurance in place? Does the company have all the proper licenses and permits in place?

- Business compliance requirements
- Licensing
- Insurance
- Permits
- Pending compliance, regulatory, lawsuits, and legal issues—by company and against company
- Environmental information, such as health and safety notices, information related to any hazardous substances, or underground storage tanks

CHAPTER 12

Financing the Deal: The Different Options

	The Strategic Playbook	The Commercial Playbook	The Operational Playbook	The Financial Playbook	The Governance Playbook	The Organizational Playbook	The Change Management Playbook
Concept Research Investment Case Negotiation Deal/Due Diligence Contract Close Integration Acceleration Next Normal	The Investment Case	Organic Revenue Growth	Cost Optimization	Deal/ Due Diligence	Regulatory	Culture Incentives	Integration Leader Change Management
	Focus		Operational Excellence: Supply Chain, Distribution, Continual Improvement	Financing	Financial	Leadership	Communication
	Plans	Customers		M&A	Board	People	Announcement
	Innovation	Marketing & Sales	Technology			Politics	Adjustments

The second component of the financial playbook is funding the deal. Your real investment is different depending on how you finance the deal.

True story. Someone (name withheld) agreed to pay $3MM for 100 percent ownership in a company within 1 month of the close of the sale. The day the sale closed, the company had $5MM in the bank. One month later, the new owner transferred $3MM from the company's accounts to the old owner.

You don't have to be a mathematical genius to figure out that new owner's real investment was not $3MM.

While funding for all your mergers and acquisitions may not be quite that favorable, do consider options for funding beyond cash including equity, seller funding or earnout, and debt, among others.

Cash

On one hand, cash is reasonable straightforward. You give the old owners money. They give you the company. Of course, there may be some wiggle room on when you give them the cash, what currency the cash is in, and other dimensions. And you separately need to source your cash, which may get into other areas of financing outside of the actual deal with the seller.

Equity

Equity deals essentially divide shares in the new, combined entity between the owners of the previous entity. Theoretically, no cash trades hands. There's no need for debt financing. The negotiation focuses the new owners' different levels of equity.

Seller Funding or Earnout

At some point, delaying when you pay the seller becomes a loan from the seller. Or if the seller has to hit some milestones or deliverables to earn part of their sale price, that becomes an earnout.

When Hal Reiter agreed to buy executive search firm Herbert Mines from its founder, Herbert Mines, they agreed on a firm price and 10-year transition. In 1993, Reiter purchased 25 percent of the firm and became president.

Over the next 5 years, Mines transitioned his main client relationships to Reiter. In 1998, Reiter purchased another 50 percent of the firm and became CEO.

Finally, in 2003, Reiter purchased the remaining 25 percent. When Reiter and Mines met for lunch for Reiter to give Mines the final check, Mines noted, "If I'd know how successful you would have been, I would have asked a higher price."

Reiter didn't miss a beat and replied, "Let's renegotiate." He ending up giving Mines substantially more money than the original contract in recognition of how helpful he had been during the transition.

Debt

Debt comes in different forms from general loans to bonds to credit lines to bridge financing to mezzanine or subordinated debt.

- General loans are when banks or others loan money to organizations in return for interest payments. This is reasonably straightforward and a good idea if the incremental cash flows enabled by the loan more than offsets the interest payments. Expect these to come with covenants that may restrict your degrees of freedom.
- Bonds are essentially public debt in which you sell bonds to the public instead of shares.
- Credit lines are agreements to loan money that can be accessed when needed.
- Bridge financing bridges the gap from deal announcement to close.
- Mezzanine or subordinated debt are loans that get paid back after other loans and therefore riskier and carrying a higher interest rate.

Guest Contributor Aaron Darr

Capital Structure Management: Someone Decided to Borrow Some Money

Regardless of the specifics, someone want(ed/s) to buy something that they don't have the cash for. This could be anything: new inventory, new equipment, a shareholder's equity stake, or another entire business. The principal issue is that you need cash, and whomever is going to lend you money is going to need confidence that they are going to get paid back (plus some return on their capital). While this description seems pedestrian, every bit of complexity in capital structure formation and management results from this simple dynamic.

The person or entity that lends you money—let's call them the *lender* for simplicity—needs to be reasonably confident that you'll be able to pay them back plus some return, usually in the form of interest.

(Continued)

If you don't pay them back, they want to be able to take something of value from you to be made whole. The type of loan you can get is going to be a result of what you have (that they can take and presumably sell for cash). Businesses usually use a combination of assets and cash flows to convince a lender they'll be paid back. Assets can be hard (e.g., land, equipment, inventory) or soft (e.g., intellectual property, patents).

If this all sounds simple, trust your judgment—it is. That said, simple does not mean easy.

For purposes of discussion, let's focus on what is required to maintain a capital structure following a transaction. There are a couple of practices for a finance leader that are good hygiene, so to speak.

1. *Review credit documentation for critical operating items*. Despite the core document usually being somewhere north of 100 pages, critical operating items center around (a) key dates, (b) definitions, and (c) reporting requirements. Leverage legal counsel to create a calendar of key dates and memo of key definitions, and review with them in detail at the onset. Beyond counsel's advice, work with your counterpart at the lender to review draft reporting prior to formal submission. In a majority of cases, any lender is aligned with initial reporting going smoothly (otherwise they look stupid, too).
   a. *Key dates:* Reporting and payment dates occur on a monthly, quarterly, and annual basis with standard timelines (e.g., 30-, 45-, 60-day deadlines). Depending on the existing cadence within the finance organization, such requirements can represent a substantial increase in tempo.
   b. *Definitions:* A number of non-GAAP terms will be key components of reporting requirements. Understanding how trial balance-level data maps onto such non-GAAP terms is important.
   c. *Reporting requirements:* Some variation of compliance certification will need to be completed, signed, and submitted on a recurring basis.
2. *Build and maintain supporting financial rigor*. With additional financial metrics to monitor and manage relative to credit-related reporting requirements, it is important to build and maintain financial analysis to supplement whatever existing financial reporting is in place. With key definitions addressed in step 1, the

next step is to put numbers to those definitions. With debt financing of some sort added to the capital structure, the business has assumed additional financial risk that needs to be appropriately managed. Said another way, debt service (i.e., interest and principal payments) has increased the amount of fixed costs in the business. The value of good hygiene here cannot be overstated.

a. *Map trial balance-level data to non-GAAP definitions*. Utilize the definitions reviewed in step 1 to build Microsoft Excel–based schedules to calculate non-GAAP terms. Certain non-GAAP terms have a number of sub-components to them. A good example of this is adjusted earnings before interest, taxes, depreciation, and amortization (EBITDA). EBITDA itself is a non-GAAP concept of cash flow; adjusted EBITDA goes a step further and excludes one-time impacts to earnings that are thought to not be ordinary course so as to more accurately represent the true earnings power of the business. Two common examples of an adjustments are (i) merger and acquisition (M&A)–related expenses and (ii) one-time consulting expenses. Since these two categories can overlap, it is important to track them at the invoice level in an Excel-based file so that you can optimize the adjusted EBITDA figure.

b. *Build Excel-based compliance certificate schedules*. Once key definitions have been built into an Excel-based reporting package, the next step is to develop Excel-based schedules for credit compliance reporting. This is as simple as replicating the compliance certifications scheduled in the credit documentation. A common metric to certify compliance is net leverage:

   Net leverage = total debt – cash / adjusted EBITDA

   which is represented as a ratio or multiple (e.g., 3.75:1 *or* 3.75x). While it is common to complete a simple compliance form—literally check a box certifying that net leverage is less than 3.75x and sign the bottom—maintaining the precision of a bottoms-up build in Excel is a best practice.

c. *Develop and maintain 13-week cash flow analysis*. Debt service, often in the form of cash payments, increases the fixed cost in the business and presents significant monthly, quarterly, or annual cash uses that need to be planned for. A direct cash

(Continued)

model to project weekly cash inflows and outflows 13 weeks (e.g., includes quarterly payments) is an incredibly valuable tool. Even with modest debt service on a business, there are times when payroll, rent, vendor payments, and debt service all align and require a finance lead to both plan ahead and manage timing. Paying a vendor a few days late is preferred to defaulting on a credit agreement by not remitting debt service payments. A 13-week cash flow model will need to be tailored to the specific cash flow profile and capital intensity of the business. That said, a few key dimensions should be considered standard: (i) cash receipts; (ii) disbursements related to fixed costs; and (iii) cash disbursements related to variable costs. The goal is to bifurcate cash receipts and disbursements into what is controllable (e.g., ability to impact timing such as paying vendors a few days late) and what has zero discretion (e.g., rent, debt service).

CHAPTER 13

Further M&A: Enabling Commercial and Operational Success

	The Strategic Playbook	The Commercial Playbook	The Operational Playbook	The Financial Playbook	The Governance Playbook	The Organizational Playbook	The Change Management Playbook
Concept	The Investment Case					Culture	Integration Leader
Research		Organic Revenue Growth	Cost Optimization	Deal/ Due Diligence			
Investment Case					Regulatory	Incentives	Change Management
Negotiation			Operational Excellence: Supply Chain, Distribution, Continual Improvement				
Deal/Due Diligence	Focus			Financing	Financial	Leadership	Communication
Contract		Customers					
Close	Plans			M&A	Board	People	Announcement
Integration		Marketing & Sales					
Acceleration	Innovation		Technology			Politics	Adjustments
Next Normal							

The third component of the financial playbook is mergers and acquisitions (M&A). Further acquisitions, mergers or joint ventures with other companies, brands, technologies, systems, and the like layered on to the new, combined platform—especially in a relatively fragmented market—can enable all the other plans. On one hand, everything in this book applies to bolt-on M&A. On the other hand, in some cases you can do smaller bolt-ons to fix discrete problems or take advantage of discrete opportunities.

Just be deliberate about your choices and what you're buying. It's easier to see if the company you're acquiring has hard assets like buildings, plant, and equipment. It's harder to see if they do not—like many service companies. For example, consulting firm A could buy consulting firm B lock, stock, and barrel, subsuming their brand, intellectual property, and people. Or they could hire away their key people.

We're right back at the beginning. The first, fundamental questions go to what you want out of an acquisition or merger, how it would fit with what you've already got, and what you're willing to give up to get it.

Buy the full consulting (or other firm) if you need everything they are and do. Buy or hire away the parts you value if you don't need the whole thing.

PART V

The Governance Playbook

CHAPTER 14

Regulatory: And the License to Play

	The Strategic Playbook	The Commercial Playbook	The Operational Playbook	The Financial Playbook	The Governance Playbook	The Organizational Playbook	The Change Management Playbook
Concept Research Investment Case Negotiation Deal/Due Diligence Contract Close Integration Acceleration Next Normal	The Investment Case	Organic Revenue Growth	Cost Optimization	Deal/ Due Diligence	Regulatory	Culture Incentives	Integration Leader Change Management
	Focus		Operational Excellence: Supply Chain, Distribution, Continual Improvement	Financing	Financial	Leadership	Communication
	Plans	Customers		M&A	Board	People	Announcement
	Innovation	Marketing & Sales	Technology			Politics	Adjustments

The governance playbook has three components: regulatory, financial, and board governance. The first is about risk management. The second is mandatory. And the third can be hugely value-adding.

The Georgia brand team walked into George's office in Tokyo.

"Bradt-san, the lawyers say our new brand name is illegal."

"OK. We're not going to argue with the lawyers. They know the law. Instead, ask them what they think, in their legal opinion, would happen if we (a) chose to break the law and (b) got caught."

This being Japan, the brand team didn't like that. But as much as they feared breaking the law, they feared George more and went back to legal.

They returned an hour later.

"Bradt-san, it happened."

"What happened?"

"We had an illegal brand name in the market and we got caught 13 years later."

"OK. What happened?"

"We had to change the name."

"Who went to jail?"

"No one."

"How much was the fine?"

"There was no fine. We just had to change the name."

"Excellent. I'm prepared to accept that risk. Go forth and launch your illegal brand name on my authority."

Of course, you're not going to do that. You're not going to do a risk–reward assessment and then knowingly violate regulations that don't really matter. Our point is the Gore-Tex waterline analogy. They're happy with people taking risks that could result in a hit above the waterline. They can fix those. They are inconsequential and reversible. But if someone takes a risk that could sink the boat—consequential and irreversible—they need to escalate that decision.

Violating some regulations result in minor fines. Fine. Violating some regulations result in regulators taking away your license to operate. Not fine.

Other key considerations as you evaluate a business for a mergers and acquisitions (M&A) or private equity (PE) deal is brand reputation and emerging regulatory trends. Among other things, pay attention to:

- Business compliance requirements
- Licensing
- Insurance
- Permits
- Pending compliance, regulatory, lawsuits, and legal issues—by company and against company
- Environmental information, such as health and safety notices, information related to any hazardous substances, or underground storage tanks
- Industry and company pricing policies
- Risks attendant to foreign operations (e.g., exchange rate fluctuation, government instability)

Guest Contributor Katherine Kirkpatrick

The current deal-making environment is filled to the brim with resurgent M&A activity globally, and people are making money hand over fist. But in those circumstances, it can be even harder to step back and evaluate whether the proper governance and compliance infrastructure is in place.

I spent a dozen years in the private sector focused exclusively on investigations, corporate compliance, white-collar defense, and regulatory matters. When I decided to make a change, I shied away from the all-important compliance-oriented positions. Why? Certainly not because those roles aren't important—they are often the most crucial. But as someone who thrives on getting the deal done, I hesitated before considering a role that would often necessitate "no, no, no."

That being said, considering that often inconvenient no is paramount. A necessary impediment to making money is often an investment in the longer-term health of the entity. The ancillary costs of distraction (along with legal fees, fines and penalties, business limitations, undue scrutiny, and so forth) should an issue arise are *significant*. Along the lines of "no one ever regrets a workout," no C-suite ultimately regrets prioritizing regulatory implications.

Right now, the regulatory environment for M&A deals globally is exciting but fraught with landmines. Regulators are considering more stringent agendas with a distinct focus on environmental and social issues, digital assets, trade, privacy, antitrust, and national security. The regulators are getting smarter and more sophisticated, so the private sector needs to outpace them by learning more about artificial intelligence and analytics. In addition to assessing the probability of deal approval, take into account aggressive regulators and new foreign direct investment regimes intended to further economic nationalism. Everything is a chess match—if you are three steps ahead, you have a much better chance of winning.

Now is the time to make money, but it is also the time to batten down the hatches and focus on diligence, quality, compliance, and proper corporate governance.

CHAPTER 15

Financial Governance: Always Necessary

	The Strategic Playbook	The Commercial Playbook	The Operational Playbook	The Financial Playbook	The Governance Playbook	The Organizational Playbook	The Change Management Playbook
Concept Research Investment Case Negotiation Deal/Due Diligence Contract Close Integration Acceleration Next Normal	The Investment Case Focus Plans Innovation	Organic Revenue Growth Customers Marketing & Sales	Cost Optimization Operational Excellence: Supply Chain, Distribution, Continual Improvement Technology	Deal/ Due Diligence Financing M&A	Regulatory Financial Board	Culture Incentives Leadership People Politics	Integration Leader Change Management Communication Announcement Adjustments

The second component of the governance playbook is financial governance, which is *always* necessary.

This is another relatively short chapter with exactly the opposite message of the last chapter. Where your regulatory governance needs merely to secure your license to play, deploy a zero-tolerance approach to financial governance. Require complete integrity and compliance.

Every one of you knows a story of some executive that used their best judgment in recognizing some revenue in some period that others might not have recognized to deliver on their commitments. Every one of you knows a story of how that executive ended up causing severe reputational damage to themselves and their company when they did it again and again and again until they got caught.

Don't do it. Don't let anyone else do it. Own the miss. Take the short-term hit. Fix the problem. Recover. Move on.

Financial

Keep a close watch on all the financial items you looked at during due diligence:

- Financials: Income statements, cash flow statements, balance sheets, general ledger, accounts payable and receivable
- Off balance sheet liabilities
- Credit report
- Tax returns—federal, state, foreign
- General accounting policies including revenue recognition
- Risks attendant to foreign operations (e.g., exchange rate fluctuation, government instability)
- Debts, their terms, and any contingent liabilities
- Gross profit margins
- Fixed and variable expenses
- Gross profits and rate of return by each product
- Inventory of all products, equipment, and real estate, including total value
- Financial projections
- Industry and company pricing policies
- Economic assumptions underlying projections (different scenarios based on price and market fluctuations)
- Capital expenditures, depreciation, and working capital arrangements
- External financing arrangements

Business Structure and Operations

Look at the business structure and operations from the perspective of regulators.

- Company's articles of incorporation and amendments
- Company's bylaws and amendments
- Investors and shareholders—shares outstanding, owners, options, warrants, rights, notes, any other potentially dilutive securities with exercise prices, and vesting provisions

- Company names and trademark brand names
- Products and services, including production cost and margins—follow the product through the key steps to understand strengths and gaps:
  - Design and innovation—especially if the company is design led. Look how they acquire ideas from others if they do that.
  - Production—looking at the whole supply chain from sourcing materials to handling materials to physically producing and managing inventory
  - Delivery and distribution—looking at the whole ecosystem of partners, allies, and contractors to understand how products and services move through the system
  - Service—looking at the guided accountability of the front-line service providers
- Supplier database, purchases by supplier
  - Share of their business
- Purchasing agreements
- Consents
  - Ensure you have consents for all key contracts
  - Customer
  - Vendor

Material Contracts

Look at contracts from the perspective of regulators.

- Nondisclosure or noncompete agreements, any guarantees
- Company purchase orders, quotes, invoices, or warranties
- Security agreements, mortgages, collateral pledges
- Letters of intent, contracts, closing transcripts from mergers or acquisitions
- Distribution agreements, sales agreements, subscription agreements
- Loan agreements, material leases, lines of credit, or promissory notes
- Contracts between officers, directors, or principals of the company
- Stock purchase agreements or other options

Product and Intellectual Property

Look at products and intellectual property from the perspective of regulators.

- Services and products: customers and application
- Company's patents, trademarks, and copyrights
- Product inventions, formulas, recipes, or technical know-how
- Rights owned data and digital information
- Work-for-hire or consulting agreements
- Who owns or controls the rights to the intellectual property?
- Has the IP been patented?

Customer Information

Look at customer information from the perspective of regulators.

- Customer databases, subscriber lists and sales records, revenue by customer
- Purchase agreements
- Customer communication
- Refund policies
- Rebates
- Contingent liabilities
- Guarantees
- Status and trends of main relationships
- Description of the competitive landscape within each market segment
- Litigation or threats of litigation
- Standard communications and correspondence
- Pending litigation or threats of litigation
- Unsatisfied judgments
- Insurance coverage and policies
- Professional licenses and permits

Employee Information

Look at employee information from the perspective of regulators.

- Employee contracts and independent contractor agreements—including noncompete, nondisclosure, severance agreements, and outsourced work to freelancers, consultants, and so forth
- Workers' compensation
- Payroll information and employee tax forms. Look for:
  - owner's either not paying themselves a fair salary or over-paying themselves to increase or decrease profits
  - leaders and managers' compensation as a data point on the strength and expected retention of leaders and managers
- Human resources policies and procedures
- Employee benefits, retirement plan, and insurance

Infrastructure, Physical Assets, and Real Estate

Look at infrastructure, physical assets, and real estate from the perspective of regulators.

- Real estate, including office locations, warehouses, current leases, and titles
- Fixed assets, including product inventory, furniture, fixtures, and equipment
- Information technology infrastructure: data centers

CHAPTER 16

The Board: And Its Multiple Roles

	The Strategic Playbook	The Commercial Playbook	The Operational Playbook	The Financial Playbook	The Governance Playbook	The Organizational Playbook	The Change Management Playbook
Concept Research Investment Case	The Investment Case	Organic Revenue Growth	Cost Optimization	Deal/ Due Diligence	Regulatory	Culture Incentives	Integration Leader Change Management
Negotiation Deal/Due Diligence	Focus		Operational Excellence: Supply Chain, Distribution, Continual Improvement	Financing	Financial	Leadership	Communication
Contract Close	Plans	Customers		M&A	Board	People	Announcement
Integration Acceleration Next Normal	Innovation	Marketing & Sales	Technology			Politics	Adjustments

The third component of the governance playbook is the board. Boards play multiple roles: part governance and part advisory. Building the right board can make a massive impact on the success of a merger or acquisition.

In general, boards are accountable for governance and oversight as highlighted in Figure 16.1. They approve strategic, annual operating (profit and loss [P&L], cash flows, balance sheet), future capability, succession, contingency, and compensation plans and are consulted and informed on everything else. More specifically:

Public boards normally have fiduciary duties of care and loyalty in the best interest of their corporations and of *all* their shareholders and stakeholders, including customers, employees, suppliers, and communities. These boards are subject to the strictest public regulation and scrutiny even beyond their traditional fiduciary responsibilities

FIGURE 16.1 Board Roles and Management

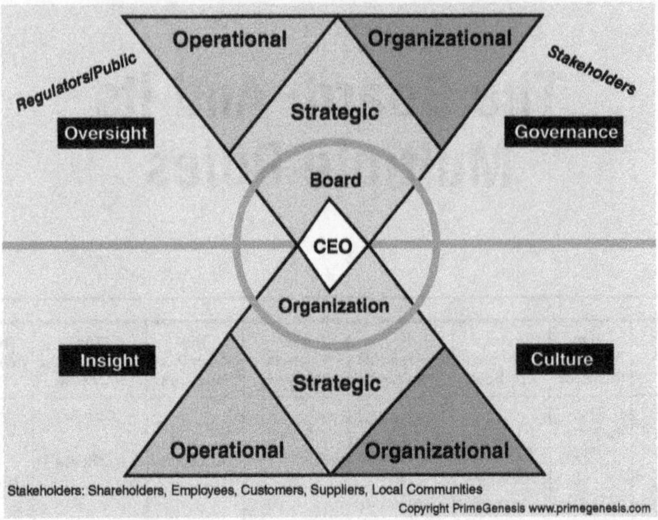

(legal, regulatory, audit, compliance, risk, and performance reporting) to their input into strategy, mergers and acquisitions (M&A), technology, culture, talent, resilience, and external communications.

Private fiduciary boards represent the owners of nonpublic companies. Although they are not subject to all the regulations and scrutiny that boards of public companies face, they are subject to many of them and must look out for the interests of *all* the owners, debt holders, and stakeholders.

Nonfiduciary boards (private or public) are really advisory boards. While the controlling owners may vest board members with some decision rights, those owners can overrule board members at any time and thus maintain the real fiduciary responsibility. Those owners may be private equity firms, families, or individuals. Their organizations may be operating with different levels of maturity. In particular, early-stage companies come with their own special sets of issues and opportunities.

Nonprofit board members serve different roles across governance, getting or giving money, representing stakeholders, making connections, and contributing their own advice or time.

RACI Terms

Leverage RACI to clarify decision rights, accountabilities, and communication protocols.

- *Approving authority:* Passes accountability to someone else, retaining approval and decision rights
- *Accountable:* The person called to account. Overall ownership of results. Drives decisions. Ensures implementation.
- *Responsible:* Does defined work (and signs off on their portion)
- *Consulted:* Provides expertise-based input (to be considered) and/or direction/concurrence (to be followed)—Two-way conversations.
- *Informed:* In advance or after the fact—One-way communication
- *Support:* Assist in completing the work

Board Roles

Be clear on board roles.

- *Air cover:* Dealing with some owners and stakeholders to free up the chief executive officer's (CEO) time
- *Accountable* for governance and oversight on behalf of owners and stakeholders (Noses in—especially through audit committee interacting directly with the chief financial officer [CFO] and so forth)
- *Approves* strategic, annual operating (P&L, cash flows, balance sheet), future capability, succession, contingency, and compensation plans.
- *Consulted* and *informed* on everything else (hands out)
- *Hire and fire the CEO*
- *Evaluate, compensate, and develop the CEO and their leadership team*

CEO Role

- *Accountable* for strategic, operating, organization plans and results, culture

Board Management

Chair accountable for board management

- Operations (committees) and board organization

CEO responsible for board management

- Prepare and brief in advance, manage meetings, follow up
- Manage board, group, one-on-one, board two-step: (1) test or consult; (2) sell

Some private equity firms *support* their portfolio companies in increasing value by providing:

- Perspective on customers, collaborators including community leaders, competitors, and conditions to drive organic growth
- Connecting company leaders with potential customers and collaborators
- Increased leverage in mergers and acquisitions to drive inorganic growth
- Perspective and resources to strengthen company infrastructure, including human capital and management team, technical and information technology, new product development, financial infrastructure for reporting, and managing cash flows
- Review commercial competitiveness of the business and advise on the strategic and operating plans

The Right Way to Divide Responsibilities Between Chair and CEO

There is no single right way to divide responsibilities among owners, chairs, CEOs, chief operations officers (COOs), and the rest of the executive team. Authority is delegated. That delegation is dependent on the business context and confidence the leaders have in one another.[1]

[1]Bradt, George, 2013, "The Right Way to Divide Responsibilities Between Chairman and CEO," *Forbes* (August 28).

Having said that, Rita's Italian Ice and Falconhead Capital—the investment firm that owns a controlling interest of the company—have a pretty good working model. Rita's executive chair of the board Mike Lorelli explained to George how they've broken down the roles:

The executive chair takes the lead on:

- Running the board of directors
- Dealing with external funding (investors and lenders)
- Joint venture pursuits and relations
- Compensation practices
- Management development
- CEO succession
- Strategic plan guidance
- M&A

The CEO takes the lead on running the company, across its:

- Strategic process
- Operating process
- Organizational process

But that's just at this moment in time. Back up a couple of years. Falconhead Capital's then CEO David Moross recruited Lorelli to represent Falconhead on the board of Rita's. Once he understood what was going on, Lorelli started recruiting for a new CEO for Rita's in March 2013 while the old CEO was still in place. As one of PrimeGenesis' partners Rob Gregory puts it, "Never fire anyone until you know who's going to do their job."

Great theory. As the situation dictated, Lorelli needed to change out both the CEO and CFO in June. So he jumped in as interim CEO. A month later, Lorelli met Jeff Moody, and they hit it off as only two ex-Pepsi employees can do. After several long conversations, a double date, and walks in the woods à la Steve Jobs and John Scully, during which they "nurtured" their relationship, Moody came onboard as CEO.

Lorelli had been conscious about managing his own transition from interim CEO to executive chair. As soon as Moody joined, Lorelli immediately vacated his CEO office and moved to an office as far away from Moody as possible. He backed off even more over time as both he and Moody became more and more comfortable in their roles.

Lorelli said, "The roles of executive chair and CEO should not be just additive but also synergistic." It's essential to have clear lines of authority. It's even better when the two share chemistry and can bounce ideas off each other. Moody described the split as "a soft division" with clear categories of responsibility but major overlaps as partners.

When it works, it works great. Think about how Bill Gates backed off and gave Steve Ballmer room to run Microsoft. Think about Ajay Banga's transition into Mastercard.

But when it doesn't work, the pain and suffering are spread across all of those people who are trying to follow their leaders. If leaders can't sort through their own responsibilities, they have no chance of providing clear direction to anyone else. And don't kid yourself—there are no secrets in any company (no matter how large or small).

In summary, here is a rough guide for dividing responsibilities between a chair and CEO:

1. Owners delegate authority to boards.
2. Chairs or lead directors run boards. (This is the only responsibility of a nonexecutive chair. Executive chairs are employees of the companies by definition and take more active roles in supporting the CEO's leadership of the company.)
3. CEOs run companies.
4. COOs, CFOs, chief human resource officers (CHROs), and others help CEOs run core operating, strategic, and organizational processes.
5. People lean in or out depending on their confidence in the ability of the people they have chosen to deal with.

Treat this as a general framework. What really matters is clear leadership that inspires and enables others. Titles don't matter. Formal divisions of responsibility don't matter. Behaviors, relationships, attitudes, values, and the environment matter. Focus on these at every level and every interaction in the organization.

How to Build Mutual Respect, Trust, and Support Between CEOs and Boards per Deloitte

Deloitte's chief executive program published a paper on "Seven Steps to a More Strategic Board." Its insights are well worth reading. They did, however, bury the lead. The seven steps add up to the importance of CEOs taking a leadership role in managing boards and building relationships rooted in "mutual respect, trust, and support." That's the lead.[2]

Deloitte's seven steps are as follows:

1. CEOs, it's really up to you. Take an active role in board management.
2. Be fearlessly transparent. Be open and humble.
3. Take advantage of tension. Grow through debate.
4. Facilitate the board experience, not just the board meeting. Build relationships over time.
5. Curate information and then curate it again. Give enough, but not too much information.
6. To chair or not to chair? Think about it very carefully. Choose your level of influence.
7. Say your piece on board composition. Build the right board over time.

Relationships rooted in "mutual respect, trust, and support" don't happen by mistake. They are built together, deliberately, and over time.

Respect

Be respectful of board members' context, strengths, roles. Give them every reason to respect you. Respect their time and help them learn enough to contribute as effectively and efficiently as possible.

Per one director, "Too much information can be just as bad as too little information." You can keep boards in the dark by giving them too little information too infrequently. You can accomplish the same end by drowning them with a board book on an iPad "and secretly hidden are 1,800 pages."

Think what, so what, now what. Then lead with the "now what" you're asking the board member to do. Do you want them thinking guidance, advice, and input or thinking governance, compliance, and

---

[2]Bradt, George, 2019, "How to Build Mutual Respect, Trust and Support Between CEOs and Boards per Deloitte," *Forbes* (July 9).

approval? Then give them your perspective on "so what." These are your conclusions from the information that leads to your request for input or approval. Finally, organize the back-up "what" data and information in a way that makes it searchable by the board members that want to dig deeper into the basis of your assumptions and logic.

Another way to respect board members is not to surprise them. No one likes surprises that make them look stupid, weak, or ill-informed. Treat your board members like they are, well, board members. Build relationships with them. Keep them informed. No excuses.

Finally, do the same future capability planning with your board that you're doing with the rest of the organization. Figure out what capabilities you're going to need in the future and then create and implement a plan to recruit board members with the talents you need and to help them acquire the knowledge and practice the skills they'll need to optimize their contributions.

Trust

At one level, this is pretty straightforward. Be trustworthy and have a bias to trust them. This is one of the keys to taking advantage of constructive disagreements. As the Deloitte paper put it:

> With a strong partnership between the board and CEO, what at first may feel like difficult conversations can become revelatory dialogues, surfacing ideas and insights that might otherwise stay buried from a desire to smooth tension and maintain civility.[3]

Support

One of the Deloitte paper's authors, Maureen Bujno, told George the key to gaining respect, trust, and support lies in CEOs being "fearlessly transparent" and "open to soliciting input." Yet Stanford Business School ex-dean Robert Joss once said, "Only 20 percent of leaders have the confidence to be open to input." Be part of that 20 percent.

---

[3]https://www2.deloitte.com/us/en/insights/topics/leadership/strategic-board-of-directors-ceo.html.

Help board members know when to provide guidance, advice, and input and when to exercise their fiduciary obligations around governance, compliance, and approvals.

The board two-step can help a lot here:

Step 1: Seek their input. Then go away so they talk among themselves or with others or give you off-the-record perspective.

Step 2: Taking into account their input and encouraging debate, seek their approval to your recommended path forward.

PART VI

The Organizational Playbook

CHAPTER 17

Culture: The Underlying Root Cause of Nearly Every Merger's Success or Failure

	The Strategic Playbook	The Commercial Playbook	The Operational Playbook	The Financial Playbook	The Governance Playbook	The Organizational Playbook	The Change Management Playbook
Concept	The Investment Case					Culture	Integration Leader
Research		Organic Revenue Growth	Cost Optimization	Deal/ Due Diligence			
Investment					Regulatory	Incentives	Change Management
Case							
Negotiation			Operational Excellence: Supply Chain, Distribution, Continual Improvement				
Deal/Due	Focus			Financing	Financial	Leadership	Communication
Diligence							
Contract		Customers					
Close	Plans			M&A	Board	People	Announcement
Integration		Marketing & Sales					
Acceleration	Innovation		Technology			Politics	Adjustments
Next Normal							

The components of the organizational playbook are culture, incentives, leadership, people, and politics. Choose the behaviors, relationships, attitudes, values, and environment that will make up your new culture. Invite people into the new culture, noting who accepts your invitation in what they say, do, and believe.

Given enough time and money, your competitors can duplicate almost everything you've got working for you. They can hire away some of your best people. They can reverse engineer your processes. They can match your service levels. Even innovation, unless embedded in the culture, can be matched. The only thing they can't duplicate is your culture.[1]

[1]Bradt, George, 2012, "Corporate Culture: The Only Truly Sustainable Competitive Advantage," *Forbes* (February 8).

Guy bumps into a competitor's star engineer at a trade event:

> "Would you come work for us if we gave you $1 million/year?"
> "I would."
> "How about $50,000/year?"
> "What do you think I am?"
> "We've already established that. Now we're negotiating."

While not everyone is for sale, enough are to make you vulnerable.

Even if you've got things patented, trademarked, or cloaked in multiple layers of secrecy, your competitors can see what you deliver, what you get done, and the core pieces of how you do it. Even if they can't duplicate what you do exactly, they can get close enough to hurt you—or take it to the next level and render your processes or products and services obsolete.

In many respects, leadership is an exercise in building culture. However you define it, culture is the glue that holds organizations together. Culture is often impacted by pivotal events, such as a new leader joining an organization, a significant external event, or—wait for it—combining organizations post–mergers and acquisitions (M&A). These moments present opportunities to accelerate culture change and deliver better results. Culture change is about bridging the gap between the current state and the desired state, which better enables a team to achieve the organization's mission and goals. The greater the cultural differences, the more difficult the adaptation or change will be. There's real power in understanding the most important cultural differences and then building a plan to bridge those gaps over time.

Jim Donald took the helm of Extended Stay Hotels as it was emerging from bankruptcy, tasked with the mandate to take the company public. He soon realized that while the company was officially out of bankruptcy, the mindset of staff was not. There was still a heads-down, play-it-safe mentality throughout the company.[2]

Donald knew that this type of behavior was not going to take them where they needed to go. It was now time for bold moves and innovative ideas. His solution was to give each employee a "get out of jail free" card. It guaranteed that as long as they were taking (safe, moral, legal) risks,

[2]*Axonify*, 2021, "'The Turnaround King' on Why Frontline Employee Engagement Is a Business Imperative" (June 4).

they would get a free pass if things went wrong. The goal? Empower employees to go out on a limb to try new things.

> "Things changed overnight. We began our march to an [intellectual property offering] IPO, and not only did we go public in less than a year, Extended Stay Hotels was just purchased last month for $6B. That's a true testament to the power of encouraging risk-taking," says Donald.
>
> "It was not magic. It was giving our employees power to make decisions. Encouraging risk taking, with the freedom to fail, is a leadership trait that most leaders are either afraid to do, or don't understand the huge upside and very little downside. Leaders today have to understand that in today's world, in our currency economy, status quo means you're going backward."

We've seen countless examples of front-line employees going above and beyond to surprise and delight customers, with just the right gesture at the right time. (Think about the legendary guest experience at brands like Southwest Airlines and Disney.) These kinds of experiences are possible only when the front line is empowered to go beyond the checklist and make decisions.

> "The right sales team, the right manufacturing team, the right frontline, should have and should demand the ability to make the decisions that could change the trajectory of the company, at the moment that decision needs to be made. Encouraging risk taking and building a culture of risk on your team is vital."

Some define culture simply as "the way we do things around here." Others conduct complex analyses to define it more scientifically. Instead, blend both schools of thought into an implementable approach that defines culture as an organization's behaviors, relationships, attitudes, values, and the environment (BRAVE). The BRAVE framework is relatively easy to apply yet offers a relatively robust way to identify, engage, and change a culture. It makes culture real, tangible, identifiable, and easy to talk about.

It's helpful to tackle the BRAVE components from the outside in with five questions, as shown in Table 17.1.

When evaluating each element of culture, think of it on a sliding scale (say 1–5), rather than in absolute terms. The specific dimensions within each cultural component may vary from situation to situation.

Table 17.1
The BRAVE Framework

Environment	Where to play	(Context)
Values	What matters and why	(Purpose)
Attitudes	How to win	(Choices)
Relationships	How to connect	(Influence)
Behaviors	What Impact	(Implementation)

Brave Cultures Are Sustainable

All music is made from the same 12 notes. All culture is made from the same five components: behaviors, relationships, attitudes, values, and environment. It's the way those notes or components are put together that makes things sing.

In sustainable, championship cultures, behaviors (the way we do things here) are inextricably linked to relationships, informed by attitudes, built on a rock-solid base of values, and completely appropriate for the environment in which the organization chooses to operate. As Simon Sinek famously pointed out, most organizations think what–how–why. Great leaders and great organizations start with why (environment and values), then look at how (attitudes and relationships) before getting to what (behaviors).

It's the context that makes it so hard to duplicate a championship culture. Because every organization's environment is different, matching someone else's behaviors, relationships, attitudes, and values will not produce the same culture.

Since you should align your culture, organization, and operations around one of four strategies, it's helpful to flesh out what the four different cultures mean. Let's work through that starting with a culture of independence in support of a design strategy.

Design: Independence

As depicted in Figure 17.1, in a design-focused organization, it's all about unleashing individual creativity and invention.[3]

[3]Bradt, George, 2018, "What It Means to Have a Culture of Independence," *Forbes* (July 3).

FIGURE 17.1 Core Focus

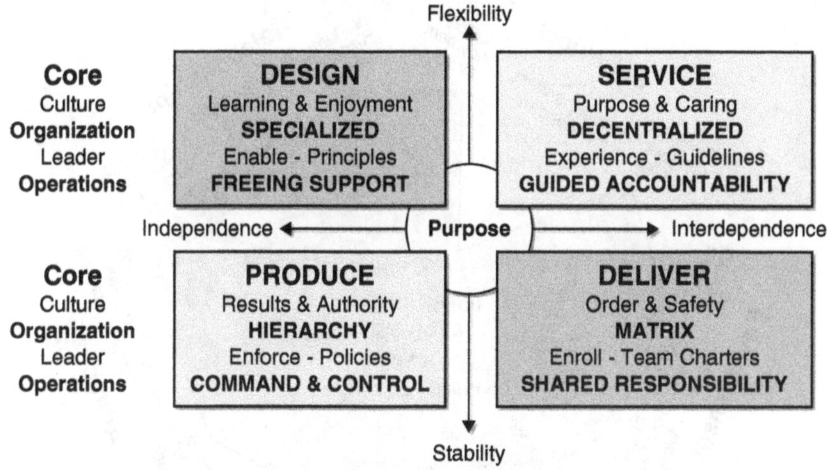

The design-focused core has five main components:

1. *Strategy:* Design or invent
2. *Culture:* Independent (and flexible, with emphasis on learning and enjoyment; Figure 17.2)
3. *Organization:* Specialized
4. *Operations:* Freeing support
5. *CEO:* Enable with principles

In *The Culture Factor*, Boris Groysberg and coauthors[4] suggest eight primary cultural styles (learning, enjoyment, results, authority, order, safety, purpose, and caring) that fall on the two dimensions of flexibility (stability and independence) and interdependence. It's a helpful construct that benefits from a fleshing out across the BRAVE dimensions of behaviors, relationships, attitudes, values, and the environment. (These are different dimensions than we're now using in the base tool. The actual dimensions are flexible.)

[4]Groysberg, Boris, et al., 2018, "The Culture Factor," *Harvard Business Review* (January).

FIGURE 17.2 Design-Focused Culture of Independence

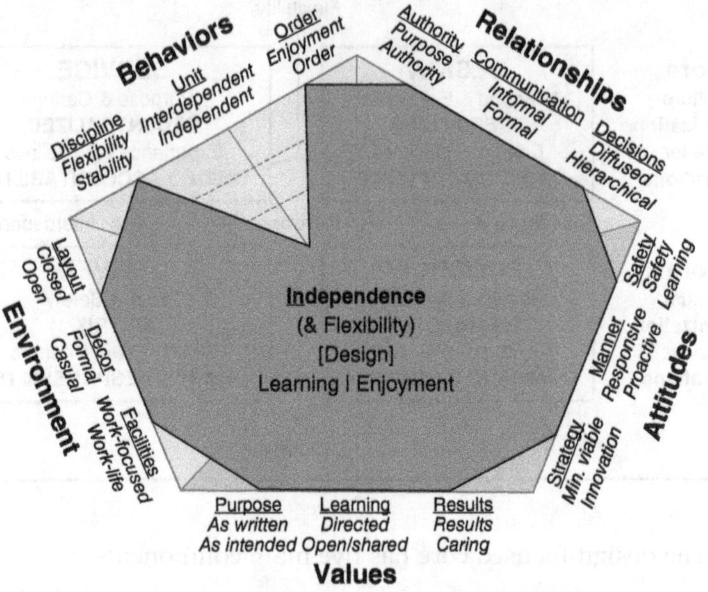

A culture of independence is on the outer edge of every BRAVE dimension. In every case it is more open, diffused, caring, flexible, informal, and casual. Expect people operating in a culture like this to care about learning and enjoyment, to be proactive and driven by their own interpretation of the intended purpose. These people will be hard to control, which is exactly what you want.

Build a culture like this to unleash creativity and invention—the first step in innovation. Innovation is the introduction of something new. You need to be innovative to stay ahead of the curve whether your primary strategy is design, production, delivery, or service. If you choose one of the latter three strategies, you may outsource your design and invention. In any case you can do a better job introducing new things with the five keys to BRAVE innovation:

1. Environment—where to play: Establish a shared definition of innovation for your organization.
2. Values—what matters and why: Aim innovation at business concepts and models.

3. Attitude—how to win: Valuable innovation is born of new, frame-breaking insights that light the way.
4. Relationships—how to connect: Learn by doing with discipline across your innovation system.
5. Behaviors—what impact: Drive an end-to-end process through to commercialization.

Independence

In the case of independence, it's not an oversimplification. Certainly, all cultures are blends of many different elements. Certainly, some people in organizations with cultures like this will and must work interdependently. While most people in these organizations will have a bias to flexibility over stability, some things must be stable and reliable. But the overriding, most important dimension is independence because the sparks of invention are inherently individual. Inventing requires freeing individuals.

Not only is each person in a culture of independence going to behave individualistically, but there is also no overall formula for the ideal independent culture. Organizations may vary their cultural preferences on scales like work-focused versus more work–life balance or formal versus informal communication or how they learn.

Purpose

The one thing that probably should not vary is attention to purpose. Chief executive officer (CEO) Tim Cook and all at Apple are clear they are "trying to change the world for the better." They care about products and people, about inventing products that help people do things they could not have done before, about infusing products with a humanity that others have never done. Their purpose is their ultimate guiding principles.

Cook sees himself as their chief enablement officer. His job is to lead the efforts to provide freeing support to Apple's inventors. As he says over and over again, his job is "to block the noise from the people who are really doing the work"—the designers and inventors.

Produce: Stability

In a culture of stability in support of a production strategy, it's all about ensuring reliability.[5]

The five core components of stability are:

1. *Strategy:* Produce and manufacture
2. *Culture:* Stable (and independent, with emphasis on results and authority; Figure 17.3)
3. *Organization:* Hierarchy
4. *Operations:* Command and control
5. *CEO:* Enforce

A culture of stability is at the inner point of every BRAVE dimension. In every case it is more results focused, authority driven,

FIGURE 17.3 Production-Focused Culture of Stability

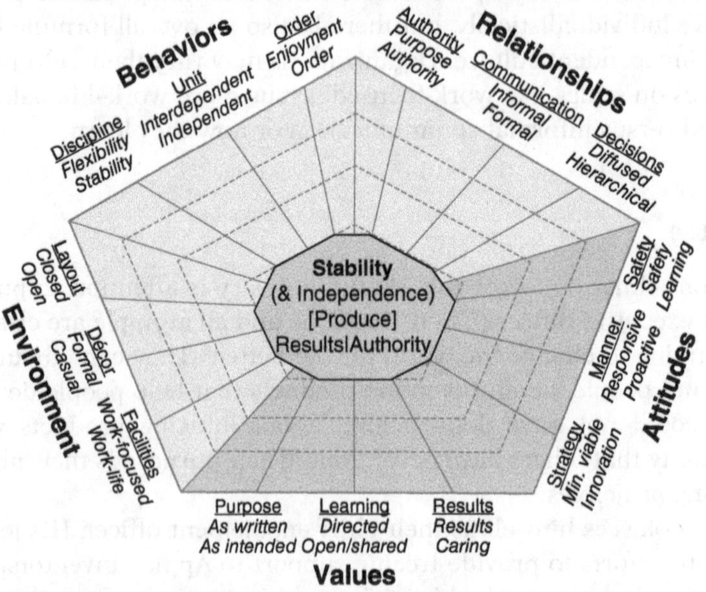

[5]Bradt, George, 2018, "What It Means to Have a Culture of Stability," *Forbes* (July 10).

formal, hierarchical, directed, and closed. Expect people operating in a culture like this to care about order and safety, to be reactive, and to follow purpose and rules as written. These people will do what you tell them to do and not much more—which is exactly what you want.

Build a culture like this to produce things consistently and reliably on an ongoing, regular basis.

Stability

In the culture of stability, don't expect flexibility or innovation. Expect compliance with the rules, with your direction. Expect people to deliver the minimum viable product every time. If you push people in a culture like this to operate more interdependently, to make decisions on their own, to be more proactive, at best they will resist and more likely, you'll break the system.

Coca-Cola is a classic example of a production company with a culture of stability. It operates with a clear hierarchy of command and control, with CEOs who see their primary task as enforcing policies. As a result, every Coca-Cola produced everywhere in the world lives up to the same high standards.

One of Coca-Cola's biggest ever innovations was the introduction of New Coke. A small Skunk Works group worked the project all the way through, leaking nothing until the last minute when the new formula was shipped to every bottler in the world for a coordinated worldwide launch. The product was superior on the dimension of initial mouth appeal, but the brand failed. As a result, the company swallowed its pride and relaunched Classic Coke.

It's an example of why stable production companies should think twice about revolutionary innovations.

Zara is another example of a stable production company. They outsource all their design by relying on copying others' designs. Their magic is that they can go from seeing a design on a fashion catwalk to producing it and getting it into their stores in 15 days.

In some ways, this is the tightest and most easily understood and managed culture. If you're leading a producing company, drive stability, independence, results, and authority. Have a bias to organize hierarchically. Do not shy away from command-and-control operations. Enforce polices for the good of all.

Deliver: Interdependence

In a culture of interdependence in support of a delivery strategy, it's all about enrolling diverse players across the ecosystem.[6]

The five core components of an interdependence culture are:

Strategy: Delivery, product supply, logistics

Culture: Interdependent (and stable, with emphasis on order and safety; Figure 17.4)

Organization: Matrix

Operations: Shared responsibility

CEO: Enroll

A culture of interdependence is a blended culture. The predominant feature is diverse people working interdependently to deliver things. Thus, individuals have to be open to differences as they deal

FIGURE 17.4 Delivery-Focused Culture of Interdependence

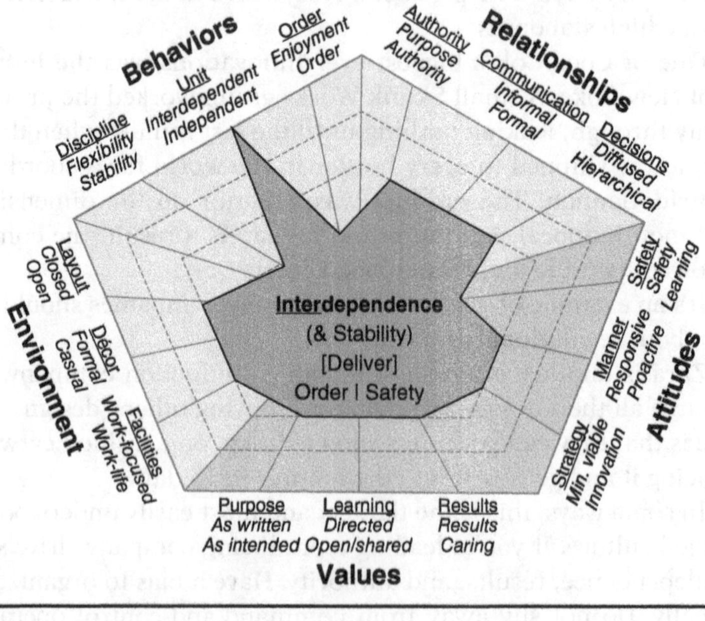

[6]Bradt, "Culture of Interdependence."

with a range of suppliers and customers. While there's generally a bias to stability, order, and safety, everything else falls in the middle. Decisions may be hierarchical or diffused. People may be proactive or responsive. They have to balance results and caring and be open to directed or shared learning.

Build a culture like this to manage logistics and product supply chains and deliver things in an orderly and safe way.

Interdependence

The opposite of independence, interdependence is all about people working together in teams. Those teams cross geographic, functional, and organizational bounds as many of the people on core delivery teams may often work for different companies. The lines between employees, contractors, suppliers, allies, partners, customers, and competitors often blur beyond recognition.

The head of one organization bumped into the head of another and told him, "We were going to name you our supplier of the year."

"Were?"

"You never returned my call when I called to tell you that. So we had to name someone else."

At the time when Sam Walton told this to Procter & Gamble's (P&G) chief executive officer (CEO) John Smale, P&G did $2 billion per year in business with Walmart. Smale got the message and moved three people to Bentonville to provide Walmart with better service.

Not long thereafter the P&G–Walmart system effectively eliminated all the people placing and receiving product orders. P&G was electronically linked into Walmart's systems, so its systems knew when every individual product left Walmart stores. It was able to ship replenishments to Walmart's distribution centers perfectly timed to go dock-to-dock from P&G's trucks to the trucks going out to stores. If there's nothing in the warehouse, warehouse turns are infinite.

Now there's a whole city of Walmart suppliers based in Bentonville, blurring the lines between organizations in Walmart's superior interdependent delivery system.

Delivery requires a broad, loose matrix organization crossing geographies, functions, products, and organizations. While you'll still want one single point of accountability for each task, project, program, or priority, the key to making this work is going to be a recognition of shared responsibilities.

Matrix organizations succeed when people work together interdependently to deliver shared objectives. They collapse when people put their own personal or functional objectives ahead of the common good. Thus, the leader's main role in an interdependent, matrix organization is to enroll people through the use of formal or informal team charters.

Service: Flexibility

In a culture of flexibility in support of a service strategy, it's all about doing whatever is required to provide the best experience for customers or guests or whatever you call them.

The five main components of flexibility in support of service are:

Strategy: Service and customer experience
Culture: Flexible (and interdependent, with emphasis on purpose and caring; Figure 17.5)
Organization: Decentralized
Operations: Guided accountability
CEO: Champion experience

FIGURE 17.5 Service-Focused Culture of Flexibility

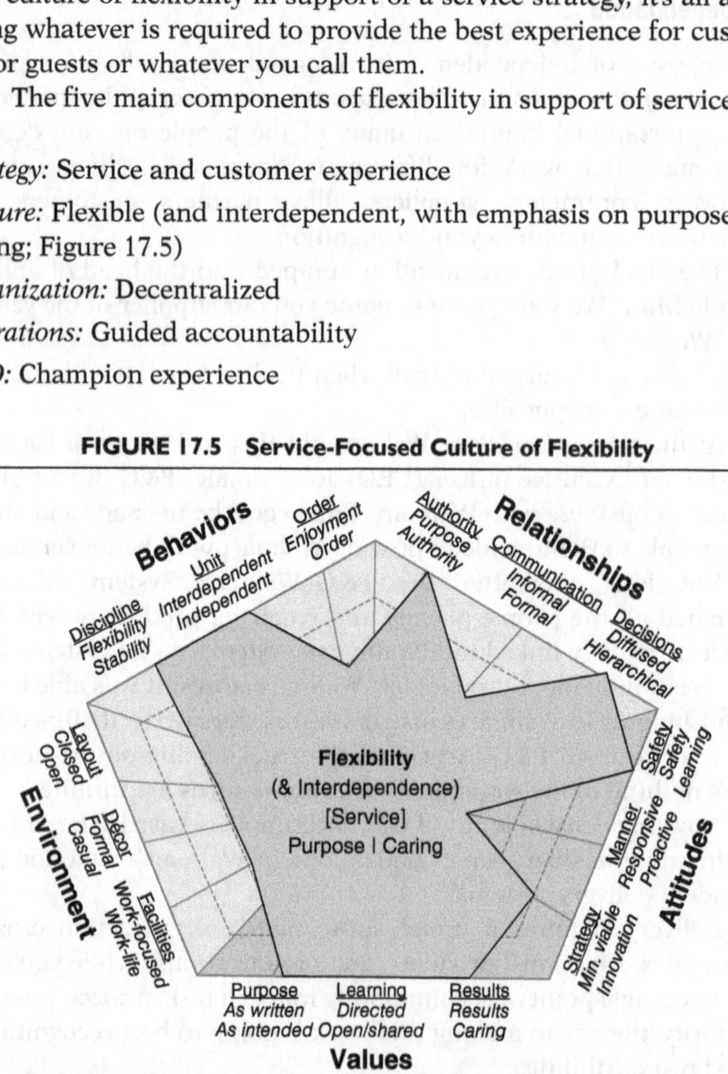

A culture of flexibility is—wait for it—flexible. Its people are going to be all over the map. When you focus people on service or customer or guest experience as a higher purpose, when you ask them to care more about customer impact than about short-term results, when you push decisions out to them, don't be surprised when your managerial authority is diminished. *Customer first* by definition means everything else second.

Cultures like this help you win with service strategies. They are counterproductive for producing and delivering and are also probably distractions for designing.

Flexibility

This culture is the opposite of stability, which suggests either outsourcing production and delivery or at least setting those functions up as separate groups with their own subcultures. There is an unavoidable conflict between people wanting to do whatever it takes to enhance customers' experience and people trying to make or deliver things in a stable, orderly, safe way.

Ritz-Carlton hotels are filled with ladies and gentlemen serving ladies and gentlemen. If you ask any bellboy to fix your broken TV, that bellboy owns that problem until it is fixed and has full authority to do whatever it takes to make you happy. To be clear, that bellboy does not have to fix the TV himself. But he does have to make sure it gets fixed and that everything that happens from that moment on enhances your experience.

Wonderful examples of retail service happen in high-end bridal boutiques. Their staffs' attitudes are all about making their customers feel like princesses for the day. Expect champagne and fawning service with wonderful gowns brought to you. These people don't design the gowns, make them, or even deliver them. Their job is to make you feel wonderful.

Leading Flexibility

Leading a culture like this is akin to steering a galloping horse. You're not really in control—and you don't want to be. You're going to have a decentralized organization. You're going to give those decentralized leaders accountability. But you're going to use things like the Ritz-Carlton's gold standards to guide that accountability. Polices are like holding the reins too tight. But letting go of the reins completely is a recipe for chaos. Deploying guiding principles is a middle way that guides your decentralized decision-makers without tripping them up.

This is why these organizations' ultimate leaders must think of themselves as chief experience officers. As such, they are keepers of purpose, the most caring people in belief, word, and deed. This is how to get people in a flexible culture to follow you and provide the service required to deliver superior customer or guest experience.

Making It Real

Whether your society is a company, family, tribe, or country, its culture is the combination of the characters of its members. While some members have more influence, all have some. So manage positive and negative deviation from true fit—especially when hiring and onboarding in general or after a merger.[7]

There are three steps to directing the culture of an organization:

1. Understand the true culture and character.
2. Focus on the most important differences.
3. Figure out the potential impact of those differences and act accordingly.

Understand the True Culture of the Society and the True Character of the New Member

The BRAVE framework allows a relatively easy, robust assessment of culture and character by looking at behaviors, relationships, attitudes, values, and the environment. Cross this with *be–do–say*. Although words matter, people's actions often don't match their words. And even if their actions do match their words but not their fundamental, underlying beliefs, they will eventually trip up and get caught. As former Goldman Sachs CEO Lloyd Blankfein told the *New York Times*' Andrew Ross Sorkin, "The character thing in the long run always came out at the worst possible time."[8]

---

[7]Bradt, George, 2021, "Culture Is the Collective Character of a Society. Manage It or Perish," *Forbes* (January 12).

[8]Sorkin, Andrew Ross, and Livni, Ephtrat, 2021, "When Business and Politics Mix, 'Character Really Counts,'" *New York Times* (January 9).

Look beyond the behaviors, relationships, attitudes, values, and environment an individual or society presents as its public face to what's really going on—the individual's true character and society's true culture. Some define character or culture as what you believe, think, say, and do when no one is listening or watching.

Focus on the Most Important Differences

The most important differences between what individuals and other members of the society believe, think, say, and do are the ones that are most different and will have the greatest impact.

An individual's preference for yellow shirts while everyone else wears white shirts is probably not an important difference. Someone's refusal to wear any clothes at all may disqualify them for an arctic exploration team.

Figure Out the Potential Impact of Those Differences and Act Accordingly

Darwin taught us that "it is not the strongest of the species that survives, nor the most intelligent, but the one most responsive to change." He's talking about species, not individuals. Species evolve over time as their stronger deviants do better and their weaker members perish.

Diversity is not a high-minded selfless act. You must bring different strengths and perspectives into your society for it to survive. The question is how much and how fast the society must and can change.

- *Level zero is no change at all.* Those societies are going to perish, so it doesn't matter how they bring new people in.
- *Level one is evolutionary change.* These societies need to add people over time whose characters differ in slight ways on just a few core dimensions from the current culture. Onboarding and nurturing them have only low levels of fit risk.
- *Level two is moderate change.* These societies need to add people who believe, think, communicate, and act differently in some important ways from the current culture in ways that enable them to influence others relatively soon. Onboarding and nurturing them have moderate fit risk. They will need help with their onboarding and support over time.

- *Level three is dramatic change*. These societies are on the path to extinction and need to add change agents who can change their cultures meaningfully and fast.

The trouble is that most change agents don't survive their own changes. Some should not. If, as Peter Drucker allegedly said, "Culture eats strategy for breakfast," it devours change agents as amuse-bouchées. The only way these stronger change agent deviants can succeed is for weaker members to perish.

Level one culture changes are relatively painless. Level two changes are uncomfortable. Level three changes are disruptive by design. Don't bring in or tolerate a level three deviant unless you're really seeking and committed to the change and prepared to work through and support the disruption. If you find yourself with a level three deviant who's having a negative impact, expel them quickly. The number one regret experienced leaders have looking back on their careers is not moving fast enough on people.

Don't join as a level three deviant unless you're sure you're going to get the support you need and can stomach the impact you will have on weaker members.

Attitude Is the Pivot Point

As you work to evolve your culture, focus on attitudes. There's a strong case to be made that IBM's near-death experience was a result of a bad attitude. It thought it was the best. It thought its customers needed it more than it needed its customers. It stopped being flexible. The big thing Lou Gerstner did was reversing that attitude. Behaviors and relationships followed.

More recently, we saw the same thing at Facebook. It has started believing its own myths and is losing the congruence between strategy and posture.

Of course, this oversimplifies things. Few things are as simple as we hope they are. Of course, you have to be in touch with your environment. Of course, you have to make sure your values are current. Of course, people and communication matter. Of course, it's all theoretical gibberish until someone actually does something that impacts someone else. Attitude is not the only lever. But it's generally the lever to pull first, using that choice or change to influence the others.

There are three steps to achieve the results you want:

1. Look back at the cultural assessments you did in due diligence for each organization.
2. Map out your aspirational culture.
3. Invite people into the new culture.

Evolving Aspirations

A recent survey of global executives suggests a need to evolve most organizations' culture by dialing up speed, more open communication, and broadening the definition of doing good for others.[9]

Let's start with the logic of evolving cultures: Culture is the only sustainable competitive advantage. You have to evolve to survive. It follows that you must evolve your culture to keep it a sustainable competitive advantage as opposed to a sustainable competitive disadvantage. Add to that the conclusions from executive search firm Cornerstone International Group's survey:

1. Speed: The speed and ubiquity of digitalization is forcing major change in business organizations:

   Decision-making is moving closer to customers

   Organizations are reforming smaller, more agile work groups.

   Talent acquisition is more specialized in order to deliver niche knowledge on Day One.

2. More open communication: Technology is re-writing boundaries:

   Globalization is enabled by technology advances across the spectrum

   Competition is no longer likely to come solely from within the core business.

   Information is now unfiltered and shared instantly across the organization.

[9]Bradt, George, 2019, "The Next Three Cultural Dimensions Almost Every Organization Should Evolve," *Forbes* (July 21).

3. Broadening the definition of doing good for others: Corporate social responsibility is driving culture change:

   The new generation of talent will only work where social expectations are being met.

   Social awareness requires evaluation of values and mission goals.

   Boards of Directors and CEOs must understand and embrace social responsibility.

As a whole, the Cornerstone Survey indicates the need to evolve cultures to dial up:

1. Intuitive, exploratory behaviors aimed at getting it right vaguely right fast and iterating (speed)
2. More informal, verbal, personalized, open communication (boundarylessness)
3. Broader definition of doing good for others that includes the entire human race (corporate social responsibility)

Post-Pandemic Changes

There are things people were in the habit of doing before the Covid pandemic that they're not doing now. Like a computer shut down prompts us to rethink previously open applications, the pandemic disrupted the inertia behind our habits, heightened our sensibilities, and gave us the opportunity to rethink our choices. This is why you must align the way you're leading with your followers' post-pandemic work–life balance, health and well-being, relationships, and sense of place in the world.[10]

Work–Life Balance and Health and Well-Being

Pandemic-driven office closures disrupted the lives of people used to commuting to and from work 5 days a week. At first it was jarring, uncomfortable, and stressful. Then people figured out the technology and how to work productively at home.

[10]Bradt, George, 2021, "How to Lead Through Post-Pandemic Changes in Sensibilities," *Forbes* (October 6).

When that happened, they discovered they didn't have to worry about getting home in time for dinner with their kids. They could spend more time with their family, more time exercising, more time relaxing, and still get all their work done.

Many liked it. All formed new habits.

Now inertia is on the side of those habits. Many are not sure they want to go back to the rat race, give up time with their families, or sacrifice their newly renewed health and well-being.

Relationships

The pandemic disrupted relationships in two ways: throwing people together or keeping them apart.

Some found themselves quarantined with people they were used to spending less time with on a regular basis. In some cases, their time together strengthened those relationships. In some cases, it made people discover things about each other they didn't like so much. Some of them will go in different directions.

Others found themselves unable to spend time with some people. As restrictions relax, they will not necessarily restart those relationships and their old habits. Instead, they'll spend time with the people they care about and let the other relationships stay dormant. It's not so much that there was anything wrong with the relationships before. It's more that the pandemic changed all of us and created new shared experiences, replacing old shared experiences.

Our Place in the World

Some things in the world at large have become harder to ignore.

The United Nations declared "Code Red for humanity" on climate change. "It's just guaranteed that it's going to get worse. Nowhere to run, nowhere to hide." This is making ever more people rethink their unsustainable habits and base more and more of their decisions on climate impact.

Social media–fueled sharing of racial, gender, LGBTQ, religious, and other injustices have made more and more aware of them across the globe. This has led many to rethink their habitual choices and biases with regard to diversity and inclusion in those lights.

The disruption in the supply chain all the way from sourcing to retail has led to many rethinking their habitual brand choices.

Now many are looking at product or brands' provenance, ethics, and how they impact the environment and treat those vulnerable to unjust treatment with new sensibilities. Customers are looking for brands to be–do–say with integrity, matching what they say with what they do with their underlying values and behaviors.

Implications for You as a Leader

Those you lead are not going to return to a pre-pandemic normal. They are going to rethink their choices either consciously or subconsciously. Fighting that is like fighting the tide. You'll lose—especially with the new generation. Instead, invest in inspiring, enabling, and empowering those you lead to do their absolute best together to realize a meaningful and rewarding shared purpose that is in line with their choices about work–life balance, health and wellness, relationship, and place in the world.

Identify the Dimensions to Evolve and Choose the Order

Part of why culture is your most sustainable advantage is that it's so hard to build and hard to change. The prescription for evolution is to move only a few dimensions at a time. Create a gap between where you want to be and where you are.

Change the Stories

Evolving culture is an exercise in changing unwritten rules. Jeff Leitner suggests the best way to do that is to encourage deviant behavior that can subvert the social norms—in the direction you want to head.

Your team needs disrupters, rebels, challengers, and deviants to help it evolve and survive.[11]

The highest-performing teams function with a minimum of disruption. They do well. But they are resistant to the changes required to evolve and survive over time. This is why you need a meaningful level

[11]Bradt, George, 2018, "In Praise of Deviants," *Forbes* (November 6).

of disruption, challenge, rebellion, and deviation on a team. The trouble with being at the peak is that the only way to go from there is down. Root out complacency and keep your team striving for a new peak.[12]

By the end of 2017, only 60 of the 1955 Fortune 500 still existed. And it continues. Witness GE's continued free fall and quarterly losses and breakup. Some members of the Fortune 500 like IBM survived near-death experiences on the way. Even Apple almost disappeared until Steve Jobs came back to reinvent the company.

At a HATCH Summit at Moonlight Basin, Montana, a recurring theme was the importance of diversity.

Darwinian Evolution

Astrobiologist Luke McKay explained how even if the odds are one in a million that one of a gazillion planets in the universe has life, the mathematical probability is that there are aliens. NASA's definition of life: "Self-sustaining chemical system capable of Darwinian evolution."

Note that Darwinian populations evolve through their mutations, which are, by definition, different from the norm. And note that the environment determines which mutations survive as opposed to the mutations picking their environment.

Differential Strengths

Kristian Ribberstrom, the Medici Group's chief experience officer, asked whether it's better to hire someone with seven critical strengths or three. If the seven strengths overlap strengths already on the team and the three are new to the team, the three are more valuable than the seven.

Different Perspectives

Creative partner Aithan Shapira discussed the need to change perspectives to give people permission to be who they are and permission to change. Most first look at only the middle 7 percent of a painting,

---

[12]Bradt, George, 2018, "Why the Highest-Performing Teams Always Fail over Time," *Forbes* (October 30).

whereas experts take in 70 percent of the same painting. He took us through the 1949 radical change in Jackson Pollock's painting style from recognizable to revolutionary and how that gave permission to other artists to change their perspective.

Deviation

Jeff Leitner and Andrew Benedict-Nelson solve problems others run away from. Their book, *See Think Solve,*[13] is an ode to deviation—an existing or new behavior so powerful that it can subvert the informal, unspoken social norm keeping problems unsolved. Teams functioning without deviation can't overcome their social norms to solve new problems.

Full Spectrum Creativity

Chris Wink, Phil Stanton, and Matt Goldman started the Blue Man Group by wandering around—literally. They dressed as the Blue Man character and wandered around to see how people reacted. Some didn't see them. Some couldn't see them. Some actively ignored them. Some thought they were cool.

They learned the character was not one but three. It's not *Blue Man*; it's the *Blue Man Group*. As Wink said, "Three is one." Their magic is in the collaboration as they put on different capes to see the world with fresh eyes, overcoming their "disabilities" of being blue men with holes in their chests and reacting to everyday situations in new ways. As depicted in Figure 17.6, their different capes include:

- The scientist who likes to test things and builds instruments
- The artist or shaman who feels things and brings them to life
- Sometimes they embrace the system as group members
- Sometimes they rebel as "tricksters"
- Some play the role of hero, pushing them toward a goal
- Some act as the innocent, bringing humanity to what they do

---

[13]Benedict-Nelson, Andrew, and Leitner, Jeff, 2018, *See Think Solve: A Simple Way to Tackle Tough Problems,* Chicago: Leitner Insights LLC.

FIGURE 17.6 Blue Men

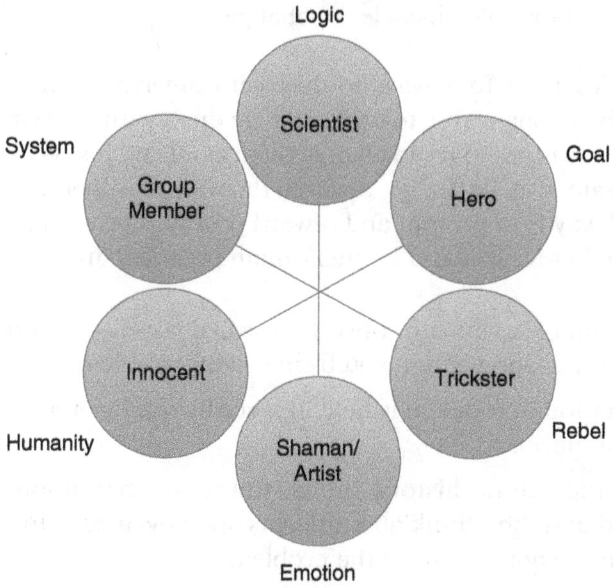

Implications

Diversity is not a goal. It's the key to survival over time. Find and nurture people with differential strengths that complement those already existing on your team, not reinforcing them. Do not push for perfect alignment of peoples' behaviors, relationships, and attitude with your existing culture. Do not bring in a complete cultural misfit like NBC did with Megyn Kelly, but do push for some evolutionary deviation on one or more dimensions.

With all that in mind, don't wiggle on purpose. Require rock-solid commitment to that. Let's explore how to get more positive deviation, drawing from Andrew Benedict-Nelson and Leitner's book *See Think Solve* on how to solve tough societal problems.

In his talks, Leitner describes culture as the unwritten rules and group expectations about what we should and shouldn't do. This is close to Seth Godin's "People like us do things like this." Leitner then goes on to suggest that unwritten rules are:

- Reinforced by social cues
- More powerful than written rules

- Virtually invisible
- Insurmountable obstacles to change

He describes four ways to deal with unwritten rules and social norms. The wrong way is to try to change them with new written rules. The easy way is not to try to change them at all and just walk away. The intermediate way is to go around them with other changes. The advanced way is to prompt and reward positive deviation.

Benedict-Nelson and Leitner's main premises are:

1. Deviant behavior can subvert the social norms—informal, unspoken rules—preventing you from solving problems.
2. Every tough problem is held in place by one or more problematic social norms.
3. See the actors, history, limits, future, configuration, and parthood and then think about norms and deviance before deviating from the norm to solve the problem.

Some definitions:

- *Actors* are the people involved in problems—directly, influencing or not.
- *History* is the stories people tell—true, false, or nonsense.
- *Limits* are explicit rules and laws that influence how people behave.
- *Future* is the set of beliefs people have about what is likely, possible, or impossible.
- *Configuration* is labels or categories people use—whether or not they actually make sense.
- *Parthood* is how your problems relate to other problems through shared actors, settings, or resources.
- *Norms* are the informal, unspoken rules that really explain what's going on.
- *Deviance* is an existing or new behavior outside the norms.

Deviance can be positive or negative, evolutionary or revolutionary, unintentional or deliberate. Positive deviations move you in desired directions where negative deviations do the opposite. Evolutionary deviations are incremental, where revolutionary deviations are major step changes. Unintentional deviations happen without foresight or planning as opposed to planned, deliberate deviations. You want positive deviations whether they are evolutionary, revolutionary, unintentional, or deliberate.

How to Get More Positive Deviance

Recall the ABCs of behavior modification: antecedents, behaviors, consequences. People do things because antecedents prompt them. They do them again because of the balance of consequences: rewarding or punishing desirable or undesirable behavior.

To get more positive deviation, start by prompting it. Hire for differential strengths to get people on your team who can do different things better than can your existing team members. Hire for differential preferences to nudge your culture in a new direction. Then explicitly invite people to challenge existing norms. It's all for naught if you don't change the balance of consequences as well.

Imagine I'm standing next to you and ask you to shake my hand. You do. I look you in the eye, smile, and say thank you. If I then ask you to shake my hand again, you likely will. You shake my hand both times because I ask you as an antecedent. You shake my hand the second time partly because the consequences of the first handshake are positive. But if I take your hand and then punch you in the face, you are less inclined to shake my hand again.

If you want positive change, you must dial up the positive consequences and dial down the negative consequences of desired behaviors and do the opposite for undesired behavior. Stop punching people in the face for doing things you want them to do—especially when it comes to positive changes that violate existing norms. And make sure others don't punish your deviants for doing things differently.

Boss comes by subordinate's desk holding a memo. "Did I ask you to write this?" "No." Boss puts the memo in the subordinate's trash bin, effectively punching him in the face for thinking on his own.

Too many people get shunned for working harder or smarter or going an extra mile for an internal or external customer by others thinking they are being made to look bad or feeling threatened in some way. Be explicit about the need for deviance and apply the ABCs to behaviors supporting or hindering that deviance as well as to the deviance itself.

At a high level, this involves:

- Understanding who's doing what: the actors, their history, limits, future beliefs, frameworks, and context
- Digging out the unwritten rules that explain the inexplicable: the norms, social situations, and actions unexplained by laws or formal, explicit rules and who keeps the actors in line
- Helping them migrate to a better way: with a deviant behavior turned into new stories

You should have mapped your current culture and the culture of the organization you're merging with or acquiring as part of your due diligence with Us for us and Ts for them in Tool 11.1. Now add an X to each line, identifying your aspirational culture. In some cases, it will be closer to your own or their existing culture. In other case, it will be something completely different.

In either case, invite everyone in both organizations to move towards your aspirational culture. Some will accept—at least with their words. Some will decline. Those declining are the easier case. Help them find other cultures, in other organizations better suited to their preferences.

Those that accept are trickier. Some of them will believe in the new culture, have the required strengths, and end up as valuable, contributing members of the new organization. Great. Some of them will say they accept, but never really sign up. Find those people as soon as practical and help them find other cultures, in other organizations better suited to their preferences.

Figure out where you're heading, and invite others to join the journey.

CHAPTER 18

Incentives: Show Me How They're Paid and I'll Tell You What They Do

	The Strategic Playbook	The Commercial Playbook	The Operational Playbook	The Financial Playbook	The Governance Playbook	The Organizational Playbook	The Change Management Playbook
Concept Research Investment Case Negotiation Deal/Due Diligence Contract Close Integration Acceleration Next Normal	The Investment Case Focus Plans Innovation	Organic Revenue Growth Customers Marketing & Sales	Cost Optimization Operational Excellence: Supply Chain, Distribution, Continual Improvement Technology	Deal/ Due Diligence Financing M&A	Regulatory Financial Board	Culture Incentives Leadership People Politics	Integration Leader Change Management Communication Announcement Adjustments

The second component of the organizational playbook is incentives, which feed right into the balance of consequences.

Michael Brown's ABCs of behavior modification provide a framework worth following. ABC stands for antecedent, behavior, consequence. People do things because an antecedent prompts that behavior. They do it again because of the balance of consequences: rewarding or punishing desirable or undesirable behavior.[1]

It's often hard to modify existing patterns of behavior because those habits have been reinforced by a poor balance of consequences.

[1]Bradt, George, 2017, "The ABCs of Changing Undesirable Behavior Habits," *Forbes* (November 15).

It's almost guaranteed that people in your organization who persist in doing things you don't want them to do are having their behavior positively reinforced.

If, as an example, employees habitually show up late for meetings, that behavior is likely positively reinforced by avoiding the negative consequence of wasting time for the few that do show up on time.

If you want to change undesirable behavior habits, change the balance of consequences. Make sure you are:

- Positively reinforcing desired behavior
- Discouraging undesirable behavior

If you are not doing this, then change the way you:

- Positively reinforce undesirable behavior
- Discouraging desired behavior

Just as the best way to eliminate recidivism in prison is to keep people from doing things that would land them in prison in the first place, the best way to eliminate undesirable behavior is to make sure it never happens to start with. This is about antecedents and prompting the right behaviors.

This is why it's so important to clarify your desired culture and reinforce it with the antecedents and consequences of behavior.

Theoretically, your mission, vision, objectives, goals, policies, guidelines, plans, and ways of leading and working all provide antecedents that prompt desirable behavior.

Theoretically, your performance management, reward, and recognition systems and practices and everyday leadership provide appropriately positive consequences to desirable behavior and negative consequences to undesirable behavior. Your compensation system is a big part of that—and especially your incentive compensation system.

The general guideline for compensation systems is to give people:

- A base salary and benefits high enough to allow them not to worry about their normal living expenses like rent, food, transportation, and medical
- Short-term incentives or bonuses that provide positive and negative consequences for doing or not doing what you want them to do over the short-term

- Long-term incentives that provide positive and negative consequences for doing or not doing what you want them to do over the long-term

In other words, tie more junior people's incentives to short-term results, middle-managers' incentives to mid-term (annual) results, and senior executives' incentives to long-term value creation.

We could write an entire book on incentives—they are so critical. Be creative and thoughtful and use the various currencies available—equity plans, long-term incentive plans (LTIP), short-term incentive plans (STIP), commission plans, specific function and role plans with a focus on tying the long- and short-term objectives, and the compensation plans together. Watch for intended consequences as people; even great leaders and managers will follow the money—except salespeople. They are different animals. The more you can make your sales compensation system work like a straight commission on sales made, the better it will work.

True story. IBM's top salesman was effectively paid on commission. One year he earned more than the chief executive officer (CEO). The next year they capped his maximum pay. He hit that maximum in 3 months, quit, and founded EDS. He was Ross Perot.

CHAPTER 19

Leadership: Starting with the Core Leadership Team

	The Strategic Playbook	The Commercial Playbook	The Operational Playbook	The Financial Playbook	The Governance Playbook	The Organizational Playbook	The Change Management Playbook
Concept **Research** **Investment Case** **Negotiation** **Deal/Due Diligence** **Contract** **Close** **Integration** **Acceleration** **Next Normal**	The Investment Case Focus Plans Innovation	Organic Revenue Growth Customers Marketing & Sales	Cost Optimization Operational Excellence: Supply Chain, Distribution, Continual Improvement Technology	Deal/ Due Diligence Financing M&A	Regulatory Financial Board	Culture Incentives Leadership People Politics	Integration Leader Change Management Communication Announcement Adjustments

The third component of the organizational play book is leadership. The only thing you can do all by yourself is fail. Successful mergers and acquisitions require an interdependent team with its members all paddling in the same direction.

Select "new" management team members based on the alignment of their motivations, strengths, and personal preferences with your vision for the new combined entity.

There are only three job interview questions. In the vast majority of cases each of the candidates for your leadership team has the strengths required to do the job. And while the main reason people fail in new leadership roles is poor fit, that's relatively difficult to assess up front. This leaves motivation as the most important criteria for selection. Be ready to probe all three interview questions, but lead with motivation.[1]

[1]Bradt, George, 2017, "Why You Should Lead with Motivation in Answering the Only Three True Job Interview Questions," *Forbes* (April 30).

Let's unpack that.

There are only three true job interview questions:

1. Will you love the job?
2. Can you do the job?
3. Can we tolerate working with you?

Every question you've ever been asked or asked others in an interview is about understanding motivation, strengths, or fit.

Lead with motivation. As Simon Sinek put it in his *TED Talk*, "People don't buy what you do. They buy why you do it."[2] It was true when he said it, and it's even truer as Millennials have become the largest cohort in the workforce and the largest cohort of leaders. And Millennials tend to be purpose-driven.

This means you should no longer choose people for what they can do. Choose for why they do it. You do care about how people's strengths can help solve problems. You also care about being able to tolerate the people working with you. But jobs are increasingly going to those with the best alignment of motivation.

The key is happiness. Happiness is good. Actually, it's three goods: doing good for others, doing things you're good at, and doing good for yourself. Everyone operates with some balance of the three—with different biases and balances. The answer to the motivation question, "Why would you want this job?" reveals that bias:[3]

- If they talk about the impact and effect they could have on others, their bias is most likely to do good for others.
- If they talk about how the job could allow them to leverage their strengths, their bias is most likely to do things they are good at.
- If they talk about how the job could fit with their own goals or progresses them toward those goals, their bias is most likely to do things that are good for them.

---

[2]Sinek, Simon, 2010, "How Great Leaders Inspire Action," *TED Talk* (May 4).
[3]Bradt, George, 2019, "Why Your First Interview Question Should Be 'Why Would You Want This Job?'" *Forbes* (January 2).

Knowing that bias informs where you should go with the interview. Essentially,

- If their bias fits with what you're looking for, go on to probe strengths and fit.
- If you're not sure, dig deeper into their motivations by going through different levels of why or impact questions until you are sure.
- If their bias does not fit with what you're looking for, end the interview. How you do this can range from going through the motions of completing the interview to letting them ask you questions, to walking out.

Order matters. Everything you do and say affects what follows. If you start your interview by probing strengths and then ask someone why they would want the job, they may try to mold their answer to fit what they infer is important to you from your questions about strengths. They may think your question is another way for you to get at strengths. Similarly, if you start your interview by probing fit and then ask about motivation, they may try to mold their question to convince you of their fit. So, start with the motivation question—without any biases.

While the world generally needs more other-focused leaders, this may not be true for your particular situation. The strongest leaders and strongest organizations over time will be, indeed, other-focused. They think outside-in, starting with the good they can do for others. They are the leaders and organizations people will want to work for over time, will want to learn from, and will want to help.

Still, you may need to focus more on strengths, building required strengths to ensure your near-term survival so you can be other-focused later. You may need to be a little more self-focused so you can attract and leverage people who think "good for me" first, so you can build some momentum.

Following are three sample answers to why someone wants the chief financial officer (CFO) job at an organization working to improve doctor–patient interactions:

1. "I see how I can contribute to improving your financial operations and help you through the coming exit to private equity investors." (Good at it)

2. "This one's a money-maker that can fund my retirement plan." (Good for me)
3. "Some of my family members' health care was compromised by poor interactions with their doctors. I want to be part of helping you fix that." (Good for others)

The choice is yours. In any case, figuring out what drives the person you're interviewing is your most important task in an interview for any role—and especially for your new leadership team. Make it your first task.

Strengths

People used to work their way up from apprentices to journeymen to master craftsmen. This involved 7-year apprenticeships as indentured servants living, eating, and working alongside master craftsmen and their families. While some of that is way out of date, some of it still makes sense.[4]

Gallup suggests strengths are made up of talent, knowledge, and skills. Adding experience and craft takes that to a different, even more valuable level. These build on each other.

- *Innate talent:* born with or not
- *Learned knowledge:* from books, classes, training
- *Practiced skills:* from intentional, deliberate repetition
- *Hard-won experience:* digested from real-world mistakes
- *Apprenticed craft:* artistic care and sensibilities absorbed from masters over time

Innate Talent

Gallup defines talent as "the natural capacity for excellence." But in *Bounce,* Matthew Syed suggests talent is a myth and that it all comes down to practice.[5] They could both be right in that it may be possible

[4]Bradt, George, 2022, "Why the Highest Level of Strength—Craft-Level Master—Requires Apprenticeship," *Forbes* (January 4).
[5]Syed, Mathew. 2011, *Bounce: The Myth of Talent and the Power of Practice* (London: Fourth Estate).

to overcome some lack of talent with deliberate practice. But having innate talent has to make it easier.

Learned Knowledge

Almost every society on the planet agrees that education is a basic human right. Investing in learning always pays off. The more people learn about a subject, the better.

Practiced Skills

As the old saying goes, "What's the best way to get to Carnegie Hall? Practice. Practice. Practice." But, as many have pointed it out, aimless, random practice gets you nowhere. Skills are built with intentional, deliberate repetition of important things so they become second nature.

Hard-Won Experience

To benefit from our mistakes, we have to be in a position to make them, understand them, and digest them so we don't repeat them. Practice works for things people do on their own. For things people do together or with an impact on others, people need experience.

Consider an orchestra preparing for a concert. Each member learns their part of the music. Each member practices to sharpen their own skills. Both are necessary, but not sufficient. They need to rehearse together to build a shared experience and make their mistakes then and not in the performance.

This is part of why U.S. President Dwight Eisenhower invaded North Africa before Europe during World War II—so his soldiers could get experience in battles they could afford to lose before engaging in the ones they could not afford to lose.

Apprenticed Craft

Craft-level artistic care and sensibilities are not innate talents. They can't be learned. You can't practice them. And while experience is important, it's not enough. Real mastery of a craft is handed down from master to apprentice over an extended period of time.

Theater legend Oscar Hammerstein handed down his craft to Stephen Sondheim. Sondheim saw Hammerstein as a surrogate father, worked as a $25-a-week gofer at age 17 on Hammerstein's show *Allegro*, and devoted himself to Hammerstein's tutorials on rhyme, characterization and storytelling, and demanding homework.

College football coaching legend Nick Saban was an apprentice to NFL coaching legend Bill Belichick of the New England Patriots for 4 years before going to the University of Alabama. Their attention to detail, systems, and processes are still so similar that players moving from Alabama to the Patriots hardly feel like they are switching coaches.

Great sushi chefs start their apprenticeships with years of rice making.

No one goes straight from medical school to being a surgeon. They spend years as residents (apprentices).

Eisenhower learned his craft as a general by serving on the general staff of several other great generals (as an apprentice) before he ever commanded armies in battle.

Implications for You

Know what you want from the people on your leadership team. Talent, knowledge, and skills always matter. Experience takes you to the next level—only if it is hard-won. Mastering a craft requires a whole different level of commitment.

General Atlantic's Talent Playbook

In their book *Talent*, General Atlantic managing director Anish Batlaw and coauthor Ram Charan note that talent is "the single most significant variable in differentiating outstanding performance from just good success," with performance defined as equity value, not just EBITDA.[6]

When George spoke with them, Charan said, "Talent is *the* value creator and competitive advantage." To that end, Batlaw and General Atlantic created a talent playbook integrally linked with the investment side of their business. That playbook has three main parts: diagnosis, strategy, and actions. As Charan pointed out, the value is in the subheads.

[6]Bradt, George, 2022, "Ram Charan and Anish Batlaw on General Atlantic's Private Equity Talent Playbook," *Forbes* (January 25).

Talent Diagnostic

General Atlantic's talent team works with its investment teams to create scorecards of the practices, processes, people, and decision-making required to enable and scale talent to achieve the investment theses. They use those scorecards to assess individuals' and the teams' potential to quadruple revenues in 3–5 years.

Charan says that's what's different versus 99.9 percent of companies—the focus on 3–5 years down the road. The key, he says, is "experience and learning agility" and understanding: (1) talent; (2) organizational structure; (3) operating rhythm; (4) culture (how people treat each other); (5) key performance indicators (KPIs); and (6) incentives and compensation and how all these are synchronized with speed and momentum.

Talent Strategy

General Atlantic's talent strategies flow from the "most important imperative of the business whether it's action on new market penetration, doing multiple M&As [mergers and acquisitions], fixing pricing, new products" or something else.

For example, Batlaw explained that the keys to realizing General Atlantic's investment thesis for Gen Z–focused fashion resale marketplace Depop were rapid expansion in the United States and superior digital marketing. They had just moved the head of the U.S. operation to London, leaving a gap in the United States. Then General Atlantic determined the core talent strategy was to fill that gap while building out digital marketing strengths in the United States at the same time.

Charan noted that "the greatest mistake is (a lack of) intellectual honesty and rigor on the most important critical priority. It can't be negotiated, downplayed, or compromised." The business strategy must start with customers. General Atlantic's value creation journey begins with choices around which customers to serve and how to serve them in a differentiated way focused on either design and innovation, production, delivery, or service.

For example, General Atlantic invested in Hemnet, Sweden's dominant online site for real estate listings. They saw expansion opportunities that "would take an aggressive new plan and a new corporate culture oriented toward product **innovation**, customer focus, and results." That customer-led focus determines the required people, culture, and infrastructure—the talent strategy.

Talent Actions

General Atlantic has learned to move quickly on people. "We found that when we made a mistake with a chief executive officer (CEO) change, the average internal rate of return (IRR) for those deals dropped by about 82 percent compared with when we got the CEO change right the first time. In addition, when a change was successfully executed within the first year of the deal, the average IRR ended up being six times greater than if the change was made after the first year."

They design the right organization for the future, leverage their talent bank of almost 5,000 pre-vetted executives, and fill positions within 6 months of a deal closing (sometimes even before).

Batlaw highlighted some things about their search process:

1. Their search and assessment criteria flow from the same scorecards they develop with the investment teams. They look hard at:

   Candidates' track records

   Strategic thinking and acumen (analytic capabilities, command of data)

   Learning agility (hunger for information and knowledge, willingness to seek out support)

   Drive for results, commercial acumen, and operations management

   Team leadership

   Interpersonal influence
2. They use reference checks not to ask people how they feel about the candidates but to validate the stories candidates told them about how they achieved success.
3. They tie incentives to future value creation, deemphasizing cash in favor of long-term incentives.

Things Change

Disciplined and consistent follow through and operations management are essential. But things change, investment theses adjust, and companies outgrow some of their leaders.

As General Atlantic's CEO Bill Ford put it, growth CEOs often "instinctively know they have people on the team who have been successful in the first chapter but who aren't equipped to support the company through its next phase of growth."

Team Synergies over Individual Strengths

Employees perform at different levels, when on different teams, in different situations, with different people. That probably makes sense to everyone. Why then do so few leaders spend so little time looking for synergies on their teams and so much time looking at individual performance? Because realizing synergies is hard work, and there has been no framework for doing so.[7]

The Skills Plus Minus Framework

Phil and Allan Maymin and Eugene Shen began their Skills Plus Minus presentation at the Massachusetts Institute of Technology (MIT) Sloan Sports Analytics Conference by asking who basketball's better point guard was from 2006 to 2008. Was it Deron Williams, who then played for the Utah Jazz, or was it Chris Paul, who played for the New Orleans Hornets at the time?

The data is inconclusive with regard to the original question, but it does show that either player would have been even more valuable had he been on *the other team*. Had the Jazz and the Hornets done a one-for-one, straight-up trade, each team would have been better off. Their stars might or might not have performed better, but the entire teams would have performed better.

The presenters looked at individual skills and events, including offensive and defensive ball handling, rebounding, and scoring. Then they looked at those skills and events in the company of other players to determine the positive and negative impact of players on each other. If two players each steal the ball from their opponents two times per game on their own but together steal the ball five times per game when they are on the court together, that's a positive synergy.

---

[7]Bradt, George, 2012, "A Framework for Turning Individuals' Strengths into Team Synergies," *Forbes* (September 18).

Applying the Skills Plus Minus Framework to Your Team

Of course, it's important to understand the strengths of the individuals on your team. That always will be important. But that's just the first step. The only way to optimize synergies on a team is to leverage differentiated individual strengths in complementary ways.

In a hypothetical example, one manager is particularly strong at managing details, one at operations, and one is particularly strong at encouraging creativity. Unfortunately, the guy with the operating strength is managing the group that needs to be creative; the more creative guy is managing a group that needed to pay attention to details; and the detail-oriented manager is trying to manage a complex operation. Moving each to the right role frees everyone up to perform better.

It's not just about the individuals. It's about the individuals in the context of the tasks that need to get done and the other individuals involved.

Let us propose a couple of steps flowing from the BRAVE leadership model:

1. Understand the context in terms of where you choose to play and what matters.
2. Determine the attitude, relationships, and behaviors required to deliver what matters.
3. Evaluate each individual's attitudinal, relationship, and behavioral strengths.
4. Structure the work in a way that allows individuals to complement each other's strengths.
5. Monitor, evaluate, and adjust along the way.

The pivot point is leveraging complementary strengths across attitudinal, relationship, and behavioral elements. The specifics of those are going to be different in each different situation. That gets us back to the initial point. But now you've got a framework. So there's no excuse not to pay as much attention to potential team synergies as you do to individuals' strengths.

Fit

Fit goes to the alignment of their personal preferences across behaviors, relationships, attitudes, values, and environment with the culture you are creating. This goes right back to your core focus. That focus and your cultural choices are inextricably linked.

One coal mining company's leadership team was split on whether they should be production or service focused. Those arguing for production focused said their essential business was moving dirt to uncover coal and they needed to be the low-cost producer. Those arguing for a service focus said that solving their utility company customers' problems was the only way to differentiate.

They wondered if they could do both.

They could not.

The required cultures were diametrically opposite. Service requires a customer-back decentralized flexibility to create more value for customers and earn a higher price. Production requires stability and a command-and-control attention to details to achieve the lowest total cost.

The critical question for this coal company was whether their best-serviced, most loyal customers could be lured away by a competitor offering them a 5 cent/ton lower price. The answer was yes, reinforcing the need for a production focus.

At a high level, as depicted in Figure 19.1:

- Design-focused organizations are generally marked by cultures of independence, flexibility, learning, and enjoyment led with freeing support.
- Produce-focused organizations are generally marked by cultures of stability, independence, results, and authority led with command and control.
- Deliver-focused organizations are generally marked by cultures of *inter*dependence, stability, order, and safety, led with shared responsibility
- Service-focused organizations are generally marked by cultures of flexibility, *inter*dependence, purpose, and caring, led with guided accountability.

FIGURE 19.1 Core Focus

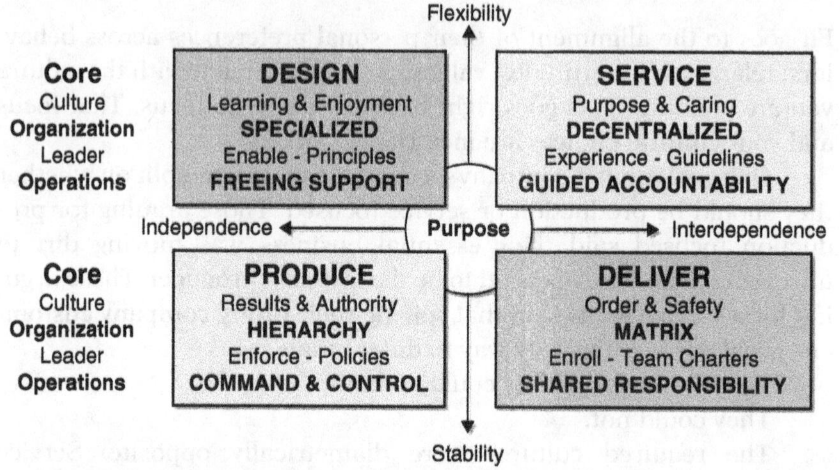

Choose leadership team members who agree with this core focus choice and can fit with this choice. In the next breath (and next chapter) you'll co-create plans.

One CEO told his people that they were going to make 90 percent of the operating decisions and that, as CEO, he was going to have to support them. He said 6 percent of decisions they'd make together and 4 percent were his to make, and he expected them to support his decisions.

The core focus decision was made as part of the investment case and confirmed during due diligence. It falls into the 4 percent of decisions that others are going to need to support. The high-level plans fall into the 6 percent of decisions that the new leadership team are going to make together. The distinction is important when it comes to inspiring, enabling, and empowering others.

For decisions that have to go through you, you're the choke point at the bottom of the funnel, controlling the flow. Conversely, when you provide clear direction, resources, bounded authority, and accountability, enabling others to make decisions, you turn the funnel into a megaphone, amplifying your influence and impact. It's one of the fundamental differences between early-stage entrepreneurs and successful leaders of larger, more complex enterprises.[8]

[8]Bradt, George, 2021, "Why and How You Should Switch to Decision-Enabling from Decision-Making," *Forbes* (April 13).

Decision-Enabling

Coca-Cola's Neville Isdell was a decision-enabler. He led by giving people:

1. *Direction* as to the desired objectives and results so everyone understood his intent.
2. *Resources*—the human, financial, technical, and operational resources—needed to succeed.
3. *Bounded authority* to make tactical decisions within the strategic boundaries and guidelines all had agreed to.
4. *Accountability* by way of standards of performance, time expectations, and positive and negative consequences of success and failure for those held to account.

It's counterintuitive, but clear direction, boundaries, and guidelines free people up to act. Knowing what you can't do lets you spend more time thinking about what you can do. Coca-Cola's people knew they couldn't mess with the core pillars of Coca-Cola. No one tried to change the secret formula. (Except once with New Coke. But that's a different story.) Global package changes were big deals. But people had tremendous flexibility with local advertising, promotions, and execution, enabling the tactical capacity to adjust quickly and decisively.

Isdell deliberately spent more time enabling others' decisions than in making decisions himself.

Here's the point. Taking the core focus discussion off the table for your new leadership team allows them to spend their time thinking through and managing how to make it work.

Executive Onboarding

The most important lesson in Bob Iger's book *The Ride of a Lifetime* is that "a little respect goes a long way, and the absence of it is often very costly." Respect yourself, colleagues, and brand.[9]

[9]Bradt, George, 2022, "Executive Onboarding Lessons from Disney's Bob Iger," *Forbes* (February 25).

Respect Yourself

A big part of self-respect is self-confidence—enough to own up to your own mistakes with confident humility. Quoting Iger:

- "You'll be more respected and trusted by the people around you if you honestly own up to your mistakes. It's impossible not to make them; but it is possible to acknowledge them, learn from them, and set an example that it's okay to get things wrong sometimes."[10]
- "You can't pretend to be someone you're not or to know something you don't."
- "You can't let humility prevent you from leading."

For example, Iger's boss at ABC sports, Roone Arledge, treated him "differently, with higher regard, it seemed, from that moment on" after he owned up to a big mistake.

Respect Colleagues

Iger learned to respect others' different strengths. Of content creators, Iger wrote, "Everything is subjective; there is often no right or wrong. The passion it takes to create something is powerful, and most creators are understandably sensitive when their vision or execution is questioned."[11]

In line with that, when he was Disney's CEO, Michael Eisner taught Iger "how to see" in a way he had not been able to do before. "Michael walked through the world with a set designer's eye, and while he wasn't a natural mentor, it felt like a kind of apprenticeship to follow him around and watch him work."

And Iger's bosses at Cap Cities, Tom Murphy and Dan Burke, "hired people who were smart and decent and hardworking, they put those people in positions of big responsibility, and they gave them the support and autonomy needed to do the job."

---

[10]Iger, Robert, 2019, *The Ride of a Lifetime: Lessons Learned from 15 Years as CEO of the Walt Disney Company* (New York: Random House).
[11]Ibid.

Respect Brand

Iger learned to get at the heart of the brand.

For example, ABC Sports told big stories in depth. "No detail was too small for Roone. Perfection was the result of getting all the little things right."

Don't confuse this with doing everything. Iger learned from branding and political consultant Scott Miller that if you have too many priorities (as in more than three), "they're no longer priorities." He went on to say, "Not only do you undermine their significance by having too many, but nobody is going to remember them all."[12]

You live your values in what you walk by as well as in what you do. When Roseanne Barr started tweeting some "thoughtless, occasionally offensive" things, Iger took her out to lunch and persuaded her to agree to stay off Twitter.

When she did not, tweeting something even more offensive, Iger fired her. It was an easy decision for him, guided by his principle that "there's nothing more important than the quality and integrity of your people and your product"—your brand.

Respectful Executive Onboarding

Respect for brand, self, colleagues—and their needs—were critical components of Iger's being able to attract and onboard the key people from Pixar, Marvel, and Lucas Films to add technology, talent, and characters propelling Disney into the future:

- Pixar's Steve Jobs, John Lasseter, and Ed Catmull needed Disney to respect the essence of Pixar.
- Ike Perlmutter needed Disney to value the Marvel team and give them the chance to thrive in their new company.
- George Lucas needed to trust that his legacy, his "baby," *Star Wars*, would be in good hands at Disney.

Iger earned their trust over time. Each of them had known Iger or known of him and how he treated others for years before they even started thinking about possible mergers.

---

[12]Ibid.

When Lucas was considering selling to Disney, Jobs told him that Iger had stood by his word. Iger had said, "It doesn't make any sense for us to buy you for what you are and then turn you into something else." He then honored the two-page "social compact" of culturally significant issues and items that Disney had promised to preserve in Pixar—and then Marvel and then *Star Wars*.

It's not an either–or choice. When onboarding executives individually or as part of a merger or acquisition, respect yourself, them, all your colleagues, and the brands.

The most up-to-date, full, editable versions of all tools are downloadable at primegenesis.com/tools.

TOOL 19.1

Team and People Assessment

Motivation. Why they want to be part of the new entity:
Strengths. Alignment of their and needed strengths:

- *Innate talent*—either born with or not
- *Learned knowledge*—from books, classes, or training
- *Practiced skills*—from deliberate repetition
- *Hard-won experience*—digested from real-world mistakes
- *Apprenticed craft*—absorbed from masters with artistic care and sensibilities

Fit. Mark your aspirational culture with an A and their preferences with a P. The closer the alignment, the better the fit:

Environment—Where Play

Workplace		
Remote, virtual, open, informal	1 – 2 – 3 – 4 – 5	In-person, closed, formal
Work-Life Balance		
Health and wellness first	1 – 2 – 3 – 4 – 5	Near-term productivity first
Enablers		
Human, interpersonal, societal	1 – 2 – 3 – 4 – 5	Technical, mechanical, scientific

Values—What Matters and Why

Focus		
Do good for others/Environmental, Social, Governance	1 – 2 – 3 – 4 – 5	Do good for selves, what good at
Risk Appetite		
Risk more, gain more (confidence)	1 – 2 – 3 – 4 – 5	Protect what have, minimize mistakes
Learning		
Open, shared, value diversity	1 – 2 – 3 – 4 – 5	Directed, individual, single-minded

(Continued)

Tool 19.1 Team and People Assessment (continued)

Attitude—How Win

Strategy		
Premium price, service, innovation	1 – 2 – 3 – 4 – 5	Low cost, low service, minimum viable
Focus		
Divergence from competitors	1 – 2 – 3 – 4 – 5	Convergence on market leader
Posture		
Proactive, breakthrough innovation	1 – 2 – 3 – 4 – 5	Responsive, reliable steady progress

Relationships—How Connect

Power, Decision-Making		
Diffused, debated—confront issues	1 – 2 – 3 – 4 – 5	Controlled, monarchical
Diversity, Equity, Inclusion		
All welcome, valued, respected	1 – 2 – 3 – 4 – 5	Bias to work with people just like us
Communication, Controls		
Informal, verbal, face to face	1 – 2 – 3 – 4 – 5	Formal, directed, written

Behaviors – What Impact

Working Units		
One organization, interdependent teams	1 – 2 – 3 – 4 – 5	Independent individuals, units
Discipline		
Fluid, flexible (guidelines)	1 – 2 – 3 – 4 – 5	Structured, disciplined (policies)
Delegation		
Inspire, enable, empower, trust	1 – 2 – 3 – 4 – 5	Narrow task-focused direction

CHAPTER 20

People: Acquire, Develop, Encourage, Plan, Transition

	The Strategic Playbook	The Commercial Playbook	The Operational Playbook	The Financial Playbook	The Governance Playbook	The Organizational Playbook	The Change Management Playbook
Concept **Research** **Investment Case** **Negotiation** **Deal/Due Diligence** **Contract** **Close** **Integration** **Acceleration** **Next Normal**	The Investment Case	Organic Revenue Growth	Cost Optimization	Deal/ Due Diligence	Regulatory	Culture Incentives	Integration Leader Change Management
	Focus		Operational Excellence: Supply Chain, Distribution, Continual Improvement	Financing	Financial	Leadership	Communication
	Plans	Customers		M&A	Board	People	Announcement
	Innovation	Marketing & Sales	Technology			Politics	Adjustments

The fourth component of the organizational playbook is people. When it comes to sorting people and roles on your team, work with a short-term, mid-term, and a long-term framework. Initially, determine whether any short-term moves should be made before or at the start, and any mid-term moves should be made in the first 100 days. Then, continue to develop teams over time.

Guest Contributor Ericka Stevens

As a young [human resources] HR professional, full of energy and optimism, I thought I had a solid plan to climb the corporate ladder. Approximately 5 years into this master plan, I was gifted 1 hour with our company's chief human resources officer. My hands were sweaty, knees were shaking as I sat across from the guru of HR. I nervously shared with him my career goals and how I aspired to lead people and culture for an organization. I asked him, "What can I do to accelerate my development and readiness for a strategic leadership role?"

He replied bluntly, "You need to walk into a fire." He further explained the precise and intense conditions surrounding how diamonds are formed. Under the pressure of approximately 725,000 pounds per square inch, and at temperatures of 2,000 to 2,200 degrees Fahrenheit, a diamond will begin to form.

The entire process sounded extremely painful. I remember thinking to myself, "There must be an easier way."

What I didn't appreciate or understand then, that I do now, is that greatness is created under extreme pressure and adversity. Under these intense circumstances, great leaders are born. While in the "fire" individuals accelerate their growth and development, and teams achieve remarkable results.

Mergers and acquisitions are high-stress, high-stakes, high-pressure events. These unique transactions can be used as a furnace to produce something extraordinary. Architects of successful mergers and acquisitions spend significant amounts of time on the financial aspects of the transaction. Employees are often an afterthought and caught in the middle of what feels like the end of the world.

I was working as a plant HR manager for a manufacturing company when our business was acquired by a global organization. Soon after the announcement, rapid changes generated fear, mistrust, and a lack of confidence. Our team's performance quickly suffered.

Combining two or more companies is often extremely difficult as cultural differences across organizations must be overcome. Employee disengagement, declining brand loyalty, and a reduction in long-term profitability are just a few negative outcomes that may emerge if efforts fail to promote respect, integrity, diversity, equity, and inclusion.

What if leaders took the same amount of time, spent on the financials, to create an environment that cultivates creativity, instead of fear, and collaboration instead of mistrust? What if leaders intentionally used this transaction as a stage to grow and showcase talent?

The 1998 science fiction disaster film *Armageddon* serves as an example of people working together to bridge a cultural divide. After a massive meteor shower obliterates the Space Shuttle Atlantis, NASA scientists discover they have 18 days before an asteroid the size of Texas impacts Earth, destroying all planetary life. A group of blue-collar, deep-core drillers collaborate with NASA astronauts to stop a gigantic asteroid on a collision course with Earth. Although the movie is fictional, *Armageddon* is a film that brilliantly highlights the magic that occurs, under extreme pressure, when a diverse group of people come together to execute a common vision.

As I continue to lead cultural transformation, I am reminded of the importance of transparency and trust. Creating an environment where people can show up every day in an authentic state, without judgment, starts with a leader's willingness to be vulnerable.

Vulnerability is a powerful way to support a trusting, positive team culture. When leaders are vulnerable, it gives permission to their team members to feel comfortable being open and honest with their concerns, questions, mistakes, and roadblocks.

A safe environment, rich with trust and respect, breeds inclusion. Inclusive organizations attract diverse talent, bringing with them unique experiences. Diversity and inclusion spark innovation and creativity. Like a greenhouse that has optimal conditions for growing plants of all kinds, the right culture allow people to convert experiences into creative solutions for today's organizational challenges, driving a stronger team performance.

Align Everything Around Your Core Focus and Burning Imperative

Start by defining the structure and set of roles that you need to realize your mission, execute your strategy, and deliver on your goals. The mission determines the makeup of the ideal organization. The resulting strategies and plans help determine what roles are required to do the things that need to be done daily to achieve the goals. This gives you a map of the roles you need to have and the roles you may need to eliminate. This is also the time to root out the role outliers.

FIGURE 20.1 Core Focus

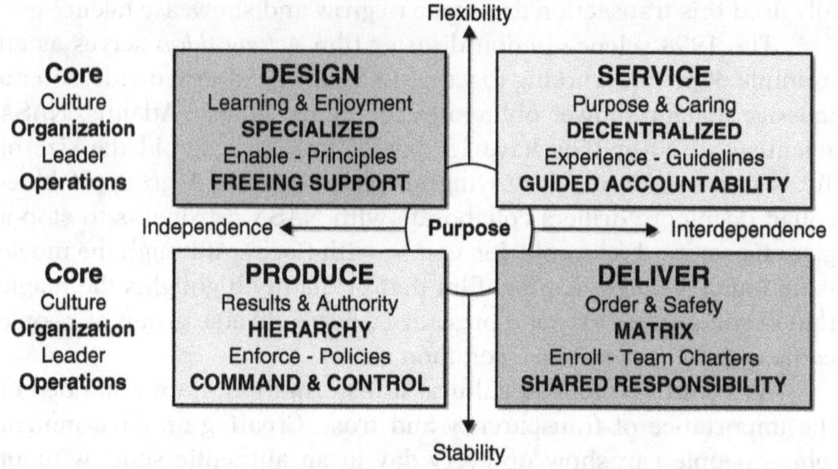

As discussed earlier and depicted in Figure 20.1, all organizations design, produce, sell, deliver, and service. The core focus of your business will indicate which one of those actions is your primary function. Once this has been identified, your first job is to align all functions to support it in terms of organization and operations.

Implement ADEPT Talent Management

Once you've determined your core focus and have aligned your purpose, organizational structure, operations approach, culture, and leadership focus to that core and your burning imperative, you'll now want to think in terms of acquiring, developing, encouraging, planning, and transitioning (ADEPT) talent to accelerate team development. The headlines are in Table 20.1.

Keep your core focus in mind as you acquire, develop, encourage, plan, and transition people.

Role Requirements

With a picture of ideal structure and roles in hand, you can now determine which roles will have the greatest impact on delivering against your mission, strategies, and goals. The roles responsible for these tasks are the critical ones. The other roles encompass tasks that can be

Table 20.1
ADEPT Framework for Talent Management

Acquire	Scope roles. Precision, depth, and clarity are essential.
	Identify prospects.
	Recruit and select the right people with the right talent for the right roles.
	Attract those people.
	Onboard them so that they can deliver better results faster.
Develop	Assess performance drivers.
	Develop skills, knowledge, experience, and craft for current and future roles.
Encourage	Provide clear direction, objectives, measures, and so on.
	Support with the resources, authority, and time required for success.
	Reinforce desired behaviors with recognition and rewards.
Plan	Monitor people's performance over time.
	Assess their situation and potential.
	Plan for future capability development, succession, and contingencies.
Transition	Migrate people to different roles to fit their needs and life stage and company needs.

done merely well enough. This is where strategy and people overlap. At this point, determine which roles need to be best in class and invested in and which roles can be maintained or outsourced.

The airline industry has historically lost buckets of money over the long term. Yet, Southwest makes money every year. Part of why it does is that it has figured out which are its critical roles. Southwest overinvests in maintenance roles so it can turn its planes around faster. It overinvests in training its flight attendants so passengers' in-air experience is fun. Conversely, it underinvests in food service and on-the-ground waiting spaces.

Identify what roles will enable you to:

- Win with capabilities that are predominant, superior, or strong compared with others.
- Play not to lose by being above average or good enough.
- Choose to outsource, ally with others, or not do at all.

Right People in the Right Role

Once you have defined the right structure and set of roles and determined the requirements for success in those roles, it is time to see whether you've got the right people in the right roles (current) and who should be placed in new roles. It's unlikely that you'll acquire a team that is perfectly set up to deliver against your Burning Imperative. If you're lucky, with a couple of small tweaks you'll be on your way to a world-class team. However, if there is a significant need for change, you may need to do a major overhaul. If so, be prepared for a lot of work and a lot of disruption. The earlier you make that assessment the better. Don't make the mistake of delaying or avoiding the people changes that need to be made while hoping that some magical transformation will occur. It won't.

For some reason, it is human nature to put off such decisions. Yet the number one regret experienced senior leaders express is not moving fast enough on people. Have a strong bias for figuring the right role sort out as early as possible and making the moves quickly. Getting the right people in the right roles with the right support is a fundamental, essential building block of a high-performing team. Without the right people in the right roles, there is no team.

Getting the right people in the right roles is guided by the team's mission, vision, and values, as well as by individuals' strengths. Strengths are necessary for success. But they are not sufficient. People must want to do well, and they must fit in. It is helpful to think in terms of strengths, motivation, and fit.

Strengths

Match the right people with the right roles. In their book *Now, Discover Your Strengths*, Marcus Buckingham and Don Clifton's core premise is that people do better when they capitalize on their own individual strengths, which comprise talent, knowledge, and skills. According to Gallup, "a strength is the ability to consistently provide near-perfect performance in a specific activity. The key to building a strength is to identify your dominant talents, then complement them by acquiring knowledge and skills pertinent to the activity." Use a tool such as Gallup's Clifton Strengths Assessment to help you better match talent to roles and as a valuable aid in career development for your team.[1]

[1]Buckingham, Marcus, and Clifton, Donald, 2001, *Now, Discover Your Strengths* (New York: Free Press).

It's useful to add hard-won experience to this base model because people learn from their failures and mistakes—hence "hard-won." In some rare cases, people take these strengths to craft-level based on their artistic caring and sensibilities. This suggests a more complete view of strengths includes innate talent, learned knowledge, practiced skills, *plus* hard-won experience and apprenticed craft.

Motivation

If you understand your people's values, your people's goals, and how they see what they are currently doing considering those goals, you have a terrific advantage in helping them find or live up to the right role for themselves and for the organization. Look at recent performance reviews, go back to your due diligence, and reflect on the observations you have made so far.

Fit

Fit is determined by how well an individual's cultural preferences match with the organization's culture. Take a hard look at attitudinal perspective, values, and biases.

Perspective is an attitude born out of how people have been trained to view and solve business problems. It is the accumulation of people's business experience as manifested in their mental models. People with a classic sales perspective may feel that they can sell any product to customers. Conversely, people with a more marketing perspective may feel the organization should modify its products and services to meet customers' needs. It's not that one perspective is better than the other—just that they are different.

It is rare for all of any individual's values to match all of the organization's values. However, it is important for most of the core values to match and for none of them to be in direct conflict with each other.

Different people behave at work in different ways. Some roles may require people with a greater sense of urgency. Some roles require people who think things through thoroughly before jumping in. If someone who tends to get a later start in the day is assigned the role of generating overnight sales reports for the group before everyone else comes in, it would force the person to work in opposition to a natural bias and would most likely be a recipe for failure (and inaccurate reports!).

When Things *Aren't* Working, Don't Wait

We've run over 50 chief executive officer (CEO) boot camps over the past 2 decades, each with 8–12 CEOs and other experts in the room. Looking back on their careers, the number one regret senior leaders have is not moving fast enough on people in the wrong roles.

Couple that with the number one thing high performers want, which is for someone to get the deadwood or other obstacles out of their way, and it's no surprise that when leaders finally do move on people in the wrong roles, they are met with others asking, "What took you so long?" And as one CEO put it, he knew some of them were thinking, "We were beginning to doubt your judgment."

Some leaders think they're being nice by waiting. They're not. At some level, people in the wrong roles know they're in the wrong roles. The sooner you can move them into the right role (either in your organization or elsewhere), the better for all involved.

How Fast Should You Move on the Team?

In a merger or acquisition, think in terms of three time frames: immediate, 100 days, and long-term.

As discussed earlier, no one is going to be able to fully engage with their new reality until you've answered the question, "What about me?" They need to know if they still have a job, what that job is, and what you want them to do.

One organization had done a series of acquisitions without fully integrating them. Finally, they announced a major restructuring, telling its people that they were going to zero base everyone's job and cascade the choices. First the CEO was going to pick his direct reports. Then those people would have 6 weeks to pick theirs, then the next level would have 6 weeks, and the next, and so on. They said the entire process was going to take a year given the number of layers and that people should keep doing their existing jobs along the way.

There were some predictable responses. Everyone started creating other options. The organization lost some of its best people along the way and suffered through tremendous stress and confusion.

What they had not predicted was the complete failure of the rollout process.

They made a choice to move from separate, geographically focused organizations to a single triple matrix cut by product line, function, and geography. But they failed to account for the massive increase in travel costs in having their product line leaders and functional leaders fly all over the world to collaborate with their geographic partners.

Six months into the process they had theoretically realigned the first four layers of the organization and decided to eliminate the product line leg of the matrix, pretty much starting their organizational thinking again. Six months after being told their jobs were in jeopardy, only 8 (8—not 8,000) of the 40,000 people in the organization felt secure in their jobs.

Of course, organizations have to evolve as things change. But you can do that in three steps:

1. *Immediate*. Do an initial role sort, announcing and making all the job moves you can before, on, or shortly after the day the deal closes. This includes eliminating redundant jobs. Shame on you if you don't do the work to get this right for 80–90 percent of the new organization.
2. *100 days*. Fill open positions in the first 100 days. This will include bringing in new people with new-to-the-organization strengths to fill newly created roles and making the remaining choices in your initial role sort.
3. *Long-term*. Implement future capability plans and continue to evolve the organization over time.

HOT TIP

Have a bias to move faster on your team than you think you should. The risks of moving too fast are nothing compared with the multiplier effect of leaving people in the wrong place too long. The number one thing that experienced leaders regret is not moving faster on their people.

Three Types of Leaders

When people see or hear *leader*, they generally think of interpersonal leaders inspiring and enabling teams. Although those interpersonal leaders are of critical import, many organizations need artistic leaders and scientific leaders as well. The common characteristic of all leaders

Table 20.2
Artistic, Scientific, and Interpersonal Leadership Characteristics

	Interpersonal	Scientific	Artistic
Where to play	Context	Problems	Media
What matters and why	Cause	Solutions	Perceptions
How to win	Rally team	Better thinking	New approach
How to connect	Hearts	Minds	Souls
What impact	Actions	Knowledge	Feelings

is that they inspire others to become better than they would on their own. Each of the three types of leaders inspire others in different ways as described next and summarized in Table 20.2.

Artistic leaders inspire by influencing feelings. They help us take new approaches to how we see, hear, taste, smell, and touch things. You can find these leaders creating new designs, new art, and the like. These people generally have no interest in ruling or guiding. They are all about changing perceptions.

Scientific leaders both guide and inspire by influencing knowledge with their thinking and ideas. You can find them creating new technologies, doing research and writing, teaching, and the like. Their ideas tend to be well thought through, supported by data and analysis, and logical. These people develop structure and frameworks that help others solve problems.

Interpersonal leaders can be found ruling, guiding, and inspiring at the head of their interpersonal cohort whether it's a team, organization, or political entity. They come in all shapes and sizes and influence actions in different ways. The common dimension across interpersonal leaders is that they are leading other people.

Ask yourself what type of leader your team needs the most in each role. Is there a certain type of leader that is needed but not yet on the team? Evaluate all team members on their leadership potential and their natural type, and you'll start to find valuable clues on how to best develop them for continued success. One hallmark of the strongest leaders is their ability to develop other leaders along the way. Develop as many as you can and when you do, you'll leave a legacy on your organization that will deliver consistent growth and inspire many lives.

Future capability planning is the primary link between your strategic process and organizational process. Use it to create a gap between your future organizational needs and current reality and a plan to fill those gaps.

Succession planning gives you a picture of the people that can take the place of current leaders when they move on—their "successors."

Contingency planning gives you a picture of how you're going to fill the gap when a leader needs to be replaced unexpectedly.

Talent management helps you optimize the potential of your existing people, developing them in place, or moving them across, down, or out as appropriate.

Create a picture of the post-merger organization, culture, capabilities, and perspectives you need to implement your strategy. This creates gaps with your pre-merger current reality. Think through the various ways to fill those gaps, including:

- Developing current people by evolving their attitudes and building knowledge, skills, experience, and craft on top of their existing talents
- Acquiring new people with required attitude, talents, and differential perspectives soon and then building their knowledge, skills, experience, and craft
- Acquiring new people with the required attitude, talent, knowledge, skills, experience, craft, and differential perspectives just in time as needed

Strategic Priorities

Confirm the organization's strategic priorities. A key piece of this is choices around where to

Win by being: Predominant or top 1 percent, superior or top 10 percent, strong or top 25 percent;

Not lose by being: Above average or competitive, good enough or scaled; or

Not do by: Outsourcing or not doing at all.

Future Culture, Capabilities, and Perspectives Required by Those Priorities

Lay out the human, financial, physical, technical, and operational organization and culture and different capabilities and perspectives required to implement those priorities. This most likely involves either a specialized, hierarchical matrix or decentralized organization:

- *Specialized* organizations enable winning invention or design. They provide freeing support to enable specialized artistic leaders to do what they do best.
- *Hierarchical* organizations enable winning production. They provide disciplined command and control so scientific leaders can focus their efforts.
- *Matrix* organizations are essential to winning distribution. They drive interdependence across the various groups involved in distributing and delivering products and services.
- *Decentralized* organizations enable winning customer service and experience. They provide flexible guidance to interpersonal leaders rallying their teams.

Existing Capabilities

Insert an assessment of your current human, financial, physical, technical and operational culture, capabilities, and perspectives based on objectively factual data and truths versus subjective, personal, cultural or political truths, opinions, assumptions, or conclusions.

Gaps

Highlight the differences between future culture, capabilities, and perspectives required and existing capabilities, culture, and perspectives.

Current people to develop/plan to develop them

Insert the output from the latest talent management reviews along with any updates since then and your due diligence, along with the current plans to develop these people to be able to fill future human capability gaps.

Sort redundancies
Where you have people in overlapping roles, choose who will stay in that role in the future and who will move to another role within the new organization or to another organization altogether.

Gaps to recruit for early on and develop/plan to develop new people
Lay out which gaps to fill first from the outside and your plan to develop those new people.

Gaps to recruit later
Identify which gaps to fill later and when and how you will fill them.

Plans to fill other gaps
Lay out plans to fill financial, physical, technical, and operational gaps.

Bosch and Seeo

Automotive industry supplier Bosch announced its acquisition of Seeo, a developer of next-generation solid-state batteries. At least some, like Lux analyst Cosmin Leslau, suggested this "acquisition has some wrinkles that make it a risky bet for Bosch." In particular, Seeo's status was "fragile," was "burning through cash," and had "technical issues."

But it was not about the business.

Linda Beckmeyer, a Bosch spokeswoman, said that Bosch has acquired all of Seeo's intellectual property plus its research staff. That's what they wanted. Not the current business. Not the current customers. Not even the current technology. They wanted Seeo's capabilities.

You can imagine the conversations.

"We need to increase our footprint in battery development."

"With our people?"

"By buying a company with people that know this space so they can help everyone in our company up their game in this area fast."

And that's just what they did.

Bosch needed battery capability much faster than it could train its existing people to get there. Instead, it filled its capability gap with the Seeo acquisition.

Summaries of Related Efforts

Succession Planning

Succession planning gives you a picture of the people who can take the place of current leaders when they move on—their successors:

1. Identify most important leadership positions.
2. Identify successors to the leaders in those positions in line with future capability plans.
3. Put in place development plans for those successors.

Contingency Planning

Contingency planning gives you a picture of how you're going to fill the gap when a leader needs to be replaced unexpectedly. For the same positions identified in succession planning, lay out plans to back-fill those leaders if there's a sudden, unexpected need by (in no particular order):

- Having the person currently supervising those leaders step in on an interim basis
- Having a peer assume supervisory responsibilities on an interim basis
- Bringing someone in from the outside to supervise on an interim basis
- Having a direct report into that position assume supervisory responsibilities—either permanently or on an interim basis

Talent Management

Talent management helps you optimize the potential of your existing people, developing them in place or moving them across, down, or out as appropriate:

1. Begin with an assessment:
   a. Results versus objectives and cultural ratings (doing the right job, the right way)

   b. Learnings and accomplishments: What worked? What needs to improve? What learned about self?
   c. Strengths: Innate talent + learned knowledge + practiced skills + hard-won experience + apprenticed craft
   d. Gaps
   e. Career interests
2. Based on assessment, map people on role appropriateness versus performance grid:
   a. If in right role and underperforming, invest to improve their performance.
   b. If in right role and effective, support in current role.
   c. If in right role and outstanding, cherish in current role.
   d. If in wrong role and underperforming, move to a better role in or out of the organization.
   e. If in wrong role and effective, move laterally to a better role for them in the organization.
   f. If in wrong role and outstanding, promote them to better role.

   Many organizations find it helpful to do some sort of calibration meeting where people managers can share their assessments of the people that work for them. This allows those managers to get input from others to refine their thinking and calibrate assessments of performance and potential across the organization.
3. Make moves as appropriate. Once you decide people have to go, move.
4. Put in place development plans, which are all about helping people develop. The trap is that some managers focus development plans exclusively on filling gaps/fixing problems. It's better to help people further develop their strengths (as well as filling gaps). Do this for each element:
   a. Strength to develop:
   b. Gaps to fill:
   c. Developmental objectives for the period—build on innate talent with learned knowledge, practiced skill, relevant experience:

d. Developmental approach and plan
   i. Learn knowledge (reading, courses, training):
   ii. Practice skills (On-the-job or other emphasis):
   iii. Gain relevant experience (activities, projects, programs, assignments, roles):
   iv. Nurture craft-level artistic caring and sensibilities
e. Resources to be deployed – managers, coaches, trainers (internal or external):
f. Responsibilities of person being developed:
g. Responsibilities of manager/coach:
h. Milestones/timing:

5. Implement and repeat.

Underperforming in Right Role: Invest

Do what it takes to define their roles, fix their management, give them the training or resources they need, and they will perform.

Effective in Right Role: Support

Invest appropriately to support in current roles, helping them continue to grow, perform, and be happy.

Outstanding in Right Role: Cherish

Overinvest to help them grow, perform, and be happy in their current roles.

Table 20.3
Appropriateness Versus Performance Grid

	Role Sort		
	Underperforming 15–20 percent	Effective 65–70 percent	Outstanding 10–15 percent
In right role	**Invest** (to improve performance)	**Support** (in current role)	**Cherish** (with extra attention)
In wrong role	**Move Out** (quickly with compassion and respect)	**Move Over** (with an onboarding plan)	**Move Up** (quickly with an onboarding plan and mentorship)

Underperforming in Wrong Role: Move Out

Treat with respect and compassion and move them out with a minimum of discretionary investment.

Effective in Wrong Role: Move Over

Find them and move them to the right role before they burn out or quit.

Outstanding in Wrong Role: Move Up

Promote them before somebody hires them away. Move them up sooner than you're comfortable and with more support to succeed in their new roles.

Or the classic nine-box (Table 20.4).

Table 20.4
Nine-Box Talent Management

Potential			
Promotable 2 or more levels	6 Wrong role?	8 Improve performance	9 Future leaders
Promotable 1 level	3 Move to other role or out?	5 Continue to develop and improve performance	7 Continue to develop and stretch
Not promotable	1 Move out	2 Nurture	4 Cherish in current position
	Below Standard	**Meets Standards**	**Exceeds Standards**
		Performance (What and How)	

Think through the people you have in place and how you can apply them best to immediate priorities and how you're going to build the organization you need to deliver ongoing, accelerated value creation.

Strong Performers and the Three Goods

Invest in your strong performers first. Way too many leaders get sucked into spending so much time dealing with underperformers that they don't pay enough attention to the people in the right roles performing particularly well until those people walk in to announce they're leaving.

Instead, treat your strong performers so "good" all along the way that they will not ever be open to the conversation about possibly leaving. Remember this is three goods:

- *Good for others:* Inspire your strong performers with the *good for others* part of your mission or purpose.
- *Good at it:* Do what it takes to remove any barriers that hinder your strong performers' ability to do more of what they are good at.
- *Good for me:* Ensure your strong performers receive the recognition and rewards they deserve. As your strong performers' knowledge, skills, and accomplishments grow, make sure the person recognizing and rewarding their new market worth is you.[2]

Position Profiles and Potential

Mapping performance and role appropriateness facilitates an urgent identification of who is in the right role and who is in the wrong role now. It is important not to confuse *role match* with *potential* because there is a significant difference between the two. Role match focuses on the current position. What's the likelihood of their performing well in their current position? Potential focuses on growth, development, and future promotions. What is required to help people move up the ladder? What is the appropriate timeline for those promotions?

Position profiles like Tool 20.3 are formalized ways to set the foundations for achievement within an organization at any given role. Every organization has its own way of doing position profiles. When done well these can be used when acquiring, evaluating, mentoring, developing, and promoting talent. The better position profiles include the key elements of the mission, vision, strengths, motivation, and fit relative to the position.

Keeping Your Head

Mergers and acquisitions are stressful for all involved. The people picking the new teams are under tremendous pressure to make the right decisions quickly. And the people waiting to be picked are under

[2]Bradt, George, 2015, "Why You Should Never Make or Take Counter Offers," *Forbes* (November 18).

similar stress and may feel like they're in purgatory until they are told what's going to happen to them.

But not you.

You're going to choose to be part of the solution instead of a pawn in the game.

Think through what you want, where you are now, and how to bridge that gap.

Think through what you want in terms of the role in which you can make the greatest contribution, do the best for others, leverage your strengths and earn the respect, appreciation, recognition, and rewards you deserve.

Think through where you are now, how people view you, and how they view others that could do the job you aspire to.

Bridge the gaps by managing how others perceive your motivation, fit, and strengths.

Regarding motivation, let the right person/decision-maker know what you want. Don't assume they know. Don't expect them to read your mind. They're desperately trying to figure out where people belong. They need your help. They should appreciate your letting them know.

Fit is code for culture and the new culture in particular. Figure out where senior leadership is taking the culture—perhaps using such sophisticated tools as asking them. Then start living the new culture now across its dimensions of behaviors, relationships, attitudes, values and environment.

When it comes to strengths, one of the best ways of interviewing for strengths is to ask people for examples of times when they've demonstrated the required strengths. Preempt that by starting to demonstrate the strengths required in the role you aspire to in your current role or by starting to do the new role even before you are asked.

Two companies were merging. Each had a regulatory group. The leader of the smaller regulatory group was expecting his group to get merged into the larger one with his own job going away. Nevertheless, he thought through what he'd do in his first 100-days leading the combined group and what he expected the combined team to get done over their first year. He put both down on paper and shared them with his senior leaders.

When it came time to pick the group leader, senior leadership chose the man with the plan. Be the person with the plan.

The most up-to-date, full, editable versions of all tools are downloadable at primegenesis.com/tools.

TOOL 20.1

Future Organizational Capability Planning

Create a picture of the organization, culture, capabilities, and perspectives you need to implement your strategy, being explicit about diversity, equity, and inclusion (DE&I) targets.

Strategic priorities. Lay out the organization's strategic priorities:

Future culture, capabilities, and perspectives required by those priorities. Lay out the human, financial, physical, technical and operational organization and culture, and different capabilities and perspectives including DE&I required to implement those priorities:

Existing capabilities. Insert an assessment of your current human, financial, physical, technical and operational culture, capabilities, and perspectives including DE&I:

Gaps. Highlight the differences between future culture, capabilities, and perspectives required and existing capabilities, culture, and perspectives including DE&I:

Current people to develop and plan to develop them. Insert the output from your latest talent management review along with any updates since then, along with your plan to develop these people to be able to fill future human capability gaps:

Gaps to recruit for early on and develop and plan to develop new people. Lay out which gaps to fill first from the outside and your plan to develop those new people:

Gaps to recruit later. Identify which gaps to fill later and when and how you will fill them:

Plans to fill other gaps. Lay out plans to fill financial, physical, technical, and operational gaps:

TOOL 20.2

Talent Management

1. Begin with an assessment:

   Results versus objectives and cultural ratings. (Doing the right job, the right way.)

   Learnings and accomplishments:

   What worked? What needs to improve? What learned about self?

   Strengths (Innate talent + learned knowledge + practiced skills + hard-won experience + apprenticed craft.)

   Gaps

   Career interests

2. Based on assessment, map people on role appropriateness versus performance grid:

	Role Sort		
	Underperforming 15–20 percent	Effective 65–70 percent	Outstanding 10–15 percent
In right role	**Invest** (to improve performance)	**Support** (in current role)	**Cherish** (with extra attention)
In wrong role	**Move Out** (quickly with compassion and respect)	**Move Over** (with an onboarding plan)	**Move Up** (quickly with an onboarding plan and mentorship)

(Continued)

Tool 20.2 Talent Management (continued)

Or the classic nine-box:

Potential			
Promotable 2 or more levels	6 Wrong role?	8 Improve performance	9 Future leaders
Promotable 1 level	3 Move to other role or out?	5 Continue to develop and improve performance	7 Continue to develop and stretch
Not promotable	1 Move out	2 Nurture	4 Cherish in current position
	Below Standard	**Meets Standards**	**Exceeds Standards**
	Performance (What and How)		

3. Make moves as appropriate.
4. Put in place development plans:
5. Implement and repeat.

TOOL 20.3

Recruiting Brief

Recruit for job title, department, compensation grade, start date

Mission and Responsibilities

Why does this position exist?

What are the objectives, goals, and desired outcomes?

What is the desired impact on the rest of the organization?

What are the specific responsibilities of the role?

What organizational relationships and interdependencies are important?

What is the vision (picture of success) for the role?

Strengths

What talents are required? (Innate)

What knowledge is required? (Learned: education, training, experience, qualifications)

What skills are required? (Practiced: technical, interpersonal, business)

What experience is required? (Hard-won)

What level of craft is required? (Artistic caring and sensibilities)

Motivation

How do the activities of the role fit with the person's likes/dislikes/ideal job criteria?

How will the person progress toward the desired long-term goal?

Fit

What are the desired behaviors, relationships, attitudes, values, environmental preferences for the role?

What are the characteristics of the company's work style?

What are the characteristics of the group's work style?

What are the characteristics of the supervisor's work style?

How well does the candidate fit with each of the above?

CHAPTER 21

Politics: What Current and New Leaders Need to Know Organizationally and Personally

	The Strategic Playbook	The Commercial Playbook	The Operational Playbook	The Financial Playbook	The Governance Playbook	The Organizational Playbook	The Change Management Playbook
Concept **Research** **Investment Case** **Negotiation** **Deal/Due Diligence** **Contract** **Close** **Integration** **Acceleration** **Next Normal**	The Investment Case	Organic Revenue Growth	Cost Optimization	Deal/ Due Diligence	Regulatory	Culture Incentives	Integration Leader Change Management
	Focus		Operational Excellence: Supply Chain, Distribution, Continual Improvement	Financing	Financial	Leadership	Communication
	Plans	Customers		M&A	Board	People	Announcement
	Innovation	Marketing & Sales	Technology			Politics	Adjustments

The fifth component of the organizational playbook is politics. Can we talk about politics? Do we have to talk about politics? Politics is inevitable in any organization of more than one person. Even if you'd like to pretend your organization is politics-free, it isn't. Even if you'd like to ignore the politics and get on with the real work, you can't. On the other hand, those who make playing politics their first priority often fail to get beyond it.

To be fair, some try to avoid the politics and the hard decisions.

Two companies merged in Japan. For all to save face, they agreed that the president of one of the companies would be the first president of the combined organization. When he retired, the president of the other company would take over. Then, each successive leader would alternate between the two companies.

And that's what they did.

For 30 years.

After 30 years, all the people who had previously worked for either one of the original companies had finally left or retired and they finally got to pick a president who thought he worked for the combined company.

And sometimes people don't even talk.

One combining company merged departments by putting them on the same floor—but kept all the old work groups together on opposite sides of the floor. You'd get off the elevator and go left to talk to someone who had previously worked for one of the merged companies and turn right to talk to someone from the other company.

They never mingled and never got to know each other. After 6 months, they were still using FedEx to send each other packages overnight—across the hall.

You read that right. Someone from FedEx would pick up a package and drive it to the local depot where it was put on a plane, flown to Memphis, sorted, put back on a plane, flown back to the originating city, put on a truck, driven back to the office building, and delivered to the recipient—50 feet from where it started.

A Different Approach

AMN Healthcare Services chief executive officer (CEO) Susan Salka said its acquisition of Medfinders was going "exceptionally well." She believed the acquisition had strengthened its position as the country's largest health care staffing company, leading to a doubling of fill rates, keeping more services "in-house," and helping win more business. She was pleased because AMN's customers, leadership, and team members saw the benefits of the merger for their businesses and for themselves.[1]

---

[1]Bradt, George, 2011, "Three Priorities in Ensuring a Smooth Merger or Acquisition," *Forbes* (July 20).

This success did not come without hard work and careful planning. The steps Salka and her team took provide insight into how to use the time before the deal closing to jump-start learning and relationships. Salka built success on a foundation of improved customer service and three priorities:

1. Early conversations with all
2. A well-resourced integration management office
3. Staying close to the process

Early Conversations

Salka and her lieutenants had early conversations with AMN's investors and laid out the benefits to its clients and the company culture. Then she spent significant time aligning the combined leadership team, investing heavily in planning and communication between the announcement and the close, and then bringing the combined sales leadership together right after the close. As Salka explained to George,

> Investing in planning and communication up front . . . so we could have as many decisions made and ready to communicate as possible. . . . That clarity and decisiveness created a lot of trust and reduced anxiety.

Integration Management Office

A merger is not business as usual. AMN established and resourced an integration management office to give it a real-time view of how things were going. As a result, they knew:

- What they were accomplishing and getting done
- How they were progressing toward their target of adding $10 million in earnings before interest, taxes, depreciation, and amortization (EBITDA)
- How well we were keeping team members motivated and inspired

Stay Close

Salka learned the importance of communicating with everyone at a personal level to get at their expectations, hopes, and fears. It's not good enough to keep tabs on what's going on; leaders must show up. As Salka put it, you need a management process:

> But even more important than that is to be out in the field listening, listening, listening to the team members, to our customers. Because you can hear one thing in a meeting and see it on paper, but if the reality or the perception is different out in the field, whether it be at one of our offices or with a customer, then what's on paper doesn't really matter. . . . You just can't spend enough time out in front of your team members listening—and sharing!

Implications

In a merger or acquisition, everybody's first question is, "What about me?" A merger or acquisition resets everyone's progress up Maslow's hierarchy of physiological, safety, belonging, self-esteem, and self-actualization needs.

As you reboot or establish new relationships with internal and external stakeholders, including customers, you're going to have to meet them where they are and move back up the hierarchy together. Remember, it's a competitive world. Play not to lose on hygiene physiological and safety factors. Then move on to belonging, self-esteem, and self-actualization benefits.

Hygiene

In the 1950s and 1960s, Fredrick Herzberg taught us about job satisfiers and job dissatisfiers.

The dissatisfiers, like company policies, supervision, relationships with supervisor and peers, work conditions, salary, status, and security, are hygiene factors that need to be good enough not to dissatisfy people. But there are severely diminished returns to taking them beyond good enough.

On the other hand, the more the better with satisfiers like achievement, recognition, the work itself, responsibility, advancement, and growth.

Maslow Hygiene Factors

In general, the first two levels of Maslow's hierarchy are hygiene factors. People's physiological and safety needs need to be met well enough for them not to be problems.

The top levels are satisfiers. The more self-esteem and self-actualization, the better.

Belonging benefits are caught in the middle. They are higher-level than hygiene factors, but often not satisfiers on their own. People want to belong to a club, tribe, or fan base. But it's only a differentiating benefit if that membership builds their self-esteem or self-actualization.

Reboot

One of the tricky things for people working through a merger or acquisition is the shift from focusing on Maslowian satisfiers to hygiene. The issue is that people generally move through Maslow's hierarchy sequentially. They can't even think about the next level up until they've satisfied the level below. And a merger or acquisition sends everyone back to thinking about physiological or safety needs.

There's a huge risk in not meeting people where they are. You can't talk about higher-order objectives with people trying to figure out if they're going to lose their job.

Happiness

Happiness is good. Actually, it's found in the pursuit of three goods: good for others, good at it, good for me. These line up with Maslow's hierarchy as physiological, safety, and belonging are about good for me (and those I care about), self-esteem is correlated with being good at what you do, and self-actualization comes from doing good for others.

Thus, the prescription for success: Win at office politics by getting alignment around a shared purpose first and then taking a principle-based approach to navigating through the politics.[2]

1. Start by reconfirming your purpose.
2. Figure out the Maslowian political landscape.
3. Take a principle-based approach to working through the politics with your allies.

Shared Purpose

Start with what matters. Call it what you want: mission, vision, cause, higher calling. There is some reason for your organization to exist, some purpose. This is why people are part of your organization and why the organizations needed to merge. Everyone in the organization should agree on this—even if they forget it from time to time.

In his work to gain passage of the 13th Amendment abolishing slavery and indentured servitude, U.S. President Abraham Lincoln went all the way back to the Declaration of Independence's unalienable rights of "life, liberty, and the pursuit of happiness." Securing those is the nation and the government's purpose. In general, all agreed with this.

Sometimes this will be hard. But find and reconfirm your organization's purpose as a starting point.

Political Landscape

Even if all agree on the purpose, they will be at different stages of Maslow's hierarchy and may have different interpretations of that purpose and different views of the best way to achieve it. Different people will have different constituencies, different allies, and different personal agendas. You cannot influence these people until you understand their context, perspectives, and needs.

Lincoln understood the different factions in the House of Representatives. Some had different priorities. Some saw different sequences of events. One of the big questions in 1865 was whether to

[2]Bradt, George, 2012, "How to Win at Office Politics," *Forbes* (December 3).

push for an end to the Civil War before pushing for the constitutional amendment or the other way around. Some congressmen had been voted out of office. They would be worrying about their next jobs. Net different people had different perspectives and different personal agendas.

Understand the political landscape.

Working Through the Politics

Taking a principle-based approach to working through the politics with your allies helps to elevate things beyond the personal. It's not about you. It's not about them. It's about working together in pursuit of a shared purpose. Try to avoid arguing about different opinions as much as possible. Instead, agree on a set of principles. Then marshal your allies to move things forward in keeping with those principles.

As depicted so well in Stephen Spielberg's film *Lincoln*, Lincoln was prepared to push all sorts of boundaries to eliminate slavery. He was prepared to work with anyone he needed, humble himself when needed, cajole when needed, bully when needed, and stay out of the way when needed. He was prepared to trade jobs for support, but not pay bribes. He was prepared to delay peace talks so he could say they had not happened yet.

Play from principles, not personal persuasion.

Think in terms of a BRAVE approach to office politics:

- Where to play (environment): understand the political field and especially where people are on their reboot up Maslow's hierarchy.
- What matters (values): your purpose and principles.
- How to win (attitude): how to navigate the politics to achieve your purpose by (1) meeting people where they are on Maslow's hierarchy, (2) helping them understand how things can be good for them, (3) helping them do what they are good at, and then (4) helping them do good for others.
- How to connect (relationships): build alliances first to keep people safe (good for me), then do things they are good at together and finally to do good for others in line with the organization's purpose.
- What impact (behaviors): make it real.

Acquired Company Leaders

The prescription is not much different for acquired company leaders—if you immediately flip from thinking about yourselves as acquired company leaders to leaders in the new, combined company.

The people evaluating you and trying to figure out your role in the new organization have the same first question, "What about me?" In other words, what role can they put you in that's best for them? Treat them like you would treat a new boss.

Portions of this framework were adapted from Kevin Coyne and Edward Coyne's article "Surviving your new CEO,"[3] and then expanded. Here are seven behaviors to keep in mind:

1. *Foundation:* Treat your new boss and new colleagues decently as human beings. Make them feel welcome, valued and valuable. Enable them to do good work. Do the job they ask you to do well—not the boss's.
2. *Attitude:* Choose to be optimistic. Believe the best about your new boss and colleagues. Focus on these positives at all times with all people.
3. *Approach:* Proactively tell your new boss and colleagues that you want to be part of the new team and follow up with actions to reinforce this.
4. *Learning:* Present realistic and honest game plans to help your boss and colleagues learn. Seek out the new boss's and your new colleagues' perspectives early and often, and be open to new directions.
5. *Expectations:* Understand and move on your new boss's agenda immediately. Know the boss's priorities. Know what the new boss thinks your priorities should be.
6. *Implementation:* Adjust to your new boss's working style immediately. This is a hard shift, not an evolution around control points, decision-making, and communication.
7. *Delivery:* Be on your "A" game. Be present and "on"—everything done by you and your team will be part of your new boss's

---

[3]Coyne, Kevin, and Coyne, Edward, 2007, "Surviving Your New CEO," *Harvard Business Review* (May).

evaluation of you. Deliver early wins that are important to your new boss and to the people they listen to. In a merger or acquisition, the score is reset. Your old wins and your team's old wins are history.

Working for a Boss Who Didn't Want You

It happens all the time. Headquarters or the owners drop someone in to help a division or portfolio company accelerate through a point of inflection like a merger, working for a boss who doesn't want them. If you're the one getting dropped in, jump-shift your loyalties immediately: (1) disengage from your previous situation; (2) engage with your new boss; and (3) do what is required to accelerate progress—in that order.[4]

Disengage

Whatever the people who put you into the job have in mind for the long term over the short term everyone needs you to help your new boss and their organization be more successful.

Be prepared for your new boss to fear the worst—that you were dropped in for a darker purpose. They may think you're there to spy on them, to shore up one of their personal weaknesses, or to replace them. As much as they try to bury those concerns, and whether they voice them or not, they are real and must be addressed before they can trust you.

Your long-term loyalty to the people that put you in to work for your new boss is best served by transferring your immediate loyalty from them to your new boss. Help them by helping your new boss. Making this is a hard shift. You no longer work for the people you used to work for. You work for your new boss and have to earn their trust. The best way to earn trust is to be trustworthy.

Be explicit with the people who put you into the job. Be clear that you're going to route communication to them through your new boss. Neither they nor you should go around your new boss in any way. You may not be able to and may not want to sever all communication links,

[4]Bradt, George, 2021, "Executive Onboarding with a Boss Who Didn't Want You," *Forbes* (December 1).

but you can make sure your new boss knows everything you're telling their bosses—ideally before you tell them. And in all cases make sure your new boss hears about communication with their bosses from you and not from them.

Engage

Choose to be optimistic. Even if they didn't choose to have you work for them, you can choose to make this the best possible experience with the best possible results for all involved. Commit to your new team's purpose, its cause. Do this explicitly with your words and actions. Adjust to your new boss's working style. Engage with your boss personally.

Regarding your game plan, don't assume that what the people who dropped you in told you or what you observed from your previous vantage point was right. Understand and move on your new boss's agenda immediately. Know your boss's priorities. Know what your new boss thinks your priorities should be. Be open and willing to do whatever it takes to move the organization forward, putting aside your own interests as appropriate.

Follow Through

Be on your "A" game. Be present and "on."

PART VII

The Change Management Playbook

CHAPTER 22

Integration Leadership: Start Here

	The Strategic Playbook	The Commercial Playbook	The Operational Playbook	The Financial Playbook	The Governance Playbook	The Organizational Playbook	The Change Management Playbook
Concept Research Investment Case Negotiation Deal/Due Diligence Contract Close Integration Acceleration Next Normal	The Investment Case Focus Plans Innovation	Organic Revenue Growth Customers Marketing & Sales	Cost Optimization Operational Excellence: Supply Chain, Distribution, Continual Improvement Technology	Deal/ Due Diligence Financing M&A	Regulatory Financial Board	Culture Incentives Leadership People Politics	Integration Leader Change Management Communication Announcement Adjustments

The first component of the change management playbook is integration leadership. The other components dig into what the integration leaders need to lead.

Stand Up Your Transition, Transformation, or Project Management Offices

Complex change management efforts through points of inflection like mergers and acquisitions or restructurings go better with people giving leaders leverage by managing the change processes. These people have different titles in different organizations. Here's one set of definitions:

Leaders inspire, enable, and empower others to do their absolute best together to realize a meaningful and rewarding shared purpose.

Deputies are second in command, empowered to act in their superiors' absence. As such, they are leaders themselves who may step in to manage some changes and processes.

Chiefs of staff give leaders increased leverage by managing them, priorities, programs, and projects, and communication. Where a deputy has some direct power, a chief of staff's power is all indirect as the voice of the leader.

A project management office (PMO) conceives potential programs and projects in line with enterprise-level priorities, helps prioritize and define those programs and projects with team charters, assembles resources, communicates and coordinates within and across programs and projects, facilitates key meetings, tracks milestones, analyzes results, and initiates appropriate process improvements.

Transformation, integration leader, chief transformation officers, as the M&A Leadership Council's Mark Herdon suggests,[1] manage chaos as the key point of contact, accelerate process by helping executive staff manage, architect success by providing focus and direction, and personally drive the change on major issues.

Going into more depth on the last three, starting with some definitions:

Enterprise-level priorities include ongoing strategic, organizational, and operational priorities and processes and the one or two most important enterprise-wide endeavors.

Programs are the main longer-term components of those priorities, generally tracked and managed monthly.

Projects are the subcomponents of programs, generally tracked and managed weekly.

Tasks are the actual work that rolls up into projects, programs, and priorities. These are generally tracked and managed at least daily by front-line supervisors.

---

[1]Herndon, Mike, 2017, "Defining the Role of the Integration Leader," https://www.mapartners.net/insights/defining-role-integration-leader (February 8).

Chief of Staff

The chief of staff gives the leader leverage by managing the leader; managing priorities, programs, and projects; and managing communication.

Managing the Leader

Manage the leader's schedule or diary in line with the leader's priorities so the leader is spending time on the most important things and not spending time on less important things. A big part of this is managing distractions—either making them go away or dealing with them. This requires the chief of staff to be a close confidant of the leader, understanding their priorities and helping them think things through.

Decision rights matter. The chief of staff needs to be clear with the leader when they are:

- Making a recommendation or request for the leader to decide or do something
- Seeking the leader's contribution/input on a decision or action they are going to make or do (They won't go forward without the leader's input.)
- Informing the leader about a decision or action they intend to make or do so the leader is aware, can learn, and can veto or change as appropriate (They will move forward unless the leader redirects you. Silence is consent.)
- Reporting to the leader about a decision or action they already made or took so the leader is aware.

Follow up for the leader. This is about influencing others' schedules or diaries in line with the leader's priorities so priority items aren't getting dropped or delayed by others.

Managing Priorities, Programs, Projects

Act as the leader's proxy or program or project manager as appropriate—especially with regard to things that cut across others' areas of responsibility. This is not about doing the work, but assembling resources, directing, and working behind the scenes to enable others to do the work.

Managing Communication

Bring issues and opportunities to the leader's attention as appropriately gathered in conversations, emails, tweets, blogs, and so forth. Help the leader think through and implement their message and communication efforts.

There are six levels of delegation:

1. Do self well
2. Do self well enough
3. Delegate and manage
4. Delegate and not manage
5. Do later
6. Do never

With this in mind, the chief of staff should help the leader assign levels to things, assist on level 1 and level 2 priorities as much as possible, and own all levels 3–6 priorities.

Meeting agendas run the gambit from simple to complex. The chief of staff should ensure there is one for every meeting or call the leader who is involved in. Every agenda should include:

- The objective of the meeting
- Meeting timing and methodology (live, video, audio)
- What the leader is being asked to do in the meeting (decide, contribute, learn)
- Meeting attendees, their role in the meeting by agenda item (decide, contribute, learn), and anything new the leader should know about their ability to decide, contribute, or learn
- Prereads for the leader and attendees to digest in advance to help them decide, contribute, or learn

Project Management Office (PMO)

The PMO's role is different than that of a program or project manager. A program or project manager defines project-specific objectives and goals, gathers data, schedules tasks, and manages the program and project's costs, budgets, and resources to deliver agreed objectives and goals.

The PMO remit is broader: part information technology (IT), part planning, finance, risk management, and resourcing, collaborating to ensure that all projects are delivered with high quality and achieve their defined outcomes. This is achieved by mapping out project goals, defining processes, workflows, methodologies, resource constraints, and project scopes.

- Help *prioritize* programs and projects based on return on investment—both direct (on their own) and indirect (as part of a larger program, priority, or process). This prioritization is a nontrivial effort as scope is always a function of resources (including force multipliers like methods, tools, and technologies) and time. Need to allocate scarce existing resources to the most important programs and projects while working to create future capabilities to expand capacity down the road.
- Help *assemble resources* in line with programs and projects' scope and move them between programs and projects as appropriate as circumstances change.
- Help *communicate* and *coordinate* within and across teams and with senior management.
- *Facilitate* key meetings:
  - Send out meeting notices, agendas, and requests for input.
    - Meeting agendas should include:
      - The objective of the meeting
      - Meeting timing and methodology (live, video, audio)
      - What people are being asked to do in the meeting as a whole (decide, contribute, learn)
      - Meeting attendees, their role in the meeting by agenda item (decide, contribute, learn)
      - Prereads for attendees to digest in advance to help all decide, contribute, or learn.
  - Facilitate, keep time, and take notes during the meeting.
  - Distribute notes after meeting.
- Work behind the scenes to enable others to do the work with methods, tools, and technologies, as well as appropriate mentoring and coaching.
- Manage the *milestone tracking* process: sending out meeting notices and requests for input, following up to ensure delivery

of required inputs, assembling and disseminating the inputs, facilitating milestone management meetings, issuing notes from the meetings.

- *Analyze* data, including project budgets, finances, risks, and resource allocation and provide appropriate reports in line with lean project management:
  - Strategize: Translate enterprise-level strategic priorities into actionable criteria.
  - Collect: Collect and develop new program and project initiatives driving continuous improvement and step-changes.
  - Decide: Make informed decisions on new program and project initiatives and program and project conflicts.
  - Execute: Put decisions to work and manage programs and projects to completion.

Team charters are great ways to get teams aligned around direction, resources, authority, and accountability as described in Chapter 9.

Transformation Officers

Most change agents don't survive their own change. Of course, the organization was at a point of inflection and needed to change. Of course, they were brought in to lead that change. But the change process is often so painful and so many "good" people have to go away that the change agent becomes an ongoing reminder of bad times. Stepping into the brighter future requires a new leader.

Thus, the job of most transformation leaders is to manage the change and then go away so the ongoing leadership can tell everyone how glad they are the transformation leaders are gone and get back to the new normal.

These transformation officers act as the leader's proxy or program or project manager as appropriate:

1. Serving as consumer or customer advocate, mapping current and aspirational customer journeys
2. Helping to design the change initiatives and new enterprise business model and architecture, providing focus and direction
3. Understanding capabilities and then pulling together and reallocating resources to the few most important initiatives

4. Leading the most important innovations and changes on major issues
5. Collaborating with all to move initiatives forward and managing chaos as key point of contact
6. Acting as the storyteller-in-chief and overcommunicating at every step of the way
7. Managing the finances and results to help executive staff manage

The *transformation and integration team* is made up of people with differential strengths:

- Head of transformation office—planning and execution
- Innovation
- Information
- Analytics
- Operations
- PMO
- + Subject matter experts: business processes, app development, GDPR, marketing, IoT, Cloud, technology architecture, user experience, story-telling, conversational brand strategy, forensics analysis, ethics compliance, digital product management

Guest Contributor Jeff Scott

Good Decisions Aren't Enough

There's an old riddle that goes like this: Five frogs are sitting on a log. Four decide to jump off. How many are left?

Answer: Five. Why? Because there's a difference between deciding and doing!

"Doing" doesn't sound hard, does it? Just do it, right? After leading more than a dozen acquisition integrations in the financial services space—where the word synergy is overused and the pace of work borders on insanity—I found the "doing" part to be complicated. Over time, I had to adapt my recipe for success to boil down to (1) fast decisions and (2) a healthy approach to engaging the team.

(Continued)

Before we discuss making fast decisions and approaching the team, let's start with the first big elephant in the room when we meet a newly acquired team. Is this a takeover or a merger? Takeovers have a place in the world of M&A, and, frankly, eliminating the products, systems, processes, and structure of the new company is easier than deeply integrating two businesses. After all, cost synergies are straightforward; product and revenue synergies are hard. If it's a takeover situation, treat the new team with dignity and respect, but don't play games trying to convince people that a takeover is an integration of equals.

After all, who do we think we're kidding? People take a cue from our actions more than our words. If our actions make it look like a takeover, we won't successfully deceive people until the point in which we don't think we need them. Fearful, uncertain, and disgruntled people are the biggest barriers to execution. Lying to them is a fast track to poor execution that leaks value as we clumsily tap dance with the team. Keep it simple with takeovers.

On the other hand, true integrations where we merge companies are a point of inflection for our businesses and require quite a bit more energy and thought.

Fast Decisions

In their book on M&A integration called *Five Frogs on a Log: A CEO's Field Guide to Accelerating the Transition in Mergers, Acquisitions, and Gut Wrenching Change* (and the source of our riddle), Mark Feldman and Michael Spratt are clear on the need for integration to focus on value drivers. Value drivers follow the Pareto principle in thinking that 20 percent of the opportunities for value creation in a deal contribute 80 percent of the total benefit of integrating companies. The focus on a small number of value drivers is critical, yet there is one more element to deciding on our focus areas—making those decisions as quickly as possible.

Someone once said, "Give me six hours to chop down a tree and I will spend four sharpening the blade." Our blade sharpening should happen during a thorough due diligence process where we can make the significant decisions on what we're going to do before day one. The how will be a co-creation process with the new team. If we leave the big decisions until after the deal is done, that will be a formula for delays and excessive compromise. This isn't an exercise in compromise, it's an exercise in doing the best thing for the business. We should respect what's been done to date (by both sides) but be careful not to try and please too many people and mix too many ingredients as we combine companies. To be fair, we likely won't have a perfect batting average on big decisions when we make them quickly, but executing well on a solid plan that is formulated quickly is better than taking forever in search of a perfect plan that pleases everyone and is difficult to execute (and, let's be honest, perfection likely doesn't exist).

A Healthy Approach to Engaging the Team

In reality, our approach to engaging the team applies both to our new team and our existing team, but the latter group most likely lacks the fear, uncertainty and doubt of the former group. Regardless, our plan should engage both groups with just a bit more emphasis on the key people from the new team.

I learned to be healthier in my approach as time went on after learning quite a few lessons. By healthy, I mean that our communications have to be clear and believable and propagated through more innovative means than email and group meetings. Healthy also means that our actions have to support our words, and we need to work hard for early wins that demonstrate the alignment of our words and actions.

Our communication plan should key off the fast decisions that we've already made so that we can be candid and clear on the direction (the what) and that the best way to execute (the how) will be a focused collaboration. One more thing is super important when communicating the game plan, it is imperative that we articulate the why. If we cannot effectively communicate why decisions were made (even if our audience doesn't like the answer), then how will people be inclined to follow us? There is a fine line between rhetoric and authentic communication and it helps if they understand why decisions were made.

Just as when my kids take advice from their cool cousin after having ignored the same advice from me, the source of perspective also matters. Malcolm Gladwell's book *The Tipping Point* explains how ideas can spread like epidemics and one key component of viral transmission of ideas is a group of people called "connectors." Connectors are those with an extraordinary knack for making friends and acquaintances and they are often the reason that we have connections of our own with others. In a business setting, we all have examples of connectors in our companies. The connectors are the people that have strong social skills, interact with many different groups, and have the

(Continued)

intelligence and team mentality that prompt everyone to respect them and what they have to say. If we want our integration ideas to stick, we must find our team of connectors (both in the existing and new business). Spend time with the connectors to help them deeply understand—and believe—the plan. If we do, everyone's understanding of our integration game plan will accelerate at an exponential rate.

Finally, everything we do communicates. Search for early ways to have our actions support our words. For starters, it is imperative that we are diligent in focusing *only* on value drivers and stop all small, tactical actions. Second, one idea to consider is the leadership for our program management office for the integration. Why not designate the best PMO person from the acquired company to lead our Integration PMO? We stand a much better chance of having a balanced view of how to execute the plan—as well as richer insight to the operations of the new company—with a new person leading the PMO. And the derivative benefit is that the new team sees that their business assets and the approach to integration will get a fair shake with one of their people in a position of power. Hopefully, they will start to believe that this just may *not* be a takeover!

CHAPTER 23

Change Management: Leading Through the Point of Inflection

	The Strategic Playbook	The Commercial Playbook	The Operational Playbook	The Financial Playbook	The Governance Playbook	The Organizational Playbook	The Change Management Playbook
Concept Research Investment Case	The Investment Case	Organic Revenue Growth	Cost Optimization	Deal/ Due Diligence	Regulatory	Culture Incentives	Integration Leader **Change Management**
Negotiation Deal/Due Diligence Contract	Focus		Operational Excellence: Supply Chain, Distribution, Continual Improvement	Financing	Financial	Leadership	Communication
Close	Plans	Customers		M&A	Board	People	Announcement
Integration Acceleration Next Normal	Innovation	Marketing & Sales	Technology			Politics	Adjustments

The second component of the change management playbook gets at change management itself—after you've got your integration leadership in place.

At a high level, once those working for you have had their "What about me?" question answered, pivot to inspiring, enabling, and empowering them.

In change management A × B × C > D, in which

A: platform for change/reason for change

B: envision self in a brighter future/goals

C: call to action so they can be part of solution

D: inertia

Note the math on this. If you leave out any of the platform for change, vision, or call to action, you're left with zero chance of overcoming inertia.

Platform for Change

The platform for change is generally an external situational change or change in ambition. These get at *why* the changes need to be made. Note, using the merger or acquisition itself as the platform for change is a cop-out. Get at the external situational change or ambition change that led to the merger or acquisition. That's the platform for change.

The external piece is important. People respond better to being asked to change in response to a change in the world than they do to being told that something about themselves needs to change.

Picture of Success

Next, you need a picture of success in which others can envision themselves. The word is *envision*, not *vision*. No one cares about your vision. They care about how it's going to impact themselves or those they care about.

Call to Action

Give people a personal call to action so they know how to be part of the solution. It's the difference between doing things to people and doing things with people.

The combination of the platform for change, picture of success, and call to action must be strong enough to overcome inertia. They are also the raw data for your message.

Message

Once you've figured these out, pull them together into a message headline and key communication points. You and your leaders will use these over and over again to drive your message in sync to get and keep your followers engaged.

But engagement is too important and dynamic a metric to live with a binary distinction between the engaged and unengaged. Instead, think of engagement in terms of four levels: committed, contributors, watchers, and detractors.

1. *Committed:* The committed are driven by the purpose, the cause, and doing good for others. They believe and will do whatever it takes to accomplish the desired results. Keep them committed with simple direct communication that touches their emotions and gets them to believe viscerally in the change you're trying to bring about together.
2. *Contributors:* The contributors are good at what they do and it shows. They enjoy their work. Their output is positive and helps keep moving the ball down the field. They are important players, but not necessarily leaders. Communicate with them directly so they understand what is required of them.
3. *Watchers:* The watchers are compliant and primarily driven by what is good for them and concerned about their basic needs. Compliant people aren't hurting the organization, but they are not primary drivers of change. They are doing what they are told and no more. The goal is to make them aware of what they need to do and make sure it gets done.
4. *Detractors:* The detractors are disengaged and have checked out emotionally. They don't believe in the platform for change, the vision, or the call to action. They won't do what the organization needs them to do. Their complete disconnect qualifies them as detractors. If they don't immediately respond to the new messaging, move them out, quickly.

Change management is about changing balances—changing the balance of committed and detractors by changing the balance of consequences. You're not going to turn detractors into committed champions—at least you're not going to change them in one step. Instead, invest in the committed champions to get them to bring the contributors along with them and eventually start picking off the watchers.

Let's dive a little deeper into what good and less good looks like for each of these.

Direction

Empowering delegation starts with clarity around what you want done. Whether you call it objectives, desired results, or something else, this is isn't about labels. It's about people knowing what you're asking them to accomplish and the intent behind that request—what will happen next after they've completed the task.

This does not look unclear, overly vague, or changeable.

Resources

It's frightening how many people think they can subvert the laws of physics. Scope is a function of resources and time. You can't increase expectations of someone without giving them more resources or tools or more time or all three. Clarify the direction and then make sure you're giving people the resources, tools, and time they need.

Yet we keep hearing people say things like "We have to do more with less." It won't work. You can do more with fewer people. But you have to compensate the lack of people resources with other resources. These could be operational, mechanical, or technological or other resources. But the basic equation always holds.

Bounded Authority

Strategos is the art of the general—arranging forces before the battle. *Taktikos* is about deploying forces in the battle. As the general, you cannot be everywhere during the battle. You can't make the tactical decisions. The analogy is clear. If you delegate direction and give people the resources and time they need, but do not give them the authority to make tactical decisions, you've given away your leverage.

"I'd love to delegate more. But I don't trust the people I would delegate to." Whose fault is that? If you don't trust them, replace them with people you do trust. Leaders are defined by their followers. If you have bad followers. You're a bad leader.

Note this is not blanket authority. It's tactical authority to make decisions within the bounds of the general's strategic choices. When Neville Isdell was group president of Coca-Cola Europe, his strategies were crystal clear. At our meetings with him, he was always fully supportive of choices we made within those strategies. And he was equally clear about redirecting us when we tried to move outside the strategic boundaries.

Accountability

The last piece of delegating and trusting is clarifying the accountability—what you're going to measure with what standards of performance and when. Couple that with clarity around consequences—both positive and negative—and making them real, and you're off to the races.

Another way to think about this is that a big part of change management is *removing barriers* to change, including:

- Unhelpful policies, procedures, or systems
- Filling tool and resource gaps
- Getting intractable detractors out of the way

Change Management at Albertsons

Jim Donald joined Albertsons as chief executive officer (CEO) in 2018 with a goal of fixing revenue and margin, updating technology, and taking the company public.[1]

To accomplish that, he'd have to make some changes.

His first priority was to get the frontline workforce—which made up 98 percent of their 275,000-strong workforce—aligned and onboard with the changes ahead.

"I learned that communicating a message consistently to the frontline solves the riddle of getting everybody moving at the same pace and in the same direction," says Donald.

"I began doing 45-second videos, three times a week, posted on the company portal for all to see, showing me doing various things like driving a semi across the country with groceries to a store. Frying chicken at a deli. Cutting meat in a cutting room with a bunch of meat cutters around me, or simply working with the overnight crew, unloading a truck."

The results were impressive.

"It flipped our culture. It spiked our revenue and it allowed us to go public (July 2021). Why did that happen? These videos created an environment where I spoke the language of all my employees from age 16 to 80."

It wasn't just about keeping employees in the loop. It was about showing frontline employees they were a valued part of the business, and their work was important to the company's success.

---

[1]*Axonify*, "'The Turnaround King' on Why Frontline Employee Engagement Is a Business Imperative" (June 4).

"By doing what I've asked others to do, I spoke the second language of the frontline. That's called communicating to the heart. That causes action. It also creates engagement. When people become engaged, they are emotionally connected to the business, and things happen very fast. Revenues grow; profits improve."

This sense of engagement was also critical to ensuring that the changes the company was going through were understood, adopted, and executed by the people on the frontlines.

"The best-laid plans don't work once they're launched if you don't have the understanding of those users that interface with the customer. It's not easy. The word change management is key here, because getting your associates at every level to understand that we're doing things differently is so critical to the success of this," says Donald. "If it's told in a way that they're always going to remember, if it's told in a way that engages them emotionally, they'll get it, and they'll execute on it."

Generate Early Wins

Early wins fuel team momentum and confidence. To that end, its essential to clearly identify and jump-start potential early wins early. Once they are widely understood, the team should overinvest to deliver them as soon as practical. In general, *early wins* are not synonymous with *big wins*. They are the early, sometimes small, yet meaningful wins that start the momentum of a winning team. They are the blasting caps, not the dynamite. They are the opening singles, not the grand-slam home run. They are the first successful test market, not the global expansion. They may be found by accelerating something that is already in progress instead of starting something new.

The early win prescription is relatively simple:

1. Select one or two early wins from your milestones list:
   a. Choose early wins that will make a meaningful external impact.
   b. Select early wins that your boss will want to talk about.
   c. Pick early wins that you are sure you can deliver.
   d. Choose early wins that will model important behaviors.
   e. Pick early wins that would not have happened if the merger or acquisition had not occurred.

2. Jump-start early wins and deliver as soon as practical:
   a. Early means early. Select them early. Communicate them early. Deliver them early.
   b. Make sure that the team understands the early wins and has bought into delivering them on time.
   c. This will give your bosses or owners the concrete results they need when someone asks how you are doing.
3. Overinvest resources to ensure that early wins are achieved on time:
   a. Do not skimp on your early wins. Allocate resources in a manner that will ensure timely delivery. Put more resources than you think you should need against these early opportunities so that your team is certain to deliver them better and faster than anyone thought was possible.
   b. Stay alert. Adjust quickly. As the leader, stay close, stay involved in the progress of your early wins, and react immediately if they start to fall even slightly off-track or behind schedule.
4. Celebrate and communicate early wins:
   a. As your early wins are achieved, celebrate the accomplishments with the entire team. This is important and should not be overlooked.
   b. Make sure that your early wins are communicated to the team and beyond as appropriate.

Early wins are sure to generate credibility, confidence, momentum, and excitement. Remember the watchers? The people who have not shown themselves to be detractors, yet, have also not stood up as strong contributors. Once early wins begin, some of the watchers will edge closer, and eventually will jump in as contributors. After all, everybody wants to be part of the winning team, right?

Manage Through the Dips

In her book *The Change Monster: The Human Forces That Fuel or Foil Corporate Transformation*, Jeanie Daniel Duck outlines five stages of change that organizations need to be prepared to manage as they embark on a change initiative. Duck refers to the change monster "as a catch-all phrase for the complex, sometimes scary, human emotions and social dynamics that usually emerge during a change effort."[2]

1. Stagnation
2. Preparation
3. Implementation
4. Determination
5. Fruition

Applying these to mergers and acquisitions:

Stagnation: Born of outdated strategy, lack of leadership, market shifts, too few products or resources, outdated technology, and so forth, this phase ends when someone in a position of power recognizes the problem, envisions a new approach, and demands change (like a merger or acquisition).

Preparation: This involves all the things we've talked about to this point from the investment case through team role sort. As we've said, expect people to be anxious, hopeful, threatened, excited, distracted, and betrayed, wondering first and foremost, "What does this mean for me." Duck makes the point that moving forward without alignment is the major cause of failure of change initiatives. Move this stage along as quickly as possible, but make sure it is complete before proceeding.

Implementation: This is the phase you're starting now. As change plans are initiated and work is beginning, be prepared for the change monster to get things fired up. To the emotions already experienced in the preparation stage will be added feelings of confusion, apathy, resentment, inadequacy, and volatility, along with relief, exhilaration, excitement and recognition. Everything is changing, but at the same time, nothing has changed yet. Communications—frequent and sent through multiple mediums—are critical during this stage.

Determination: Expect this later, when all your efforts are becoming evident at the same time the organization may be feeling change fatigue. It takes a lot of energy for people to rethink how they do their work and change their ways. If they see signs of success, they'll be

[2]Duck, Jeanie Daniel, 2001, *The Change Monster* (New York: Random House).

energized and keep up their momentum and contributions, even in the face of fatigue.

However, if they sense an attitude of doubt, they will switch gears, go back to watching, and dispassionately go through the change motions without expectations for the desired results.

Again, the wrath of the change monster is stirring. Leaders must be careful to manage the expectations, energy, and experiences of their employees. Not all the early wins will work. Not everything is going to be a success. Where negative events occur, acknowledge and learn from them. When employees come together to confront and conquer the change monster, they are usually rewarded with the path to fruition.

Fruition: Eventually, all the hard work will pay off. It's a time to celebrate and acknowledge the transformed organization, highlighting the big and small wins, as well as lessons learned. However, "the success of fruition brings the organization full circle, because the territory on the far side of fruition is a new period of stagnation."

Institutionalize the changes and your new culture, base systems, and processes. And start preparing for the next step change.

Guest Contributor Dennis Stratton

Aligning an Organization After a Major Strategic Pivot

Business Imperative

For over a decade, this financial services institution pursued an aggressive strategy based on growth through acquisition. The success of this strategy hinged not only on identifying and buying appropriate businesses but quickly integrating them into their own operations, with a clear and unequivocal emphasis on optimizing efficiencies while minimizing costs.

This strategy was brilliantly executed. As a result, the organization enlarged its operational footprint and gained market share in chunks. This was great in terms of fulfilling the strategy—but not so good in terms of the impact on customers—and community, or good will. It was only natural that in the process of execution, much of the acquired base felt steamrolled by a big, impersonal machine.

(Continued)

Especially in markets where they had been most aggressive, their favorability numbers took a substantial hit. They recognized the need to develop a *new* strategy specifically targeting the customer experience. Furthermore, if they wanted to fully leverage the gains of acquisition and deliver the most shareholder value possible, they would need to be just as focused and aggressive in accomplishing this new strategy as they had been with the old.

This business unit had responsibility for the branch banks as well as many of the home- and community-focused franchises and was a high-profile, high-impact leverage point for this critical shift. In the new strategy, this unit would be a major force in shaping employee satisfaction, customer loyalty, and the creation of real shareholder value.

Leadership Response

The unit engaged Stratton Consulting Group (Stratton) to help its leadership team understand the full scope of the challenge and create the changes needed for quickly transforming their business. Stratton began by assessing their current state. Following a review of relevant internal data, implementation of the Denison Culture Survey, and completion of several executive level interviews, Stratton debriefed executives on key findings and then helped them to examine the implications and plan for effective actions.

The client recognized that the institution's shift in strategy would require a corresponding shift in people's fundamental beliefs about and approach to the business. The senior leadership team needed to create a new strategic context within which people defined reality and made decisions about how best to create value for the business. They needed to articulate a compelling new direction that would not only redirect people's attention but actively encourage and engage their commitment in making the necessary changes. In short order, they needed to establish a new operating culture that could promote organic growth, reestablish customer favorability as a competitive advantage, and provide optimal value to shareholders, customers, and employees.

Interrupting the Skepticism

Because of people's long-term experience of the "acquisition and efficiency" strategy, there was a deeply instilled skepticism about the change. Leaders therefore faced the paradoxical challenge of having to overcome the powerful legacy of past success. People were predisposed to believe that, regardless of what leaders might say about change, the company's old operating style was the one that would ultimately be encouraged, reinforced, and valued. This meant that leaders would have to be particularly rigorous—not only in articulating a compelling case for change but also in demonstrating their unshakeable commitment to those changes. They would have to lead by example, demonstrating new behaviors while openly declaring and displaying a personal passion for the new mission and strategy.

In a watershed offsite visioning session, Stratton's facilitative approach, processes, and focus enabled senior leaders to fully appreciate the scope of personal and organizational changes involved. They collaboratively crafted leadership messages and identified key actions to promote their new strategic direction while simultaneously creating breakthroughs in their team outlooks and relationships. Follow-up coaching helped individuals manage the sometimes difficult transitions required of them as leaders in the newly customer-centric organization.

Accelerating Toward Success

Given the erosion of the company's favorability and the abundance of fast-paced, opportunistic competitors, leaders knew that they had to move quickly—the customers wouldn't wait. Stratton designed and facilitated a series of 2-day leadership forums to extend ownership of the mandate and help mobilize the wider leadership team in tackling the challenges and implications involved.

To create the necessary speed and agility, there was a real need to break down old barriers and strengthen relationships throughout the organization. Many behaviors and operational habits that had been rewarded in the past were now unacceptable. Top organizational leaders were encouraged, therefore, to focus on critical elements in the plan to achieve major breakthroughs in the whats and hows of their performance.

These sessions also provided an opportunity to develop key measurements and indicators of success organized along four key criteria:

- Accuracy and reliability of service
- Ease of doing business
- Problem resolution
- Caring for customers

(Continued)

Mid-level managers were identified as being key pivot points in the organization, instrumental in shifting behaviors, influencing attitudes, and managing the direct customer interface. By providing a newly defined leadership context for their work, combined with new tools and training in their use, these managers were enlisted in the work of transforming the customer experience on the front lines.

Results

This company had a strong record of successful execution, so the business unit's underlying ability to change was never really in question. The core issue was whether the people who needed to execute on the new strategy would accept the logic, legitimacy, and leadership commitment behind it. By taking the time to consider this aspect of the challenge and to thoughtfully manage the *meaning* of the leadership messages concerning a more customer-centric approach, they made swift strides.

An organization that was initially reticent and skeptical about such sweeping changes has now embraced the need for customer favorability as a strategic imperative.

- Customer favorability is embraced as a *key measure* to be monitored closely by the board of directors.
- The entire *marketing strategy* has shifted its message to the new mission: easy to do business.
- A new organization structure is being redesigned to enable more effective leadership and governance specific to customer-centricity.
- Customer favorability in key markets has begun to shift positively.

The most up-to-date, full, editable versions of all tools are down loadable at primegenesis.com/tools.

TOOL 23.1

Alignment Workshop

Prework

- Communicate decisions already made
  - Organization
  - Roles, accountabilities, measures

Workshop

Decide

- Mandates, roles, accountabilities, resourcing and capability needs, and cross-functional support areas
- Discuss: individual and shared accountabilities, decision rights, operating rhythm
- Communication rollout

Roll Out to Subgroups

- Operating rhythm and governance
- Performance management
- Talent management
- Incentives

Measure Success and Engagement

CHAPTER 24

Communication: Everything Communicates

	The Strategic Playbook	The Commercial Playbook	The Operational Playbook	The Financial Playbook	The Governance Playbook	The Organizational Playbook	The Change Management Playbook
Concept Research Investment Case	The Investment Case	Organic Revenue Growth	Cost Optimization	Deal/ Due Diligence	Regulatory	Culture Incentives	Integration Leader Change Management
Negotiation Deal/Due Diligence	Focus		Operational Excellence: Supply Chain, Distribution, Continual Improvement	Financing	Financial	Leadership	Communication
Contract Close	Plans	Customers		M&A	Board	People	Announcement
Integration Acceleration Next Normal	Innovation	Marketing & Sales	Technology			Politics	Adjustments

The third component and backbone of the change management playbook is communication. Be deliberate about your ongoing communication efforts as you cycle through the five BRAVE questions again and again.

Everything communicates. Everything. Even the things you don't do and don't say send powerful signals to everybody in the organization observing you.[1]

Because we live amid a communication revolution, the guidelines for communicating are changing dramatically. As much as you would like to treat communication as a logical, sequential, ongoing communication campaign, in many cases you must manage it as an iterative set of concurrent conversations.

[1]Bradt, George, Check, Jayme, and Lawler, John, 2022, *The New Leader's 100-Day Action Plan* (Hoboken, NJ: Wiley).

Guest Contributor Michael Ovalles

It is perplexing to see how communications is typically at the bottom of the priorities in most merger and acquisition (M&A) scenarios. Unfortunately, organizations focus heavily on closing the deal and on operationalizing it (with a heavy focus on return on investment [ROI]) falling over and over on the same trap: lack of or insufficient communication with both internal and external stakeholders.

Unfortunately, the lack of or poor communication has profound implications on the success of an M&A strategy as stakeholders will always fill information gaps with perceptions and unreliable data points, resulting in a narrowed or mistaken understanding of the objectives of the deal and its implications to the broader organization and to the individual.

Lack or insufficient communication will cause confusion (vendor: "To whom should I send my invoice now?"), drive anxiety (employee: "what's going to happen to my job?"), and eventually despair (stakeholders: I can't deal with this anymore. I give up). Lack of or insufficient communication will inevitably result in unhappy customers and vendors and the loss of great talent.

Organizations want to avoid this situation and its consequences.

Owning the narrative of an active M&A agenda in a transparent manner and with clear communications is a prerequisite for the organization to successfully assimilate the gargantuan change that comes from planning, closing, and integrating a new business.

Leadership needs to actively share the vision and empower the next management layer to ensure both the acquirer and the target understand the go-forward vision and priorities of the combined organization as well as the overall business strategy.

Tactically, this is best achieved by equipping key leaders from across the business to serve as communicators, and build a plan for how, when, and what topics they own.

A cadence of normal-course communication with a variety of channels to engage employees and other stakeholders is required so as to ensure information is cascading down and sinking in.

Lastly, an integration management office (IMO) has to be empowered to operate as the central nerve of the organization: inputs from and to the IMO are critical to inform the communication plan.

Each subsequent integration should be better understood by the organization, and while there will always be "losers" and "winners" as long as people are treated with respect, the surviving organization will value the rationale for change and embrace the journey ahead.

Use Your Communication to Drive Engagement

There's an ever-strengthening body of evidence that engaged employees produce better results.[2] Engagement is too important and dynamic a metric to live with a binary distinction between the engaged and unengaged. Instead, think of engagement in terms of four levels: committed, contributors, watchers, and detractors, as discussed in Chapter 23.

Consider What Drives Happiness

People on your team want to be happy. Everyone finds happiness by some combination of:

1. Doing good for others
2. Doing things they are good at
3. Doing good for themselves

In the work environment, the committed are motivated by all three elements and therefore are usually among the happiest team members. The contributors are motivated by elements two and three, and the compliant are motivated by element three. Sadly, the disengaged are not finding happiness in any element.

Different people are motivated more by one bucket than by another. The more focused someone is on doing good for others, the more likely that the other elements of happiness fall into place as well.

Mother Teresa was almost exclusively focused on doing good for others; while she did that, she also became very good at what she did, and her work was good for her.

Great artists, such as cellist Yo-Yo Ma, may not care about the impact they make on others or their own rewards; they just want to pursue their art for the sake of the art, because it brings them joy to do what they are good at.

Some Hollywood producers and actors are driven more by doing what's good for themselves, money and fame, rather than the quality of the films they create.

---

[2]Crabtree, Steve, 2013, "Worldwide, 13% of Employees Are Engaged at Work," *Gallup* (October 8).

Maslow's Needs

The core of Maslow's theory is that there is a hierarchy of needs.[3] At the bottom, people must satisfy their physiological and safety needs. With those in place, they can move on to belonging and esteem. Then, ultimately, they can tackle needs for self-actualization.

Add Maslow's hierarchy to the happiness and engagement frameworks, mix in a little communication planning, and out pops an approach that weaves all three together (Table 24.1).

Table 24.1
Communication Engagement Levels

Needs (Maslow)	Happiness Driver	Communication Approach	Communication Result	Engagement Level
Self-actualization	Good for others	Emotional	Belief	Committed
Belonging and esteem	Good at it	Direct	Understanding	Contributing
Physiological and safety	Good for me	Indirect	Awareness	Compliant

Satisfaction

The late Fredrick Herzberg was one of the first psychologists whose research focused heavily on business management. He was widely known for his two-factor theory on employee motivation in the workplace. According to Herzberg, the two components that drove satisfaction were hygiene factors and motivation factors.

Hygiene is probably not what you're thinking. But let's not fault Herzberg for a poor choice of words. The hygiene factors were considered things like company policies, supervisor quality, working conditions, salary, status of co-worker relations and security. The hygiene factors need to be good enough not to dissatisfy people. But there are severely diminished returns to taking them beyond good enough.

[3]Maslow, Abraham H., 1943, "A Theory of Human Motivation," *Psychological Review* 50 (4): 370–96.

The motivating factors were considered things like achievement, recognition, the work itself, responsibility, advancement, and growth. Improving these factors increased job satisfaction. The more they were increased, the better the satisfaction.

In Herzberg's theory, job dissatisfaction was influenced by hygiene factors, while job satisfaction was influenced by motivating factors.

Maslow Hygiene and Motivating Factors

In general, the first two levels of Maslow's hierarchy are hygiene factors. People's physiological and safety needs need to be met well enough for those needs not to be problems.

The top levels are motivating factors. The more self-esteem and self-actualization, the better.

Belonging benefits are caught in the middle. They are higher-level than hygiene factors, but often not motivators on their own. People want to belong to a club, tribe, or fan base. But it only matters if that membership builds their self-esteem or self-actualization.

Implications for You as a Transformational Leader

Those you lead are always going to be evolving. This is especially true after a merger or a crisis or a rapid shift in circumstances, like the rapid and massive move to remote work, when everyone's progress up Maslow's hierarchy of physiological, safety, belonging, self-esteem, and self-actualization slips or stalls.

When that happens, you need to re-boot your relationships with them.

Meet them where they are in Maslow's hierarchy. Fighting basic needs is like fighting the tide. You'll lose.

Align the way you influence with their shifted attitudes on work/life balance, health and wellness, relationship, place in the world, and other things.

Then, help them move back up Maslow's hierarchy to where they were or beyond.

Become the Narrator-in-Chief

Allen Schoer, the founder and chair of the TAI Group, a leadership consultancy, has an interesting take on the power of stories. He suggests that:

- Stories yield narrative.
- Narrative yields meaning.
- Meaning yields alignment.
- Alignment yields performance.

Stories matter, if you choose the right ones. With the right stories, you can influence but not control those committed to the cause. But you are not going to be the only one telling the stories that communicate the message. Others are going to tell their own stories in their own ways. So you're not the only storyteller, but you can be the narrator-in-chief, guiding others to choose stories that are in line with the core message.

Touch Points

Touch points are moments at which your target audiences are *touched* or reached by your message. Effective communication must include multiple touch points in multiple venues. Determine both the number of people you reach and the frequency with which you touch them. For the key individuals and groups that you want to touch, map out a series of media methods to do so, including face-to-face conversations, phone calls, videoconferences, notes, emails, texts, and more general mass and social media communications.

Monitor and Adjust

You are going to lose control of the communication as soon as you start. As people relate what they've heard to others, they will apply their own filters and biases. Shame on you if you're not ready for that and have not considered diversity, equity, and inclusion (DE&I). Have a system in place to monitor how your message is being translated. Be ready to capitalize on opportunities and head off issues that could derail your momentum. Although you can't prepare for every eventuality, if you think through a range of scenarios, you're more likely to use those contingency plans as a starting point for your response. Determine how you will measure the success of the message. Just getting it out to the audience does not mean that you've been successful. Be sure you know how and at what frequency you will measure whether your message is being received as intended.

Repeat the Message Repeat the Message

In your communication efforts, repetition is essential. We'll say it again; repetition is essential. In other words, you're going to have to create different ways and times to repeat the same message over and over again. You'll get bored of your own message well before the critical mass has internalized it, but don't shy away from repeating it. Do not ever let your boredom show; make sure you keep your energy and excitement levels high regarding the message. When you're done, do it again, fitting it into the right context for each audience each time.

Celebrate Early Wins

Somewhere along the way, you will have identified an early win. As part of this campaign, you will have overinvested to deliver that win. When it is complete, celebrate it, and celebrate it publicly. This is all about giving the team confidence in itself. So, invest your time to make the team members feel great.

Reinforce

There is going to be a crisis of confidence at some point. At that point the team will question whether you're really serious about these changes and whether the changes you are making are going to stick. Be ready for the crisis and use that moment to reinforce your efforts.

The first thing you need is an early warning system to see the crisis developing. By this time, you should be able to tap other eyes and ears throughout the organization to get an on-the-street read of the situation. These are going to be people who feel safe telling you what's really going on. They might be administrative staff, those outside your direct line of reports, or people far enough removed from you that they don't feel threatened telling you the truth. Whoever they are, you need to identify them and cultivate them. You'll often find these in the "committed" group we discussed earlier.

The main sign of the impending crisis will be the naysayers or detractors raising their heads and their objections again or more boldly. It is likely they will go quiet during the period of initial enthusiasm after the launch of the burning imperative. But they will usually find it impossible to stay quiet forever. Their return to nay-saying will be the first signs of the crisis, and their point of view will spread if you don't cut it off.

So hit the restart button fast. Make it clear that you are committed to the changes. Regroup your core team to confirm its commitment. Positively recognize the committed and contributors, those making an effort to drive the team change imperative. And take action against the blocking coalitions, with negative consequences ranging from feedback to moving people off the team if they are hindrances to business and cultural progress. Some good steps at this point may include:

- Regrouping with your core team to gather input and adjust as appropriate
- Leading *all-hands* meetings, videoconferences, or calls to highlight progress and reinforce the burning imperative
- Sending a follow-up note confirming the commitment to the burning imperative
- Making follow-up phone calls with each individual on the core team.
- Reinforcing the burning imperative at each key milestone with core team, their teams, and others
- Holding meetings or one-on-ones with key people or groups at a level below your direct reports
- Making field or plant visits
- Implementing a structured plan to measure the effectiveness of your communications
- Introducing a reward and recognition program to reinforce strong performance and supporting behaviors

At Charley Shimanski's first conference when he took over in 2010 as head of the American Red Cross's disaster response operations, he hosted 140 disaster response directors and other colleagues.

It was a master class in communication. Shimanski was everywhere: on the stage introducing speakers, speaking himself, reconnecting with old friends, hugging people who had gone through tough response engagements. He owned the room and reinforced the attendees' passion for the cause. His message flowed from every action, every message, and every pore of his being.

When asked about how he prepared for a session like that, Shimanski explained that he doesn't think about what he's going to say and he doesn't think about what he wants his audience to hear. Instead, he thinks about how he wants them to feel. "I wanted them to feel that they are at the core of what we do, that our success is on their shoulders. I wanted them to feel proud."

On one hand, not everyone has a cause as generally meaningful as the Red Cross's disaster response mission: "Provide relief to victims of disasters and help people prevent, prepare for, and respond to emergencies." But you *do* have a cause that is meaningful to you and to the people you're leading. If it didn't matter, you wouldn't be there. Be. Do. Say. Communicate the message in what you say. Communicate it in what you do. Make it your own. Do that and those following you will commit to it. You'll all feel proud.

Think about communicating top-down, bottom-up, and across.

In any case, it's all about treating people with respect.

On any communication:

- Make sure those emotionally impacted hear one-on-one in a way that respects their emotions.
- Make sure those directly impacted hear in a small-enough group to be able to ask questions and get answers.

Communication about:

- Long-term issues and opportunities should come from senior leadership at least quarterly regarding organization-wide priorities and results
- Mid-term issues and opportunities should come from middle management monthly regarding progress on major programs
- Short-term issues and opportunities should come from direct supervisors weekly regarding progress on projects and daily regarding progress on tasks

Continually look for changes in context (Where play?)

Reinforcing what matters and why (What matters and why?)

Reevaluating choices in light of new information (How win?)

Strengthening connections—especially across (How connect?)

Drowning out undesirable behavior by dialing up recognition and rewards for desired behaviors (What impact?)

You may want to dig into these areas with leading questions.

Before you object to leading questions per se, generally discouraged in direct questioning in a court of law or by neutral journalists, consider their appropriateness as a leadership tool. If a leader directs someone to do something, the best they can hope for is compliance. If they ask completely open questions, they might get any answer. But if they ask leading questions, they can lead their followers to get to the right answer and direction themselves.[4]

Findlaw defines a leading question as "one that leads a witness to an answer." Media College defines a leading question as one "which subtly prompts the respondent to answer in a particular way" and goes on to say that "leading questions are generally undesirable as they result in false or slanted information."

But that's exactly what leaders are trying to do: lead or prompt their followers to an answer in a particular way with frameworks for thinking that influence choices and prompt the highest impact actions.

A lot of organizations have used Toyota's 5 Whys technique to drill down into the root causes of problems in their Six Sigma work. Root causes analysis is a critical step in defining, measuring, analyzing, improving, and controlling. Other questions can lead people through other frameworks.

By now you've guessed that BRAVE questions are one such framework. Let's dig into other questions across behaviors, relationships, attitudes, values, and environment, looking outside in and starting with environment.

---

[4]Bradt, George, 2021, "How Leading Questions Help Leaders Lead," *Forbes* (December 21).

Next-Level BRAVE Questions

Environment: Where play
Dig in here to challenge possibilities. Ask "What could happen?" to get at the context, situation, and platform for change. Dig into understand the current reality, potential scenarios, and options.

Ask "What do we know?" "What if?" "What else could we do?"

Don't shy away from the 99 percent questions, being open to being surprised: "I'm almost positive I know the answer, but. . . ."

Values: What matters and why
These questions are designed to clarify motivation. Ask "What do we want and why?" to get at mission, vision, and values. You're trying to get at what we won't give up along the way.

This is a good place to deploy "Why?" questions to dig in and "What would that do?" to move up benefits ladders.

Attitude: How win
How win questions guide interdependencies. Ask "How do we get there?" What you're probing for is what's in the way or what's holding us back and then thinking about how we overcome barriers and bridge the gaps. Ask "What other options might we consider?" Be on the lookout for strategic linkages and unintended consequences.

Ultimately, you're leading the group to choices.

Relationships: How connect
Connection questions are about expanding influence organizationally. Ask "How do we bring others along?" Ask "Whose help do we need?" And "How do we persuade them to join our cause?"

Here you're leading the group to enhance its influence—the indirect or intangible effect they have on others, based on what they do, how they do it, how they communicate it, and who they are.

Behaviors: What impact
Impact questions get at what we're actually going to do operationally. Ask about deliverables, steps, and contingency plans. Impact is the direct and observable effect the group has on the entities you deal with.

Bias

What we believe to be true is often a product of having a bias. In an article on asking the right questions, Gary Cohen, president and cofounder of ACI Telecentrics, points out five biases that can unduly influence leadership and decision-making. Make sure your questions remove rather than reinforce these.

1. *Negative bias:* A negative experience has a larger impact on your memory and leads you to believe that certain roads are to be avoided to a greater degree than a quantitative analysis would demonstrate.
2. *Frequency bias:* Hearing or seeing something repeatedly over time makes you more inclined to believe it.
3. *Recent Bias:* When making a decision, something you learned just recently will often carry more weight than information you learned a while ago.
4. *Attachment bias:* Leaders can very easily become overly conservative and avoid making the right decision simply because they don't want to disrupt the status quo which they helped achieve.
5. *Escalation bias:* When you start down a path, you look for evidence to support your direction and, at your peril, choose to ignore warning signs.

Communication and Presentation Planning

Much of this is based on work by Speakeasy's Sandy Linver, also laid out in her book *Speak and Get Results*.[5] Tool 24.1 can help you organize your communication and planning efforts, as summarized in Figure 24.1

FIGURE 24.1

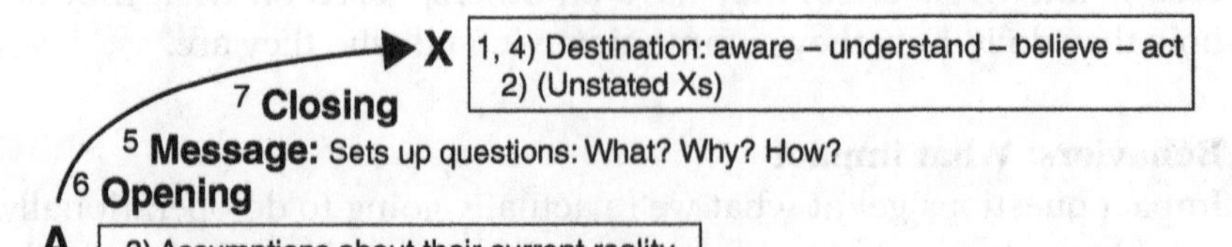

[5]Linver, Sandy, 1994, *Speak and Get Results* (New York: Simon and Schuster).

Identify Your Destination

Think through what impact you want to make on your audience. How do you want them to react? How do you want them to feel? What do you want them to do? Get specific about what you want them to be aware of, understand, believe, say, and do.

Be Explicit About Unstated Xs

Think through how you want your audience to think and feel about you (hidden X).

Assess Current Reality

Figure out where your audience is now and how they got there. What are they aware of, understand, believe? Which aspects of that help? Which get in the way? Consider potential obstacles, negative rumors, hecklers or other sabotage, legal requirements, and unintended consequences of what you say or do. Think about hidden influencers. Scenario planning is often helpful.

Reevaluate Destination in Light of Assumptions About Audience

Now go back and relook at your destination. Given what you just laid out about the current reality, can you still get all the way to the target you set in section 1? Or do you need to get there in steps?

Bridge the Gap with Your Organizing Concept or Message

This is key—choosing what to communicate to bridge the gap between the current reality or platform for change and your destination vision. Think through what people need to be aware of, understand (rationally), believe, and feel (emotionally) to answer the call to action and move from the current reality to that destination. This spawns your organizing concept (strategy) and message (words.)

Your organizing concept and message sets up questions, likely including

1. Why should anyone listen to you?
2. How should they think about what you're saying?
3. What actions should they take?

These are closely related to ethos, pathos, and logos. Ethos gets at the intentions and competence of the speaker and their empathy with the audience (*me*). Pathos is about the feelings the speaker engenders in the audience (*you*). Logos is about evidence and facts that will win the audience over, leading them to action (*us*).

Ideally, you'll communicate emotionally, rationally, and inspirationally:

- Emotionally establishing an emotional connection with your audience (ethos and pathos)
- Rationally laying out the brutal facts of the current reality as a platform for change (logos I)
- Inspirationally pointing the way to a vision of a better future with a call to action (logos II)

These form the heart of your communication, pulling in the right personal stories to establish your intentions and competence, the right illustrations to connect with the audience, and the right evidence, facts, and clear next steps to compel them to action. ("Right" means necessary and sufficient.)

Craft your message based on what people need to be aware of, understand, believe, and feel to move from current reality to the desired destination.

Platform for change:

Vision of a better future:

Call to action:

=> Organizing Concept/Message headline:

Answer three questions in your communication points:

1. Why anyone should listen to you (ethos/me—setting up emotional connection)
2. How they should think and feel about what you're saying (pathos/you—driving emotional connection)
3. What they should do next (logos/we—rational evidence leading to inspirational action)

Prepare the Opening

To frame and capture their attention. Default option for "presenting" to senior executives should probably be a one-page or one-slide executive summary that makes all your main points. A good format for that (and the basic flow of your presentation) is as follows:

1. Headline message	(i.e., "Seeking your agreement to buy X")
2. Situation, problem, platform for change	(Company X is siphoning off customers)
3. Desired impact, solution, vision of a better future	(Buy, merge, protect our base, and grow)
4. Plan, next steps, call to action	(Offer $XXB all-cash. Give specific steps.)

Prepare the Closing

To cement your message, knowing that people remember what they see first and last more than what comes in the middle.

Deliver the Communication

Implement with the best vehicles in the optimum combination with the best timing—in person or virtual, synchronous or asynchronous. Get clear on who and what influences whom. This is where you pull in your amplifiers. And don't forget to plan out how you can best plant the follow-up seeds.

What are the best vehicles to reach your audience or constituents?

What is the optimum combination?

What is the best timing to release the message?

Who and what influences whom—amplifiers?

How do you best plant the follow-up seeds?

The most up-to-date, full, editable versions of all tools are downloadable at primegenesis.com/tools.

TOOL 24.1

Communication and Presentation Planning

1. **Identify your destination**. Impact on audience: aware, understand, believe, feel, say, do
2. **Be explicit about unstated Xs.** How audience should think and feel about you (hidden X)
3. **Assess current reality.** Where audience is now, obstacles, rumors, influencers
4. **Reevaluate destination in light of assumptions about audience.** Required steps
5. **Bridge the gap with your organizing concept/message**
6. **Prepare opening.** To capture their attention
7. **Prepare closing.** To cement your message
8. **Deliver the communication.**

CHAPTER 25

Announcement Cascade: Emotional, Direct, Indirect

	The Strategic Playbook	The Commercial Playbook	The Operational Playbook	The Financial Playbook	The Governance Playbook	The Organizational Playbook	The Change Management Playbook
Concept Research Investment Case Negotiation Deal/Due Diligence Contract Close Integration Acceleration Next Normal	The Investment Case Focus Plans Innovation	Organic Revenue Growth Customers Marketing & Sales	Cost Optimization Operational Excellence: Supply Chain, Distribution, Continual Improvement Technology	Deal/ Due Diligence Financing M&A	Regulatory Financial Board	Culture Incentives Leadership People Politics	Integration Leader Change Management Communication Announcement Adjustments

The fourth component of the change management playbook is the announcement. The announcement of a merger or acquisition will impact different people differently. Some will be emotionally impacted. Some will be directly impacted. Some will be indirectly impacted. Some will be less impacted. Manage how they hear the news differently while making sure to answer the only question anyone will have: "How does this affect me?"

Internal and External Stakeholders

Start by identifying *all* the stakeholders impacted by your announcement and how they are going to feel about the announcement. Classify them as emotionally, directly, indirectly, or less impacted based on how much the announcement affects them or people with whom they are close.

Emotionally impacted: People being moved out of a job or are at risk of that, who have allies or friends being moved out of a job or are at risk, see someone else getting or potentially getting a role they might have wanted, or see this transition as particularly important to their own success are all likely to be emotionally impacted by the announcement. It's useful to tell these people one-on-one, giving them a chance to vent their emotions without being embarrassed in front of others.

Directly impacted: People working directly with new leaders or going to be working directly with new leaders—as direct reports, peers, suppliers, customers are, by definition, directly impacted. Tell these people in small groups, allowing them to ask questions.

Indirectly impacted: Those not emotionally or directly impacted can find out in large groups.

Less impacted: The less impacted can learn the news via email or broad announcement.

Message

Think through your message, working through the following as depicted in Table 25.1

Table 25.1
Messaging

Platform for change:	Headline:
Vision:	Message Points:
Call to Action:	

Platform for change: Note what will make your audience realize they need to change.

Vision: Lay out a brighter future—that your audience can picture themselves in.

Call to action: Note actions the audience can take.

Headline: Note short phrase that conveys the essence of your message. (Bumper sticker length.)

Message points: Answer three questions in your communication points:

1. Why anyone should listen to you (Ethos)
2. How they should think and feel about what you're saying (Pathos)
3. What they should do next (logos)

Along the way and through every step, your communication should be emotional, rational, and inspirational:

- *Emotional:* Connect with your audience, empathizing with how the merger or acquisition is affecting them personally.
- *Rational:* Lay out the hard facts of the situation in detail with a calm, composed, polite, and authoritative tone and manner.
- *Inspirational:* Inspire others by thinking ahead, painting an optimistic view of the future, and calling people to practical actions they can take to be part of the solution, which will instill confidence and calm in them.

Pre-Announcement Timeline

Every person you tell about an impending change increases the likelihood of the news leaking before you're ready. Thus, order matters. Start with the people who must hear the news directly from you. From there, work your way out.

Plan out whom you're going to tell when. Understand the risk of leaks increases with each additional person you tell. You're going to lose control of your communication at some point. So try to tell those that you most want to hear directly from you first. The general prescription is to tell:

1. Those emotionally impacted one-on-one first so they can be emotional in private
2. Those directly impacted in a small group next so they can ask questions
3. Those indirectly impacted in a large group so they hear it from you
4. Those less impacted through some sort of mass or electronic media—the "formal" announcement

Formal Announcement

Plan out when and how you're going to deliver the formal announcement (Table 25.2).

Table 25.2

Message delivery	
Method:	Timing:

Post-Announcement Timeline

There will be some people who you did not or could not get to before the announcement. They are still emotionally, directly, indirectly, or less impacted. Treat them as you would have before the announcement, understanding that you've lost your chance to position the announcement so you may have to correct some erroneous assumptions on their parts.

Here's an example announcement cascade timeline:

- One-on-one conversations with those emotionally impacted—early morning
- Small group meetings with those directly impacted—late morning
- Formal announcement, concurrent with large group meeting with those indirectly impacted—midday
- Follow-up conversations with those who were surprisingly emotionally impacted (there are almost always some)—afternoon

Managing Your Reaction and Response to Announcements

If you're on the receiving end of the announcement of a merger or acquisition, the emotional, rational, inspirational framework works in reverse.

- *Emotional:* Don't waste energy trying to fight your emotions. Accept them and own them. They are neither good nor bad. They just are. Take a moment. Appreciate them. And move on.

- *Rational:* Think through what has already been decided and is not going to change, what is best current thinking that you can influence, and what remains to be decided. These are the whats that kick off your what—so what—now what thinking. (This is the first part of the Stockdale paradox: confronting the most brutal facts of your current reality, whatever they might be.)
- *Inspirational:* Rally yourself by jumping into so what and now what thinking. You can't control what's already happened or been decided—but you can control how you react to those.

Think through how you might deal with what has already been decided, how you might influence current best thinking and things remaining to be decided. (So what?)

Choose to be *optimistic*. This is the second part of the Stockdale paradox, faith that you will prevail in the end—which you can never afford to lose.

Focus your energy on the few most important things you can do to be part of the solution.

David and Goliath

The head of contracts and pricing at one company learned they were merging with a larger company. The new, combined senior leadership team had been announced and would be figuring out how to merge the teams reporting into them over the next few months.

This leader realized that the new organization would not need two separate contracts and pricing teams and therefore would not need two heads of contracts and pricing.

Emotionally, he was scared. He liked his job. He liked his company. He liked his lifestyle. He didn't want to lose any of those.

Rationally, he realized his company was going to change and his current job was most likely going away. There was no opportunity to change the merger decision. There was an opportunity to influence whether his job was going to go away.

Inspirationally, he thought it through and concluded that his job should go away. He decided not to try to save his job but instead to position himself as a candidate to be head of a combined pricing and contracts function—even though he currently led a smaller group than did the current head of pricing and contracts in the "other" organization.

He led his current team through a future-focused imperative workshop to lay out:

- The *mission* of the new, combined pricing and contracts group (P&CII)
- A *vision* of success for P&CII
- A set of *objectives* for P&CII around optimizing profitability through pricing, minimizing risk through contracting and pulling these together effectively, efficiently, and rapidly
- Specific *goals*, essentially quantifying those objectives for P&CII
- An overarching *strategy* for P&CII
- *Strategic priorities* flowing from that strategy
- The *capabilities and enablers* required to drive those strategic priorities—including a new, combined organization chart (with no names in boxes yet) laying out choices around where to
  - *Win* by being: predominant or top 1 percent, superior or top 10 percent, and strong or top 25 percent;
  - *Not lose* by being: above average and competitive, good enough and scaled; or
  - *Not do* by: outsourcing or not doing at all.
- *Culture* choices for P&CII around behaviors, relationships, attitudes, values, and the environment
- An *implementation plan* with projected dates around when and how to
  - Assess the current people in both organizations
  - Choose who filled which boxes now
  - Announce those choices
  - Help those chosen come to their own decisions about whether to be part of P&CII
  - Help backup candidates come to their own decisions about whether to be part of P&CII
  - Help those either not chosen or opting out secure and prepare for their new futures
  - Accommodate work needs of the members of P&CII
  - Assimilate members into a combined team
  - Step-down this imperative into subgroup imperatives to accelerate success

You've already figure out how this story ends. On seeing this plan and the lack of a plan from the leader of pricing and contracts in the larger organization, senior leadership decided to make this leader the leader of P&CII.

TOOL 25.1

Announcement Cascade

1. **Stakeholders** (Internal and external—emotionally, directly, indirectly or less impacted):
2. **Message:**
3. **Pre-Announcement Timeline** (One-on-ones, small groups, large groups):
4. **Formal Announcement** (Method, timing):
5. **Post-Announcement Timeline** (one-on-ones, small groups, large groups, mass)

TOOL 25.2

Press Interviews

Prepare

Objective: What do you want out of the interaction?

Anticipate questions: Know interviewer, audience, and their interest factors (competition, conflict, controversy, consequences, familiar person, heartstrings, humor, problem, progress, success, unknown, unusual, wants and needs)

Approach: What way do you choose to go about achieving the objective? There are always different ways to get there. Consider them and choose one. This will lead to:

Key communication points:

Key points you want to drive (three maximum). This will allow you to do more than just answer questions (merely cues for your key points). These points need:

Support: Facts, personal experience, contrast–compare, analogy, expert opinion, analysis, definition, statistics, and examples

Deliver

Be clear, concise, complete (do one thing well,) constructive, credible, controversial, captivating, correct (must correct significant errors on the part of interviewer or press)

Be yourself, liked, prepared, enthusiastic, specific, anecdotal, a listener, a bridge, cool

Follow Through

Deliver on commitments.

Think through what worked particularly well and less well to improve for the future.

CHAPTER 26

Adjustments: Because You'll Need Them

	The Strategic Playbook	The Commercial Playbook	The Operational Playbook	The Financial Playbook	The Governance Playbook	The Organizational Playbook	The Change Management Playbook
Concept	The Investment Case					Culture	Integration Leader
Research		Organic Revenue Growth	Cost Optimization	Deal/ Due Diligence			
Investment					Regulatory	Incentives	Change Management
Case							
Negotiation							
Deal/Due	Focus		Operational Excellence: Supply Chain, Distribution, Continual Improvement	Financing	Financial	Leadership	Communication
Diligence							
Contract		Customers					
Close	Plans			M&A	Board	People	Announcement
Integration		Marketing & Sales					
Acceleration	Innovation		Technology			Politics	Adjustments
Next Normal							

The fifth component of the change management playbook is adjustments. Things change.

Once you've implemented systems to track; assess; adjust daily, weekly, monthly, quarterly, and annually; and thought through your ongoing communication, don't confuse communicating with operating cadences. Do avoid the public company sprint to do things just ahead of quarterly earnings calls, instead, staying ahead of the curve at all times.

Ideally you will have put in place a balanced scorecard to look at destination, objectives, strategic links, initiatives, and measures by the following segments:

- *Financial* (e.g., revenue, cash flow, earnings before interest, taxes, depreciation, and amortization [EBITDA], return on investment [ROI])

- *Customer* (e.g., sales from new products, on-time delivery, share, customer concentration)
- *Internal business processes* (e.g., cycle time, unit cost, yield, new product development)
- *Learning and growth* (e.g., time to market, product life cycle)

Recall, you'll likely want to follow up

- Daily for individual *tasks* done by workers (or more frequently in a crisis)
- Weekly for *projects* managed by first-line supervisors and made up of tasks
- Monthly for *programs* managed by middle managers, made up of discrete projects
- Quarterly with overall *business reviews* so senior leadership can adjust priorities and resource allocations along the way for things like information technology, infrastructure improvements, new product launches, hiring, and the like
- Annually for *core process cycle* perhaps doing talent reviews in Q1, strategic planning in Q2, future capability planning in Q3, and operational plans in Q4

Focus on strategic, organizational, and operational issues and opportunities with appropriate governance and culture as your foundation.

Strategic Process

The strategic process is about the creation and allocation of the right resources to the right places in the right way over time. It comes from the Greek *strategos* and is the art of the general, arranging forces *before* battle. Think in terms of broad choices for how to achieve objectives.

Planning
Annual strategic reassessment and plan (looking out 3–5 years)

Implementation
Through organizational and operational processes

The organizational process is about people—acquiring, developing, encouraging, planning, and transitioning them. You can't get from strategy to execution without people. The strongest organizations have *tactical capacity*—"a team's ability to work under difficult, challenging conditions and to translate strategies into tactical actions decisively, rapidly, and effectively."[1]

The core strategic organizational processes are laid out in Table 26.1.

Table 26.1
Strategic Organizational Planning Processes

Planning:	Future Capabilities	How to bridge gaps from current reality to future needs
	Succession	How to backfill leaders over time
	Contingency	How to fill surprise vacancies
Implementation:	Programs, projects and tasks to acquire, develop, encourage and transition people	
	Develop innate talent with learned knowledge, practices skills, relevant experience.	

Operational Process

The operational process is about making things happen—executional tactics. This comes from the Greek *taktikos*, the art of deploying forces *during* battle. This includes tasks that roll up into projects that in turn roll up into programs to design, build, sell, deliver, or support products or services.

Planning

Annual operating plan with monthly and quarterly reviews and updates (rolling quarterly?)

Programs and projects planned as appropriate

[1]Bradt, George, Check, Jayme, and Lawler, John, 2022, *The New Leader's 100-Day Action Plan* (Hoboken, NJ: Wiley).

Implementation

Tasks: Performed and managed in real time and daily

Projects: Interdependent tasks rolled up into projects tracked and managed weekly

Programs: Interdependent projects rolled up into programs tracked and managed monthly

Governance Process

The governance process is about ensuring compliance with laws, regulations, and policies. This process is generally owned by the board.

Culture is made up of behaviors, relationships, attitudes, values, and the environment. Consider rolling quarterly planning. Each quarter:

Prior quarter: Capture key learnings, implications for future.

What happened? Facts

So what? Conclusions about why what happened happened

Now what? Changes to future strategies and plans

If, for example, you were doing this exercise in Q2 2023 the prior quarter would be Q1 2023. This learning would be directly applicable to the plans three quarters out—Q1 2014.

- *Current quarter:* Update progress. Understand potential misses. Realign resources to optimize overall results. These will be tactical adjustments.
- *Next quarter:* Finalize goals. Ensure resources in place. Final check on milestones: what's getting done by whom, when, with what support?
- *Two quarters out:* Nearly finalize goals. Ensure longer lead-time items being worked. At this point, plans should be set.
- *Three to four quarters out:* Update general plans including things that need to be done more than four quarters out to be ready to implement in planning horizon.
- *Five to six quarters out:* Initial targets set. This allows for a rolling general overview of the next 18 months.

If, for example, you were doing this exercise in Q2 2015, the 18-month read would include all of 2016—three to six quarters out. So you could set initial targets for the following year in Q2 and have your plans ready in Q4. Thus, the rolling quarterly planning process makes annual planning redundant.

With that as context, be disciplined about adjusting along the way in four key areas:[2]

1. *Your leadership:* Periodically gain feedback on your own leadership. Take a moment and determine what you should keep, stop, and start doing to be even more effective with your direct report team and the organization as a whole.
2. *People:* Decide how you are going to evolve your people practices in line with changing circumstances.
3. *Practices: milestone management, long-term planning, and program management:* Assess whether you've been measuring the right things and have built adequate practices to develop and implement your plans.
4. *Culture:* As your insights on the culture become sharper, zero in on the biggest gaps and implement a plan to create and maintain the winning culture that will become your greatest competitive advantage.

Adjust and Advance Your Leadership

Take a three-step approach to adjusting and advancing your leadership.

Step 1: Assess your effectiveness as a leader, defining areas you need to adjust to be more effective.

- Refer to whatever documents you have available—your original 100-day plan, your milestone management document, your culture-change tracking forms, your progress on increasing diversity, or your recent financial results—and assess how you have performed versus the goals that you (and your board and your boss) set.

---

[2]Ibid.

- Rate yourself green if you are on track, yellow if you are at risk (yet have a solid plan to get back on track), and red if you will miss (and do not have a solid plan to get back on track). Ask your boss to do the same to identify disconnects in perceptions or expectations.
- Next, collect 360-degree feedback on your performance from your critical stakeholders up, across, and down. (Answer the same questions yourself so you can compare your own thoughts with others'). Doing this will help you:
  - See how others feel
  - Highlight disconnects between how you and others see you
  - Model the behavior of seeking and considering personal input from others
- Questions:
  - What are you doing that is particularly effective that you should *keep* doing?
  - What are you doing that gets in the way of your effectiveness that you should *stop* doing?
  - What else do you do to be even more effective that you should *start* doing?

Step 2: Prepare a leadership development plan.

- The plan should specify not only *what* to focus on to drive results but also *how* you need to communicate and lead the members of your team to drive engagement.
- Informed by the outputs from the self-assessment and 360-degree feedback, build your development plan. Define key deliverables across strategic, operational, and organizational matters and key leadership habits you need to strengthen to become even more effective.

Step 3: Identify support partners to help you refine your plan and stay on track.

- Start by leveraging your boss to ensure you stay on track with priorities. Establish a rolling agenda with the right balance of fixed and changeable items, and establish a regular communication cadence.

- If one of your needs is for greater organizational planning, utilize your assistant or chief of staff to ensure your time is being managed toward the key items.
- If it's behavioral coaching you need, enroll a trusted mentor or former boss, a board member, your human resources (HR) partner, an external coach, or a consultant.
- In any case, find the support to help you turn your desire into action and your action into habits. You will evolve and become an even better leader for the effort.

Develop Your Team

As appropriate, dial up your focus on developing your people as individuals, and your team as a whole, ensuring that they are positioned for longer-term success.

Set in motion a process to align the longer-term organizational development plans with the longer-term (3-plus years) strategic plan. Consider these four components:

1. *Future capability development planning* starting with the long-term strategy and then looking at what human capabilities you're going to need over time to implement that long-term plan.
2. *Succession planning* starting with the people you have in place in key roles and laying out who can take their places over time. Some of those potential successors may require development.
3. *Contingency planning* evaluating who can jump in and fill a position if one of your leaders is unable to fulfill the role for some reason. Some of these seat fillers may be permanent. Some may be on interim assignments. Some may be outsiders brought in for a short period.
4. *Performance management and talent reviews* monitoring the progress of individual development plans, and helping people maximize their potential by giving the appropriate people the training to build their knowledge, projects where they can practice and build skills, and assignments to gather experience.

Schedule these four processes to be done on an annual basis.

Enhance Practices: Milestone Management, Program Management, and Long-Term Planning

Milestone Management

By now, you should be well on your way to tracking milestones to keep the team focused on the most important deliverables, as a team. You should be doing this monthly, unless milestones are falling off target, in which case you should increase the frequency until the milestones are back on track.

Periodically pause to evaluate your tracking process. Is it working as planned? Are we tracking the right milestones? Are our meetings efficient and focusing on the most important issues? Analyze, and adjust as necessary.

Long-Term Planning

You'll also want to ensure that you have the proper balance between long-term thinking and short-term execution. Consider blending in longer-term issues (talent reviews, strategic planning and reviews, future capability, succession and contingency planning, operational reviews) on a quarterly meeting schedule to ensure that each is addressed at last once annually.

The idea is to have a meeting every month with time added once each quarter to deal with longer-term issues. It is a cycle with each piece feeding into the next. Use the calendar shown in Table 26.1 as a starting point, and then adjust it to meet your organizational needs without dropping any key pieces.

Leverage Tool 26.1 for business reviews.

Table 26.1
Prototypical Quarterly Meeting Flow

Monthly:	**Milestone update and adjustments**
Middle month each quarter:	Business review and adjustments plus a deep dive on a special topic
Special Topics:	
Q1:	Talent reviews
Q2:	Strategic review and planning
Q3:	Future capability, succession, and contingency planning
Q4:	Operational review and planning

Evolve Your Culture

Periodically pause to consider whether you can evolve the organization even more assertively to your target culture with a three-part approach.

First, make sure you and your leadership team are aligned on the specific values and behaviors you are attempting to embed into the culture.

Second, work with your leadership team to evaluate where you are as an organization against the dimensions of a culture: behaviors, relationships, attitudes, values, and the environment (BRAVE). Identify where you believe you need to focus as a team to move closer to the desired state.

Third, now that you and your leadership team are aligned on BRAVE and clear about where you need to evolve across those components, begin to make changes in business processes that reflect where you are heading. Reinforce the changes by ensuring your core people processes work for you to embed the desired culture over time.

Performance Feedback and Reward and Recognition

Provide feedback not only on measurable results but also on demonstrated behaviors in line with the target culture. Do this in the moment of the behavior as frequently as possible.

Publicly recognize those who've not only delivered concrete results but also demonstrated desired behaviors.

Internal Communication

An active internal communications program is the lifeblood of a cultural evolution. First, get your messages clear on what you wish to reinforce about the culture you are driving. If people need to work more closely as a team to solve customer problems, institute a lunch and learn or similar program to share information and get on the same page. Or encourage leadership team members to invite peers to their staff meeting to share news from their departments. If you are trying to evolve the team and the culture to a more aggressive posture in the market, celebrate examples where team members were assertive, took a risk, and won the business.

The ideas will flow; just be sure you do map your messages to your audiences, and have a continuous and multimedia approach to communicating culture.

Adjust to the Inevitable Surprises

John Wooden, the legendary coach of University of California at Los Angeles (UCLA) basketball, whose teams won an astounding 10 U.S. National Collegiate Athletic Association championships, said: "Things turn out the best for the people who make the best of the ways things turn out."

As a leader, it is up to you to make the best of how things turn out. No matter how well you have planned your merger, no matter how disciplined you are in your follow-up, some things will be different from what you expected. Often your ability to keep moving forward while reacting to the unexpected or the unplanned will be the determining factor in whether your transition is deemed a success or failure.

One of the main advantages to starting early and deploying the building blocks of tactical capacity quickly is that you and your team will be ready that much sooner to adjust to changing circumstances and surprises. Remember, the ability to respond flexibly and fluidly is a hallmark of a team with tactical capacity. The preceding annual, quarterly, and monthly meeting schedule will enable your team to recognize and react to the changes that might impact your team over time.

Not all surprises are equal. Your first job is to sort them out to guide your own and your team's response. If it is a minor, temporary blip, keep your team focused on its existing priorities. If it is minor, but enduring, factor it into your ongoing people, plans, and practices evolution.

Major surprises are a different game. If they're temporary, you'll want to move into crisis or incident management. If they're enduring, you'll need to react and make some fundamental changes to deal with the new reality. When you're evaluating change, use Table 26.2 to help guide you to an appropriate measured response.

Table 26.2
Change Map

Type	Temporary Impact	Enduring Impact
Minor Change	**Downplay:** Control and stay focused on priorities	**Evolve:** Factor into ongoing team evolution
Major change	**Manage:** Deploy incident management response plan	**Restart:** Requires a fundamental redeployment

Major and Enduring

Consequential changes that are enduring (i.e., irreversible) require a fundamental restart. These can be material changes in things such as customer needs, collaborators' direction, competitors' strategies, or the economic, political, or social environment in which you operate. They can be internal changes, such as reorganizations, future acquisitions, or spin-offs; getting a new boss; or your boss getting a new boss.

Whatever the change, if it's major and enduring, hit a restart button. Go right back to the beginning; do a full situation analysis; identify the key stakeholders; relook at your message; restart your communication plan; and get your people, plans, and practices realigned around the new purpose. Remember, the fittest adapt best.

Major but Temporary

Major but temporary surprises start out either good or bad. They don't necessarily stay that way. Just as a crisis handled well can turn into a good thing, a major event handled poorly can easily turn into a serious crisis. The difference comes down to how well you prepared in advance, implemented the response, and learned and improved for the next time.

In a crisis or disaster, teams need a way to get done in hours what normally takes weeks or months. This requires an iterative instead of sequential approach. That disciplined iteration is detailed as follows.

Leadership is about inspiring, enabling, and empowering others. Enhance that with the idea that "It is better to be vaguely right than precisely wrong." Then add Charles Darwin's point that "it is not the strongest of the species that survives, nor the most intelligent, but the one most responsive to change."[3] Add them all up and you get leading through a crisis being about inspiring, enabling, and empowering others to get things vaguely right quickly, and then adapt along the way—with clarity around direction, leadership, and roles.[4]

[3]Attributed to Charles Darwin.

[4]Bradt, George, 2019, "Learnings from Boeing's 737 Max, Coca-Cola, and Procter & Gamble on Crisis Management," *Forbes* (March 21).

This plays out in three steps of a disciplined iteration that should be aligned with the overall purpose:

1. *Prepare in advance:* The better you have anticipated possible scenarios, the more prepared you are, and the more confidence you will have when crises strike.
2. *React to events:* The reason you prepared is so that you all can react quickly and flexibly to the situation you face. Don't overthink this. Do what you prepared to do.
3. *Bridge the gaps:* In a crisis, there is inevitably a gap between the desired and current state. Rectify that by bridging those gaps in the:
   - Situation—implement a response to the current crisis
   - Response—improve capabilities to respond to future crises
   - Prevention—reduce the risk of future crises happening

Along the way, keep the ultimate purpose in mind. It needs to inform and frame everything you do over the short, mid-, and long term as you lead through a crisis instead of merely out of a crisis. Crises change your organization. Be sure the choices you make during crises change you in ways that move you toward your purpose and aspirational culture and not away from your core vision and values.

Let's delve deeper into each of these key steps.

Prepare in Advance

Preparing in advance is about building general capabilities and capacity—not specific situational knowledge. For the most part, there is a finite set of the most likely and most devastating types of crises and disasters that are worth preparing for. Think them through. Run the drills. Capture the general lessons so people can apply them flexibly to the specific situations they encounter.[5] Have resources ready to be deployed when those disasters strike.

---

[5]John Harrald argues the need for both discipline (structure, doctrine, process) and agility (creativity, improvisation, adaptability) in Harrald, John, 2006, "Agility and Discipline: Critical Success Factors for Disaster Response," *ANNALS of the American Academy of Political and Social Science* 604: 256.

- Establish crisis management protocols, explicitly including early communication protocols
- Identify and train crisis management teams (with clear leadership and roles)
- Preposition human, financial, and operational resources

Threats may be one or more of the following, often in combination:

- *Physical:* top priority—deal with these first. May be:
  - Natural: earthquakes, landslides, volcanic eruptions, floods, cyclones, epidemics
  - Man-made: stampedes, fires, transport accidents, industrial accidents, oil spills, nuclear explosions/radiation, war, deliberate attacks
- *Reputational:* second priority—deal with these after physical but before financial threats. May result from:
  - How physical threats and crises are handled
  - Choices made by you or others in your organization, outside interventions, or sudden awareness of things already there that previously went unnoticed.
- *Financial:* third priority. Come from disruptions in your value chain and can be:
  - Supply or product or resources (including cash)
  - Manufacturing, issues
  - Selling or demand disruptions
  - Service breaks

Now, back to three things you should do to prepare.

Establish Crisis Management Protocols

Plan who's going to do what when in a crisis. In general, you'll want first responders to deal with immediate physical threats to people and property. They should

1. Secure the scene to eliminate further threats to others and themselves

2. Provide immediate assistance to those hurt or injured or set up a triage system to focus on those that can most benefit from help
3. Trigger your communication protocols

There are two parts to your communication protocols. Part I protocols deal with physical issues. Part II protocols deal with reputational issues.

Part I protocols spell out who gets informed when (with lots of redundant back-ups built in). These should have a bias to inform more people faster.

Part II protocols are about formal, external communication. At a minimum, the one, single, primary spokesperson (and back-up) message and communication points should be crystal clear. It's a good guideline to follow three over-arching ideas from the Forbes Agency Council's 13 Golden Rules of PR Crisis Management.

- Develop strong organizational brand culture to ward off self-inflicted crises and be better ready to deal with others.
- Monitor, plan, and communicate, and be ever on the lookout for potential crises. When they hit, be proactive and transparent, get ahead of the story, and be ready for the social media backlash.
- Take responsibility. Own your own crisis in a human way. Seek first to understand, avoiding knee-jerk reactions, apologize, then take action that helps, not fuels the fire.

Identify and Train Crisis Management Teams

Protocols are useless if people haven't been trained to apply them. Make sure your first responders are trained in first aid and triage. Make sure your communicators are trained in communicating in a crisis so people know whom to contact when and when to trigger crisis management protocols.

One of the learnings from the Boeing 737 Max crashes is that their crisis management protocols should have been triggered years before they were. It seems that some knew there was a potential problem and chose not to deal with it.

Prepositioning Human, Financial, and Operational Resources

People need direction, training and resources. Make sure there's a site leader at each of your sites with access to cash. Make sure your first responders have working first-aid kits.

React to Events

Our fight-or-flight instincts evolved to equip us for moments like this. If the team has the capabilities and capacity in place, turn it loose to respond to the events. This is where all the hard work of preparation pays off.

A big part of this is knowing when and how to react without under- or overreacting.

Bridge the Gaps

While first responders should react in line with their training, keep in mind that random, instinctual, uncoordinated actions by multiple groups exacerbate chaos. Stopping everything until excruciatingly detailed situation assessments have been fed into excruciatingly detailed plans that get approved by excruciatingly excessive layers of management leads to things happening excruciatingly too late.

The preferred methodology is to pause before you accelerate to get thinking and plans vaguely right quickly. Then, get going to bridge the gaps with a combination of discipline (structure, doctrine, process) and agility (creativity, improvisation, adaptability).[6]

Situational questions (keeping in mind the physical, political, emotional context)

- What do we know and not know about what happened and its impact (facts)?
- What are the implications of what we know and don't know (conclusions)?

---

[6]Ibid.

- What do we predict may happen (scenarios)?
- What resources and capabilities do we have at our disposal (assets)? Gaps?
- What aspects of the situation can we turn to our advantage?

Objectives and Intent

Armed with answers to those questions, think through and choose the situational objectives and intent. What are the desired outcomes of leading through the crisis? What is the desired end state? This is a critical component of direction and a big deal.

Priorities

The Red Cross provides relief to victims of disasters. In doing that, the prioritization of shelter, food, water, medicine, and emotional support varies by the type of disaster. If someone's home is destroyed by a fire in the winter, shelter takes precedence. On the other hand, if a reservoir gets contaminated, the critical priority is getting people clean water.

These examples illustrate the importance of thinking through the priorities for each individual situation and each stage of a developing crisis. The choices for isolating, containing, controlling, and stabilizing the immediate situation likely will be different than the priorities for the mid-term response, which is more about getting resources in the right place and then delivering the required support over time. Those in turn will be different from the priorities involved in repairing the damage from the crisis or disaster and preventing its reoccurrence.

Get the answer to the question, "Where do we focus our efforts first?" and the priority choices start to become clear. Then, get them communicated to all, perhaps starting with a set of meetings to:

- Recap current situation and needs and what has already been accomplished
- Agree on objectives, intent, priorities, and phasing of priorities
- Agree on action plans, milestones, role sort, communication points, plans, and protocols

A crisis is better managed by using an iterative approach than by using the more sequential approach. This is why we recommend early meetings to jump-start strategic, operational, and organizational processes all at the same time, getting things vaguely right quickly and then adapting to new information along the way.

Bridge the Gap Between the Desired and Current State

Support team members in implementing plans while gathering more information concurrently.

Complete situation assessment and mid-term prioritization and plans.

Conduct milestone update sessions daily or more frequently as appropriate.

> Update progress on action plans with focus on wins, learning, areas needing help
>
> Update situation assessment
>
> Adjust plans iteratively, reinforcing the expectation of continuous adjustment.

Overcommunicate at every step of the way to all the main constituencies. Your message and main communication points will evolve as the situation and your information about the situation evolve. This makes the need that much greater for frequent communication updates within the organization, with partner organizations, and the public. Funneling as much as possible through one spokesperson will reduce misinformation. Do not underestimate the importance of this.

Along the way and through every step, your communication should be emotional, rational, and inspirational:

- *Emotional:* Connect with your audience, empathizing with how the crisis is affecting them personally.
- *Rational:* Lay out the hard facts of the current situation in detail with a calm, composed, polite, and authoritative tone and manner.
- *Inspirational:* Inspire others by thinking ahead, painting an optimistic view of the future, and calling people to practical actions they can take to be part of the solution, which will instill confidence and calm in them.

Remember the airplane that crash-landed in the Hudson River? First officer Jeff Skiles was the "pilot in charge" of the airplane when it took off, ran into a flock of birds, and lost both its engines. At that point, Captain Chesley Sullenberger chose to take over. With his command "my aircraft," followed by Skiles' "your aircraft," control (and leadership) was passed to "Sully," who safely landed the plane. Only one pilot can be in charge at a time. Two people trying to steer the same plane at the same time simply does not work.

The same is true for crisis and disaster management. Only one person can be the "pilot in charge" of any effort or component at a time. A critical part of implementation is clarifying and reclarifying who is doing what, and who is making what decisions at what point—especially as changing conditions dictate changes in roles and decision-making authority within and across organizations. Make sure the handoffs are as clean as the one on Sully and Skiles's flight.

After-Action Review

At the end of the crisis, conduct an after-action review looking at:

- What actually happened? How did that compare with what we expected to happen?
- What impact did we have? How did that compare with our objectives?
- What did we do particularly effectively that we should do again?
- What can we do even better the next time in terms of risk mitigation and response?

The most up-to-date, full, editable versions of all tools are downloadable at primegenesis.com/tools.

TOOL 26.1

Management Cadence

Q1 Talent Review
Business review and adjustment
Priority programs (monthly) and projects (weekly)

Q2 Strategic Plan
Business review and adjustment
Priority programs (monthly) and projects (weekly)

Q3 Future Capability, Succession, and Contingency Planning
Business review and adjustment
Priority programs (monthly) and projects (weekly)

Q4 Operating Plan
Business review and adjustment
Priority programs (monthly) and projects (weekly)

Rolling quarterly planning. Each quarter:

- Prior quarter: Capture key learnings and implications for future.
- Current quarter: Update progress. Understand potential misses. Realign resources to optimize overall results.
- Next quarter: Finalize goals. Ensure resources in place.
- Two quarters out: Nearly finalize goals. Ensure longer lead-time items being worked.
- Three to four quarters out: Update general plans including things that need to be done more than four quarters out to be ready to implement in planning horizon.
- Five to six quarters out: Initial targets set.

PART VIII

Prototypical Order

CHAPTER 27

Prototypical Order

Parts of the seven different playbooks need to be deployed at different times in different mergers or acquisitions. Here's one prototypical chronology.

Prototypical Chronology: An Example

Concept

Start with the strategic playbook and tie the strategic plan into the investment case. Your initial concept need not be any more than vaguely right and include early thinking on where you might play and how you might win—focus. Be thinking in terms of customers, people and capabilities, and costs even at the concept stage. Keep a close eye on the competitors, disruptive technologies, and emerging trends.

	The Strategic Playbook	The Commercial Playbook	The Operational Playbook	The Financial Playbook	The Governance Playbook	The Organizational Playbook	The Change Management Playbook
Concept	The Investment Case					Culture	Integration Leader
Research Investment Case		Organic Revenue Growth	Cost Optimization	Deal/ Due Diligence	Regulatory	Incentives	Change Management
Negotiation Deal/Due Diligence	Focus		Operational Excellence: Supply Chain, Distribution, Continual Improvement	Financing	Financial	Leadership	Communication
Contract Close	Plans	Customers		M&A	Board	People	Announcement
Integration Acceleration Next Normal	Innovation	Marketing & Sales	Technology			Politics	Adjustments

Research

As you do your initial research, look for potential targets with the right customers, people, capabilities and culture, and cost optimization opportunities. Look for evidence of strengths in innovation, technology, and operations. And pay attention to the regulatory environment.

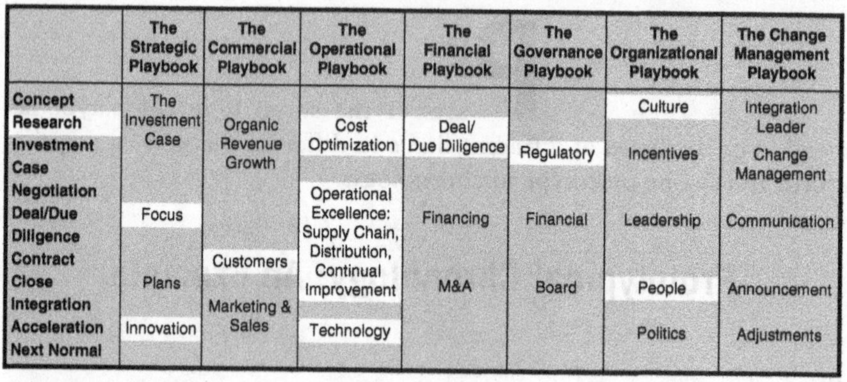

You may find the following tools helpful here:

3.1 Situation Analysis Checklist
3.2 SWOT
11.1 Culture

Investment Case

The investment case is where you dig in

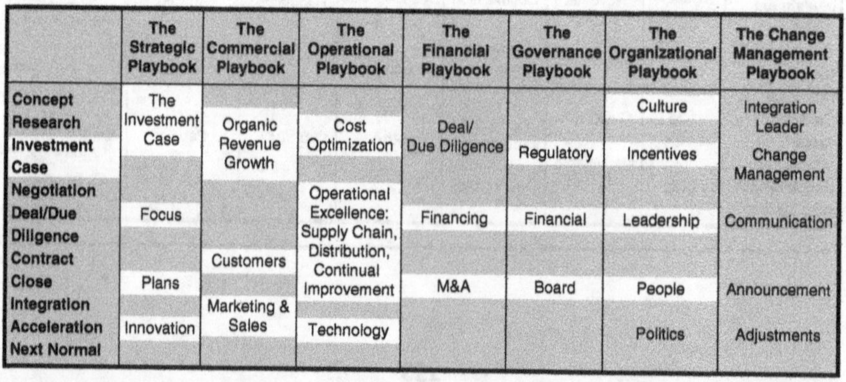

You may find the following tools helpful here:

1.1 Investment Case
3.1 Situation Analysis Checklist
3.2 SWOT
3.3 Business Planning
4.1 BRAVE Innovation
7.1 Purchase/Sales Funnel Management
7.2 Marketing Planning
11.1 Culture

Negotiation, Deal, Due Diligence, Contract

Here's where the chronology becomes a myth. Ideally, you'd negotiate, do a deal, do some due diligence, and then lock your contract. In the real world, expect to move back and forth between the steps in anything but a linear fashion. Certainly, the investment case, financing, finances, and regulatory considerations will come into play. At the same time, if you're negotiating with people you're going to be working with going forward, pay attention to how you're building relationships with them as part of your future leadership and culture. You can't be one person during negotiations and then another after the deal is done.

	The Strategic Playbook	The Commercial Playbook	The Operational Playbook	The Financial Playbook	The Governance Playbook	The Organizational Playbook	The Change Management Playbook
Concept Research Investment Case	The Investment Case	Organic Revenue Growth	Cost Optimization	Deal/ Due Diligence	Regulatory	Culture Incentives	Integration Leader Change Management
Negotiation Deal/Due Diligence Contract	Focus	Customers	Operational Excellence: Supply Chain, Distribution, Continual Improvement	Financing	Financial	Leadership	Communication
Close Integration Acceleration Next Normal	Plans Innovation	Marketing & Sales	Technology	M&A	Board	People Politics	Announcement Adjustments

You may find the following tools helpful here:

1.1 Investment Case

11.2 Negotiating

Close

The world changes and resets at the close.

Pre-close mandatories are getting your *financing* in place and *regulatory* clearance.

You're going to be much better off if you have:

- Stood up your *board*
- Prepared to go with the early parts of your *financial playbook*—like paying employees and providing stay *incentives* to the key players you can't lose yet
- Stood up an *integration leader*, transformation office, or PMO and thought through your *change management* approach
- Some current best thinking on the future *culture*
- Thought through your *communication* plan and started an *announcement* cascade

And if possible—which it won't be in many cases—you can accelerate things if you have:

- Selected the *leadership* team; and
- Co-created some of the aforementioned with them even before the close.

In any case, be mindful of the *politics* and know that every *person's* only question is, "What does this mean for me?"

	The Strategic Playbook	The Commercial Playbook	The Operational Playbook	The Financial Playbook	The Governance Playbook	The Organizational Playbook	The Change Management Playbook
Concept						Culture	Integration Leader
Research	The Investment Case		Cost Optimization	Deal/ Due Diligence			
Investment		Organic Revenue Growth			Regulatory	Incentives	Change Management
Case							
Negotiation							
Deal/Due	Focus			Financing	Financial	Leadership	Communication
Diligence			Operational Excellence: Supply Chain, Distribution, Continual Improvement				
Contract		Customers					
Close	Plans			M&A	Board	People	Announcement
Integration		Marketing & Sales					
Acceleration	Innovation		Technology			Politics	Adjustments
Next Normal							

Integration

We wrote this book to help you bring sense to the complexities of integration.

	The Strategic Playbook	The Commercial Playbook	The Operational Playbook	The Financial Playbook	The Governance Playbook	The Organizational Playbook	The Change Management Playbook
Concept						Culture	Integration Leader
Research	The Investment Case		Cost Optimization	Deal/ Due Diligence			
Investment		Organic Revenue Growth			Regulatory	Incentives	Change Management
Case							
Negotiation							
Deal/Due	Focus			Financing	Financial	Leadership	Communication
Diligence			Operational Excellence: Supply Chain, Distribution, Continual Improvement				
Contract		Customers					
Close	Plans			M&A	Board	People	Announcement
Integration		Marketing & Sales					
Acceleration	Innovation		Technology			Politics	Adjustments
Next Normal							

You may find the following tools helpful here:

19.1 Team and People Assessment
20.1 Future Organizational Capability Planning
20.2 Talent Management
20.3 Recruiting Brief
23.1 Alignment Workshop

Acceleration

A quick look at the difference between the integration and acceleration stages indicates you can stop worrying about financing and start thinking about future M&A. True. But that underplays the importance of staying focused on all the big and little things you and your team have to do to realize the investment case. Don't blink. This is a marathon, not a sprint.

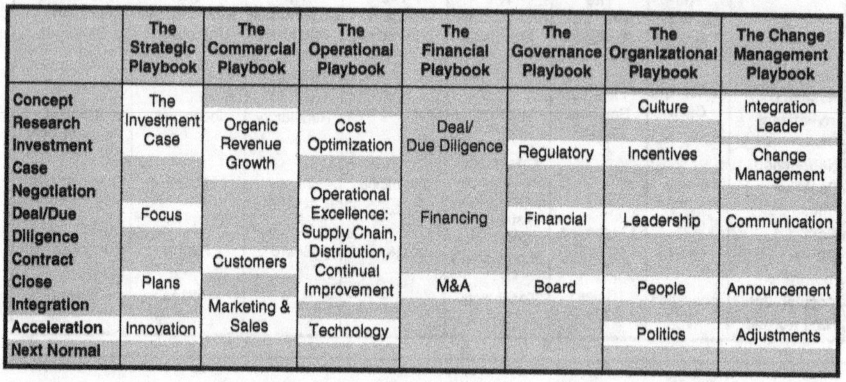

You may find the following tools helpful here:

23.2 Change Management
24.1 Communication Planning

25.1 Announcement Cascade

26.1 Management Cadence

Next Normal

This book is your playbook to create value leading through a merger or acquisition. For whom? It could be for you or the current owners in the form of dividends. It could be for a strategic buyer as a way to complement their business strengths. It could be for an economic buyer as a platform for future value creation by them.

In the latter cases you essentially want to flip the investment case and build the case for others strategically, organizationally, and operationally.

Strategically

Build a track record of sustainable organic revenue growth, and paint a picture of where future organic revenue growth will come from in terms of

- A new product pipeline
- Servicing the customers
- Innovation pipeline and track record
- Pricing upside
- New channels
- New geographies

Separately, build a record of successfully integrating other mergers and acquisitions, and paint a picture of where future mergers and acquisitions could come from.

Organizationally

Build a "buyable" management team. This means a high-performing team capable of managing at least another doubling of revenue.

Build capabilities valuable to potential investors. This, in turn, may look like

- Product development capabilities in a design-focused organization
- Manufacturing black belts in a production-focused organization
- Ecosystem enrollers in a distribution-focused organization
- Customer experience experts in a service-focused organization

Operationally

Put in place a buyable infrastructure:

- Assets
- Data
- IT systems
- Financial reporting
- Processes

Personally

If you're part of the leadership team, make yourself invaluable to the next owners by doing the job the organization needs you to do the way the organization needs you to do it.

ABOUT THE AUTHORS

George Bradt has led the revolution in how people start new jobs. He progressed through sales, marketing, and general management around the world at companies including Procter & Gamble, Coca-Cola, and J.D. Power's Power Information Network spin-off as chief executive.

Now he is chair of PrimeGenesis, the executive onboarding and transition acceleration group he founded in 2002 to accelerate complex transitions for leaders and teams. Since then, George and his partners have reduced new leader failure rates from 40 percent to less than 10 percent through a single-minded focus on helping them and their teams deliver better results faster over their first 100 days.

A graduate of Harvard and Wharton (MBA), George is coauthor of 11 books on leadership and onboarding, over 750 columns for Forbes, and 19 plays and musicals (book, lyrics, and music).

Other leadership and onboarding books by George include:

- *The New Leader's 100-Day Action Plan* (Wiley, five editions, 2006–2022)
- *Onboarding: How to Get Your New Employees Up to Speed in Half the Time* (Wiley, 2009)
- *The Total Onboarding Program: An Integrated Approach* (Wiley/Pfeiffer, 2010)
- *Influence and Impact: Discover and Excel at What Your Organization Needs from You the Most* (Wiley, 2021)
- *First-Time Leader* (Wiley, 2014)
- *Point of Inflection* (GHP Press, 2022)
- *CEO Boot Camp* (GHP Press, 2019)
- *The New Job 100 Day Plan* (GHP Press, 2012)
- *The New Leader's Playbook* (GHP Press, one volume each year 2011–2021)
- *Executive Onboarding* (GHP Press, four volumes, 2020)

Jeffrey P. Pritchett is a senior operating executive with more than 25 years of general management, finance, commercial and operations experience at both public and private companies across a variety of industries.

He is a member of the executive leadership team of Cerberus Operations and Advisory Company, the proprietary operating platform of Cerberus Capital Management ("Cerberus"), a global leader in investing with more than $55 billion of assets. In this role, Jeff works closely with the firm's investment leaders on new opportunities and overseeing resource deployment, growth, and value creation across Cerberus' businesses.

He leads strategic initiatives across Cerberus' global real estate and credit strategies. Most recently, he served as the chief executive officer of FirstKey Homes, a leader in residential real estate management, where he was instrumental in enhancing resident experience, driving scalable growth, and developing a best-in-class leadership team.

Jeff also serves on the board of directors of Pace Industries, North America's leader in full-service aluminum, zinc, and magnesium die casting manufacturing; Imagine Group, a marketing solutions company delivering premier graphic services; Tenet Equity, an internally managed net lease platform; and FL2 Partners, a real estate and property management company focused on Brazil residential investments.

His experience with growing businesses, merger and acquisitions, integrations, and strategic initiatives is extensive. He served as executive chair of the board of directors for TransCentra, where he led the growth of the business and sale to SouceHOV. He also led the operating diligence and integration/synergy plan for the $9 billion merger of Albertsons Companies and Safeway.

In addition to his expansive work with Cerberus, Jeff has been on several other boards of directors. Most recently Jeff was a member of the board and chair of the audit committee for Champion One, where he previously served as chief operating officer. He partnered with A&M Capital Partners and the management team at Champion One to grow the business organically and through M&A, which led to the successful sale of the business to a strategic competitor.

Prior to that, he served as managing partner at MLV Management, providing board, executive leadership, and advisory services and led transformations, accelerated growth, and maximized value for investment management firms. He was executive vice president, chief financial officer, and head of operations at InnerWorkings, Inc. (NASDAQ: INWK). He held leadership positions at Vertis Communications, including senior vice president and interim chief financial officer, and led the sale of Vertis to Quad/Graphics, Inc. (NYSE: QUAD). He also held a variety of senior roles at General Motors and Delphi Automotive.

Jeff graduated from Walsh College and received his MBA from Purdue University.

GUEST CONTRIBUTORS

Karl Bailliez, senior operating executive and finance practice leader (COAC) at Cerberus Capital Management. In Chapter 11 on The Deal/ Due Diligence: Financial Due Diligence

Aaron Darr, private equity investor. In Chapter 12 on Capital Structure Management

Katherine Kirkpatrick, general counsel at Maple Finance. In Chapter 14 on Regulatory: The Regulatory Environment

Michael Ovalles, senior managing director, business transformation, Office of the CFOO Solutions Practice at FTI Consulting. In Chapter 24 on Communication: Owning the Narrative

Jeff Scott, partner at PrimeGenesis Executive Onboarding and Transition Acceleration. In Chapter 22 on Integration Leadership: Good Decisions Aren't Enough

Ericka Stephens, chief human resources officer at Pace Industries. In Chapter 20 on People: Cultural Transformation

Dennis Stratton, president and managing partner at Stratton Consulting Group. In Chapter 23 on Change Management: Aligning an Organization After a Major Strategic Pivot

BIBLIOGRAPHY

Batlaw, Anish, and Charan, Ram 2022. *Talent: The Market Cap Multiplier*. Oakton, VA: Ideapress.

Benedict-Nelson, Andrew, and Leitner, Jeff. 2018, *See Think Solve: A Simple Way to Tackle Tough Problems*. Chicago: Leitner Insights.

Berman, William, and Bradt, George. 2021. *Influence and Impact: Discover and Excel at What Your Organization Needs from You Most*. Hoboken, NJ: John Wiley & Sons.

Bradt, George. 2011–2022. *The New Leader's Playbook*. Articles on www .Forbes.com.

Bradt, George, and Bancroft, Ed. 2010. *The Total Onboarding Program: An Integrated Approach to Recruiting, Hiring, and Accelerating Talent Facilitators*. San Francisco: Pfeiffer.

Bradt, George, Check, Jayme, and Lawler, John. 2022. *The New Leader's 100-Day Action Plan*. Hoboken, NJ: John Wiley & Sons.

Bradt, George, and Davis, Gillian. 2014. *First-Time Leader: Foundational Tools for Inspiring and Enabling Your New Team*. Hoboken, NJ: John Wiley & Sons.

Bradt, George, and Scott, Jeff. 2022. *Point of Inflection: Frameworks and Tools to Accelerate Team Results*. Stamford, CT: GHP

Bradt, George, and Vonnegut, Mary. 2009. *Onboarding: How to Get Your New Employees Up to Speed in Half the Time*. Hoboken, NJ: John Wiley & Sons.

Buckingham, Marcus, and Clifton, Donald. 2001. *Now, Discover Your Strengths*. New York: Free Press.

Charan, Ram, Drotter, Stephen, and Noel, James. 2001. *The Leadership Pipeline: How to Build the Leadership-Powered Company*. San Francisco: Jossey-Bass.

Covey, Steven. 1989. *The 7 Habits of Highly Effective People*. New York: Simon & Schuster.

Coyne, Kevin, and Coyne, Edward. 2007. "Surviving Your New CEO." *Harvard Business Review*, May.

Deutsch, Clay, and West, Andy. 2010. *Perspectives on Merger Integration*. McKinsey.

De Smet, Aaron, Kleinman, Sarah, and Weerda, Kirsten. 2019. "The Helix Organization," *McKinsey Quarterly*, October 3.

Duck, Jeannie Daniel. 2001. *The Change Monster: The Human Forces That Fuel or Foil Corporate Transformation and Change*. New York: Three Rivers Press.

Guber, Peter. 2008. "The Four Truths of the Storyteller." *Harvard Business Review*, January.

Groysberg, Boris, Hill, Andrew, and Johnson, Toby. 2018. "Which of These People Is Your Future CEO? The Different Ways Military Experience Prepares Managers for Leadership." *Harvard Business Review*, November.

Hastings, Reed. 2009. "Culture." *SlideShare*. August 1. http://www.slideshare.net/reed2001/culture-1798664.

Heffernan, Margaret. 2012. "Why Mergers Fail." *CBS Money Watch*, April 24. http://www.cbsnews.com/news/why-mergers-fail/.

Iger, Robert. 2019. *The Ride of a Lifetime: Lessons Learned from 15 Years as CEO of the Walt Disney Company*. New York: Random House.

Linver, Sandy. 1983. *Speak and Get Results: The Complete Guide to Speeches and Presentations That Work in Any Business Situation*. With Nick Taylor. New York: Summit.

Maslow, Abraham H. 1943. "A Theory of Human Motivation." *Psychological Review* 50 (4): 370–96.

Neilson, Gary L., Martin, Karla L., and Powers, Elizabeth. 2008, "The Secrets to Successful Strategy Execution." *Harvard Business Review*, June, 60.

Porter, Michael E. 1985. *Competitive Advantage: Creating and Sustaining Superior Performance*. New York: Simon and Schuster

Schein, Edgar. 1985. *Organizational Culture and Leadership*. San Francisco: Jossey-Bass.

Senge, Peter M. 1990. *The Fifth Discipline: The Art and Practice of the Learning Organization*. New York: Doubleday/Currency.

Syed, Mathew. 1994. *The Fifth Discipline Fieldbook: Strategies and Tools for Building a Learning Organization*. Boston: Nicholas Brealey.

Syed, Mathew. 2011. *Bounce: The Myth of Talent and the Power of Practice*. London: Fourth Estate.

West, Andy, and Rudnicki, Jeff. 2020. "A Winning Formula for Deal Synergies." *Inside the Strategy Room*. Podcast, May 8.

INDEX